Knowledge Utilization
in Residential
Child and Youth Care Practice

Knowledge Utilization in Residential Child and Youth Care Practice

edited by
JEROME BEKER
ZVI EISIKOVITS

Child Welfare League of America
Washington, D.C.

CHILD WELFARE LEAGUE OF AMERICA, INC.
440 First Street, NW, Suite 310, Washington, DC 20001-2085

CURRENT PRINTING (last digit)
10 9 8 7 6 5 4 3 2 1

Cover design by Chad Bruce
Text design by Rose Jacobowitz

Printed in the United States of America

ISBN # 0-87868-427-1

Library of Congress Cataloging-in-Publication Data
Knowledge utilization in residential child and youth care practice /
    edited by Jerome Beker, Zvi Eisikovits.
        p.   cm.
    Includes bibliographical references (p.   ) and index.
    ISBN 0-87868-427-1 (paper)   : $28.95
        1. Children—Institutional care—United States.   2. Group homes
for children—United States.   3. Child care workers—United States.
4. Social work with youth—United States.   I. Beker, Jerome.
II. Eisikovits, Zvi.   III. Title: Child and youth care practice.
HV863.K66   1991
362.7'32'0973—dc20   90-15002
                                                               CIP

To our children,
Josh, David, and Nir,
and to all children and youths,
everywhere

Contents

Acknowledgments

The editors gratefully acknowledge the contributions of so many of our distinguished colleagues, whom we are pleased to be able to call friends as well, to this book and to the Study Group on Knowledge Utilization in Residential Child and Youth Care that provided and refined most of its content. Special thanks go to Edna Guttmann, who helped both with the organization of the Study Group and in the preparation of the book, and to Emily Beker, whose assistance in the final preparation of the manuscript for the publisher was invaluable. The Study Group was made possible by contributions in cash and in kind from Bet Rutenberg in Haifa, Israel, where it was convened; from Haifa University and its Richard Crossman Chair in Social Work and Social Policy in the School of Social Work; from the University of Minnesota through its Center for Youth Development and Research, College of Human Ecology (formerly Home Economics), and Office of International Programs; from an anonymous contributor; and from the home institutions of many of the participants that enabled them to be involved. We also appreciate the efforts of the many office assistants who helped along the way. Finally, we want to acknowledge, with appreciation and love, the support of our families while the work was in progress.

THE EDITORS

Foreword

Beker, Eisikovits, and their contributors provide much food for thought to those concerned with group care and treatment for troubled and troublesome youths. Differences aside—and there are many among this international group of distinguished authors—all seem to proceed from the conviction that the "powerful environment" of Wolins can in fact be used positively to redirect, challenge, and stimulate the lives of both residents and staff, and that group care settings have a vital function to fulfill in the overall continuum of services.

This belief is refreshing at a time, at least in the United States, when much of conventional wisdom portrays group care settings more as part of the problem than part of the solution and, in fact, views them as essentially unreformable. In no small way, this pessimistic view has to do with the woefully inadequate and uneven quality of group care and treatment in public and voluntary agencies alike, recognized abuse and neglect of both the individual and the institutional variety, escalating costs, and rather modest outcomes as reflected in extant research. One consequence of this pessimism has been generally lowered expectations for group care services and relative inattention—at least as measured in government and foundation research priorities—to understanding and improving the quality of residential care and treatment provision. This attitude is a far cry from the critical thinking and brilliant insights inspired by the work of Bettelheim and Redl and Wineman over forty years ago, still frequently cited in the present volume.

Beker, Eisikovits, and their colleagues seek to challenge the conventional wisdom about group care as simply a problem waiting to be solved and offer fresh insights and, most important, some new conceptual lenses for analyzing the residential environment. Among the most significant of these are the notions of developmental, ecological, and experiential perspectives in understanding the potential of the milieu as a powerful environment for change.

Those seeking simple solutions will be frustrated by this book: it forces us to think critically about the relations that ought to obtain among youths, their families, caring staff, and the external environment. It asks the American reader to "stretch" his or her view to include international examples of staff roles and treatment organization. If short on specific program recommendations, the book makes a major contribution by identifying some of the key terms and issues in the debate over what residential care provision *ought* to look like.

In short, this is a thoughtful book written by thoughtful people, who share a passion for helping troubled youths gain a greater share of mastery over their own lives. It is, finally, a hopeful book, written from the conviction that fortune will indeed favor the prepared mind and that knowledge and understanding should precede action in the design, implementation, and evaluation of residential care settings. It is neither *Love is Not Enough* nor *The Aggressive Child*, nor does it purport to be, but if carefully read, argued, and taken seriously, it may well stimulate some nascent Bettelheim or Redl to create for a coming generation what these giants created for theirs.

JAMES K. WHITTAKER
The University of Washington

Introduction

Knowledge utilization can be viewed as an approach to practice involving reflective action. It is the process on which practitioners must depend for their continued growth as effective child and youth care workers, as well as that on which the growth of the field depends. Since our knowledge base is constantly growing and the situations in which it can be applied are in constant flux as well, attempting to utilize knowledge systematically in child and youth care work is always a dynamic process.

To elucidate these fundamentals, the editors present a knowledge utilization approach in Chapter 1 that assumes an interactive process between the field and its workers as two mutually dependent entities. The examples there and the chapters that follow illustrate the process in action in as many of the critical domains of residential child and youth care practice as possible, with, we believe, implications in many cases for nonresidential settings as well. It is hoped that the specifics will not only be helpful in themselves but will also serve as a springboard to propel the reader toward ever more effective practice and to illustrate how this practice may advance the field.

Reflected in the book are a number of theoretical and practical perspectives that have been chosen purposefully by the editors in the belief that these represent the most productive directions for the field at this time. For example, the field has moved away from the medical model to become more ecologically defined, developmentally oriented, and competency-based—perspectives that are explored in depth in the chapters by Henry Maier and Anthony Maluccio and reflected throughout the volume. The idea that workers, too, are people and can be effective only to the extent that they are aware of and use their own humanity is central to the contribution of Edna Guttmann in Chapter 4.

The next section considers direct work with children, including the role of the direct care worker in establishing a growth-oriented environment (Anita Weiner) and in helping young people to develop the feeling and the reality of social competence (Shunit Reiter and Diane Bryen). Both chapters view their topics integratively, in the context of the more general or theoretical ones that precede them. Herbert Barnes then focuses on the purposive use of program and program activities, highlighting a participatory philosophy as reflected in specific approaches. The section concludes with in-depth consideration of three essential elements from an ecological perspective that are outside the day-to-day living group: vocational development (Yecheskel Taler), the family (Karen Vander Ven), and the school (Yitzhak Kashti and Mordecai Arieli).

The residential setting as context is the focus of the section that follows, beginning with Leon Fulcher's discussion of the nature of teamwork in such a situation and its implications for the worker. Robert Friedmann concentrates on the setting as part of an organization, with all of the implications of that aspect for the direct care worker and how that role can be performed most effectively. Yochanan Wozner follows with his discussion of how, in such a context, program integration can best be developed.

In the final section, the contributors step back from direct practice and day-to-day interaction to examine even more reflectively what occurs and its implications for program enhancement in the future. In this sense, Rivka Eisikovits views the direct care worker as a qualitative researcher as well, and Don Peters and Ron Madle explore staff development. In the Epilogue, the editors provide a brief conceptual umbrella in the form of three variables that underlie the entire book: developmental approach, ecological orientation, and experiential awareness and methodology.

We recognize that child and youth care work cannot succeed as other than a human enterprise; professionalism and knowledge utilization must be applied without diluting the human connection. Each chapter seeks to reflect this essential foundation as it points the way toward more effective practice, and readers are asked to keep it before them as they weigh the application of the perspectives and approaches presented throughout the book. Thus, we hope that workers will be able to perform with ever-increasing sensitivity even as they do so with ever-greater expertise.

JEROME BEKER
ZVI EISIKOVITS

Part 1

Theoretical and Conceptual

Foundations

1

The Known and the Used in Residential

Child and Youth Care Work

ZVI EISIKOVITS
JEROME BEKER
EDNA GUTTMANN

Ignorance is the curse of God
Knowledge the wing wherewith we fly to heaven.
    Wm. Shakespeare, *Henry VI*, Part II, Act IV, Scene 7

Residential child and youth care work has access to this Shakespearean wing, the means to fly, yet the occupation is, too frequently, still not flying. Indeed, it sometimes seems unable to get off the ground! How can we make these wings—knowledge—an integral part of practice so that the field can "take off" in its reach for increasingly effective service to children and youths? The knowledge we need is available, but we rarely use it.

The history of knowledge in child care is beyond the scope of this chapter, but it is important to note that the early residential child and youth care worker was intuitive and ad hoc, improvising practice as situations arose. The worker performed many functions simultaneously or in rapid succession, such as caring, building relationships, setting norms, and "societal-representing" [Maier 1978]. The job was done spontaneously, based primarily on immediate perception of the situation and on accumulated "practice wisdom" [Schlick 1974] without theoretical interpretation or much generalization from practice. A great deal of high-quality child-care work surely resulted, with the emphasis on concern for the children rather than on using knowledge systematically to enhance their development. Heidigger [1962] has referred to this as the "intuitive" approach.

In recent decades, it has become apparent in residential child and youth care, as in other human service occupations, that intuition alone, like love alone [Bettelheim 1950], is insufficient, as essential as both may be to effective service in this field. In addition, partly in an effort to justify their existence as well as to improve their practice, human service personnel have begun to address highly charged professional and political questions: What is unique about us? What is our expertise? What can we do better than others? How? In what settings? To phrase it differently, the movement toward professionalization in a range of human service occupations is under way. In this context, residential child and youth care workers are among those who have turned to knowledge as a core component of professional identity [Eisikovits et al. 1986; Ritzer 1972; Schein 1971]. This knowledge concerns both direct care of children and youths and such broader aspects of residential care as organizational functioning, teamwork, and social change.

Various theoretical orientations have made significant contributions to the knowledge base in the field. Such leading psychoanalytically oriented figures as Aichhorn [1935] and Bettelheim [1955] helped us to understand many facets in the origin of, and effective response to, childhood disorders in the context of the residential setting. The interplay between the individual child's behavior and that of the group, and how these factors influence mental health, were closely scrutinized. Various treatment approaches were developed, such as the child guidance model (ego-supportive psychiatric treatment) and milieu therapy using the "life space interview" [Redl 1966]. Redl and Wineman [1957] conceptualized both children's behavior and treatment interventions in group care settings in practice terms.

Behaviorism contributed to the knowledge base from its perspective as well, wherein the interplay between the environment and individual learning in shaping external behavior was stressed. Behavior modification techniques (e.g., withholding and dispensing social reinforcers, teaching alternative behaviors) were developed and widely implemented in residential care settings [e.g., Ashen 1973; Bandura 1977; Lazarus 1976].

Knowledge drawn from developmental psychology helped to provide an understanding of the role of developmental stages in determining what an individual can learn at a given time in life, as well as how stage progression can be facilitated. For example, Erikson's [1950] psychosocial developmental stages are useful in helping one to understand what can realistically be expected of children or youth at various stages and the appropriateness of specific program options for particular clients. Similarly, Piaget's [1958] stages of cognitive development are useful heuristic devices in assessing levels of problem-solving ability. Kohlberg's [1969] theory of moral development was successfully implemented in residential care by the development of the "just community," which aimed to foster the moral development of its members. Maier [1978] brought practice perspectives to bear on developmental theory.

Educational perspectives have also contributed to knowledge development and implementation in residential child and youth care, notably including the Re-ED model [Hobbs 1974; Lewis 1971] and the variety of educateur perspectives developed in western Europe and French Canada [Linton 1971, 1973]. Allied knowledge has been appropriated for the field from such areas as organizational functioning [Etzioni 1975; Hage 1965; Hall 1977; Hasenfeld and English, 1974], teamwork [Barker and Briggs 1969; Brill 1976; Fulcher 1981; Garner 1977, 1980, 1982; Vander Ven 1979] theories related to societal change, and the role as well as the strategies used by change agents [Appelbaum 1970; Havelock and Havelock 1973; LaPiere 1965].

One could continue at length enumerating the rich array of theoretical influences that have contributed to the available knowledge base of the child and youth care field. All are relevant and needed, but few have an exclusive relationship to the field of residential child and youth care. This is the case in the helping professions in general: they draw largely on shared knowledge, and the uniqueness of each results from how it reformulates, recombines, and expands on such knowledge to meet its particular needs.

The child and youth care field has done relatively little, however, to make its particular adaptation of knowledge explicit. Existing knowledge has usually been presented in ways that have little, if anything, to do with the worker's background, expectations, cognitive maps, and ability to respond in a particular situation. At present, relevant knowledge in child and youth care is just starting to be filtered through to the worker. Nevertheless, too little effort is being invested in helping direct care workers to become knowledge utilizers, and the existence of pertinent knowledge has relatively little to do with how most present-day child and youth care workers go about their daily tasks.

Making Knowledge Usable

It is the objective of this book to assist in making relevant knowledge usable in the field and to show how such knowledge can be helpful to those involved in direct practice. This chapter provides a conceptual framework for that process, starting with an examination of the state of the art in the use of knowledge in child and youth care and proceeding with a more formal definition of knowledge utilization and a discussion of applicable utilization literature. These considerations provide the needed theoretical foundation for a knowledge utilization model, which is presented next, followed by a case example. The chapter concludes with an examination of the "craft" model as an approach to individualized practice in the context of needed commonalities and consistency and a brief overview linking this chapter to those that follow.

What is known and what is used in child and youth care? Figure 1 portrays what is known versus what is not known and what is used versus what is not used as two dimensions of a matrix, designed to illuminate the objective of making child and youth care knowledge usable. What we are seeking to do is to analyze movement from knowing but not using such knowledge (item 2) to knowing and using it (item 1). Furthermore, an attempt will be made to show how new knowledge can be imparted so as to be more fully usable.

What is intuitively known may not be known (or even true) from a conceptual point of view. It is used, yet it cannot be theoretically explained or interpreted; it is a product of experience that has not been examined systematically. Thus, practice based on intuitive knowledge (item 3) can be referred to as unknown but used. Although the process of verification, that is, turning intuition into knowledge, is essential, it is beyond the focus of this chapter or of the book. Those who study practitioners and direct practice are engaged in this effort, in which a basic consideration is to factor in the idiosyncratic aspects of the individuals and interactions involved. That which is both unknown and not used (item 4) remains to be experientially and empirically discovered and then used.

		Known		Unknown
Used	1.	Knowledge known and used	3.	Knowledge unknown but used (Intuitive)
Not Used	2.	Knowledge known but not used	4.	Knowledge unknown and not used

Figure 1. The Known and Unknown, Used and Not Used, in Child and Youth Care Work.

As child and youth care work has moved beyond the intuitive toward a professional orientation, it has generally been assumed that knowledge development would almost automatically result in knowledge utilization or application; that is to say, the movement of a topic from item 4 to item 2 (of Figure 1) would normally move it to item 1 as well. In reality, however, we are frequently faced with child and youth care knowledge that is stuck in item 2 (known but not used). For example, a variety of cyclical theories of child and youth development have been developed (see Maier, Chapter 2 in this book), their crucial importance for successful child and youth care work is known, yet they have had little influence on how most direct care workers go about their everyday work. This knowledge is quietly resting in the category of item 2. Thus, the assumption that turning the unknown into the known would lead directly to effective knowledge utilization has proven to be unwarranted. To make knowledge useable, then, we should try to understand why this assumption has failed and search for ways to promote implementation.

Why is it that newly developed knowledge is not necessarily used in practice? To answer this question, we turn to the philosophy of knowledge. Knowledge, defined as a "structure of ideas" [Feibleman 1976], can be divided into two types. First is the familiar "knowledge-at-hand" [Schutz 1967] in everyday use. Second is theoretical, abstract knowledge, somewhat more remote from one's daily experience. We refer to the first type as "tacit knowledge" [Polanyi 1966]; the second is "abstract knowledge."

Tacit knowledge emerges inductively from "sense experience" [Hume 1928; Locke 1964] through the systematic development of generalizations from everyday life occurrences [Argyris and Schon 1974; Bloom 1975]. As it emerges from experience, we have it in our immediate consciousness; we own it; it belongs to us. It is our knowledge-at-hand.

Abstract knowledge, however, comes either from the abstraction of empirically based data or from the integration of existing ideas in a creator's mind. Thus, it is objective to the knower, who has acquired it from outside sources and is known through theoretical concepts, principles, and statements [Foucault 1972; Schlick 1979]. Child and youth care workers own and use tacit knowledge created as they go about their everyday work; to facilitate its greater utilization, all that may be needed is to make its existence explicit. But abstract knowledge is remote from everyday child and youth care experiences; it does not become tacit, and thereby also used, merely by virtue of its relevance. It is necessary to take another step to transform it from abstract to tacit. *The dual process of creating tacit knowledge by making abstract knowledge tacit and making tacit knowledge explicit is the process of knowledge utilization.*

Ideally, then, in any given situation, workers will respond spontaneously on the basis of explicit, conscious tacit knowledge, including transformed abstract knowledge that has been incorporated into their practice. For example, we instantly use tacit knowledge to apply the brakes when an emergency appears on the road ahead. While learning to drive, however, the process is slower; we may need to think about where the brake is and how to use it—an example of abstract knowledge that has not become tacit. At the even more primitive level of driving intuitively, we might not have known what to do at all, unless we had puzzled it out before by trial and error, and even then we might be unclear about the difference between the functions of the regular and the emergency brake. So it is with knowledge utilization in child and youth care work.

To clarify further the themes embedded within the idea of knowledge utilization, we now briefly discuss the literature about it before turning to the presentation of an explicit, seven-step model of the process of knowledge utilization in child and youth care and a practice example.

Knowledge Utilization as Described in Human Service Literature

During the 1960s, with increased specialization and wide proliferation of programs in the human service fields, the issue of utilizing relevant abstract knowledge became a burning one. An inventory and categorization of relevant abstract knowledge, developed at a conference concerning the body of social work knowledge, included such categories as normal behavior; abnormality and deviation; growth, maturation, and change; and the helping relationship itself [Thomas 1964]. There was general agreement that these types of knowledge should be applied on the interpersonal, group, organizational, community, and broader societal levels.

In the light of such a high degree of specificity and consensus regarding the "what," that is, the content of knowledge, it seems notable that the "how," that is, the process of utilization, was seldom addressed, and then only in piecemeal fashion. A few approaches to utilization have, however, been suggested in the literature of the human service professions. Guba [1968], for example, proposed that the utilization of knowledge be the task of the practitioner, who, he indicated, should implement researchers' suggestions without interpretation.

In the 1970s, the issue came to be mentioned as the "science of knowledge utilization" [Havelock and Havelock 1973], and its scope was broadened considerably. The focus was placed on identifying factors that have the potential to facilitate knowledge utilization. Among those suggested were such group and organizational factors as organizational structure, communication processes, and decision-making strategies [Bennis et al. 1969; Zaltman et al. 1973] and such individual factors as the level of interest and work commitment [Larsen 1980].

Other studies suggested means by which practitioners could be encouraged to undertake research and to use empirically generated knowledge. Ideas included translating research findings into "practice metaphors" [Feldman 1980], doing research within human service organizations [Thomas 1980], teaching practitioners to collect and analyze data, and defining research problems in terms of practice tasks [Tripodi and Epstein 1978]. Some authors even suggested including the capacity to utilize research among the requirements for certification [e.g., Yin 1976]. Starting from these rather generic ideas, concern with knowledge utilization began to focus on different areas of practice. The domains in which the "science of knowledge utilization" was tried included organizational work [Kilman 1981; Zaltman 1977] and policy development [Caplan 1975; Rich 1981; Weiss 1977].

Thus, the process of knowledge utilization has been the focus of much attention in recent years, particularly in terms of approaches to utilization, factors facilitating it, and its types and their relationship to occupational focus; however, the specifics of how to use knowledge more effectively in a particular occupational or practice setting largely remain to be explored.

Two major approaches to the specifics of how to utilize knowledge have been developed. The first is experiential. Bloom [1975] describes the "scientific practice" of social work, and Glaser and Strauss [1967] discuss the concept of "grounded theory," both essentially descriptions of the experiential modality. The process begins with putting events into sets or categories, then integrating categories that possess the same properties. This procedure is closely related to the critical incident technique [Flanagan 1954], which has been used similarly by Goodrich and Boomer [1958]. Generic concepts emerge from these categories, which by their interrelatedness lead to abstractions. Although this means of knowledge utilization has the advantage of tying newly developed knowledge to the user's experiences, it fails to answer the question of how to utilize already existing, rather than newly created, knowledge.

The second modality is deductive; that is, abstractions derived from theories are operationalized into hypotheses through logical deduction. These hypotheses are in turn validated or changed through the process of being tested against some practical or empirical reality [Wallace 1971]. The potential advantage of choosing this avenue of utilization lies in the ability to use existing knowledge; its shortcoming is that it is detached from the user's concrete experience.

Attempts have been made to carry the first modality further [Lindblom and Cohen 1979], based on the idea of bringing commonsense knowledge to higher levels of abstraction [Schutz 1967]. These efforts have, by and large, been conceptual, without describing the process by which commonsense knowledge arising from experience can become abstract knowledge.

Furthermore, if our purpose is to utilize existing knowledge, rather than to create new knowledge, then neither the experiential nor the deductive approach alone will do. In that case, we need to integrate both, which is the purpose of this chapter. The experiential and deductive perspectives are interwoven into a seven-step, process-oriented model of knowledge utilization in residential child and youth care work.

An effort has been made to organize each of the chapters that follow in accordance with this model. Most begin with open-ended problems arising from child-care workers' everyday experiences. These problems are first conceptualized inductively, and existing knowledge is applied to their analysis. Finally, they are resolved. The movement from concrete, everyday problems to their conceptualization, to abstract knowledge, and back to find solutions is the process of knowledge utilization.

Toward a Process Model of Knowledge Utilization

What follows dissects the process of knowledge utilization into its component parts. By its very nature, however, this dissection changes the rhythm of the process and may be misleading. In actual practice, the rhythm is faster and boundaries between stages are blurred. The model can be viewed as a "road map" [Baizerman et al. 1976], as is presented schematically in Figure 2. Key points in it are described below, followed by a case example of the process in action.

The importance of spontaneity and immediacy in child and youth care work is widely recognized and is often suggested as a reason why knowledge utilization, or conceptual practice, is impractical and/or undesirable. Certainly it is true in many situations that a deliberate process of reflection through the steps just outlined would not be feasible: Mary is running, screaming, toward the open window, or Tom is about to hit Spike with the bat. But even immediate responses are usually the product of an implicit process of weighing action options and choosing one, and many situations not only permit but require time for observation and reflection if they are to be handled most effectively. The most important point here, however, is that, given a reasonable fund of experience and grounded theoretical knowledge, the practitioner can learn to go through the indicated steps almost automatically and with great speed, just as one converts driving a car from a conscious, labored process at the beginning to a virtually unconscious one with time and practice. This is the objective of the process to be described, but it does need to be done consciously, mechanically, and with help at the beginning.

1. Experiencing an Incident

At any given time, a number of events are occurring around us. Some pass unnoticed, or we are only vaguely aware of them; we single out others for our attention or, as Goffman [1974] called it, we choose to "frame" some events by attending to them. When a child-care worker experiences a sense of discontinuity in the stream of his or her working life or becomes aware of something that is occurring (e.g., Jane is getting angry, or Jack is sitting alone in the corner), an event is perceived to have "happened": an "incident" is born. The sense of discontinuity is experienced as an alteration of both one's inner world and one's environment (as is discussed more fully in Chapter 4).

This sense is what we define as "experience" [Schutz 1967]. It is what strikes us first and alters the sense of continuity in our bodily sensations, in our awareness of time and space, and in our emotional world. Recognition of this change signals the beginning of a *reflective* stage, which can vary in duration from being virtually instantaneous to being an extended, rather deliberate and considered process. This stage is an essential component in becoming conscious of one's experience and thereby in the process of knowledge utilization.

2. Grasping

As events around us "strike" us and we become aware of them and what they do to us, it may be said that they constitute our sense of "what is happening," and we begin to impute meanings to them. This immediate awareness is usually combined with some understanding of the context within which the event is meaningful. Our reflection on the incident in its context leads to consideration of its familiarity: Did this or something like it happen before? Did it happen under similar circumstances? Based on familiar situations, we search for patterns, and categories of experience emerge. We are now in the process of placing the event in the context of a typology grounded in our previous experiences. Thus, one recalls (and possibly re-experiences) one's previous reactions to "this kind of situation": When certain things occur in a certain way, so and so happens and this is how I experience it. At the end of this stage, which may be virtually instantaneous, one has *grasped* the happening but has neither weighed action nor actually done something (acted).

3. Identifying and Weighing Options for Action

Once we grasp the situation identified in the present, we can begin to decide what to do next. The implicit question is, "Based on what I understand about what is happening and how it fits with what has happened before, what are my possibilities for action in relation to this incident and what are their likely consequences?" Thus, we are cognitively identifying various options for action based, inevitably, on our previous experience in the field and our life experience in general, as well as on the factors of personality and temperament that color how we see the world. An experienced worker is likely to have an advantage over a novice in the number of options that will come to mind. The options that

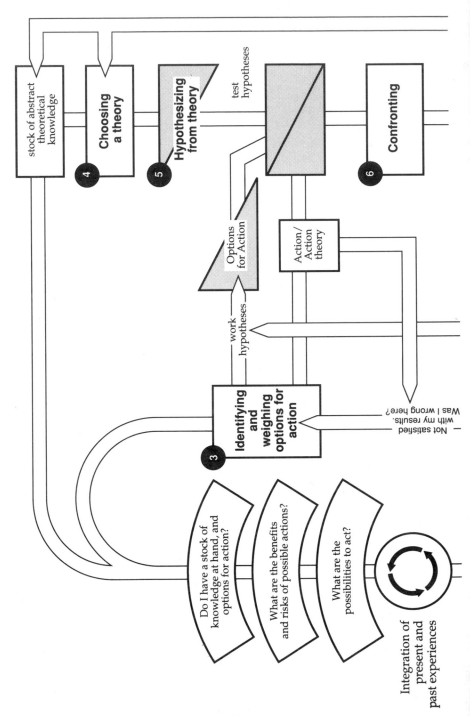

stock of abstract theoretical knowledge

Choosing a theory ④

Hypothesizing from theory ⑤

test hypotheses

Confronting ⑥

Options for Action

Action / Action theory

work hypotheses

Identifying and weighing options for action ③

— Not satisfied with my results. Was I wrong here?

Do I have a stock of knowledge at hand, and options for action?

What are the benefits and risks of possible actions?

What are the possibilities to act?

Integration of present and past experiences

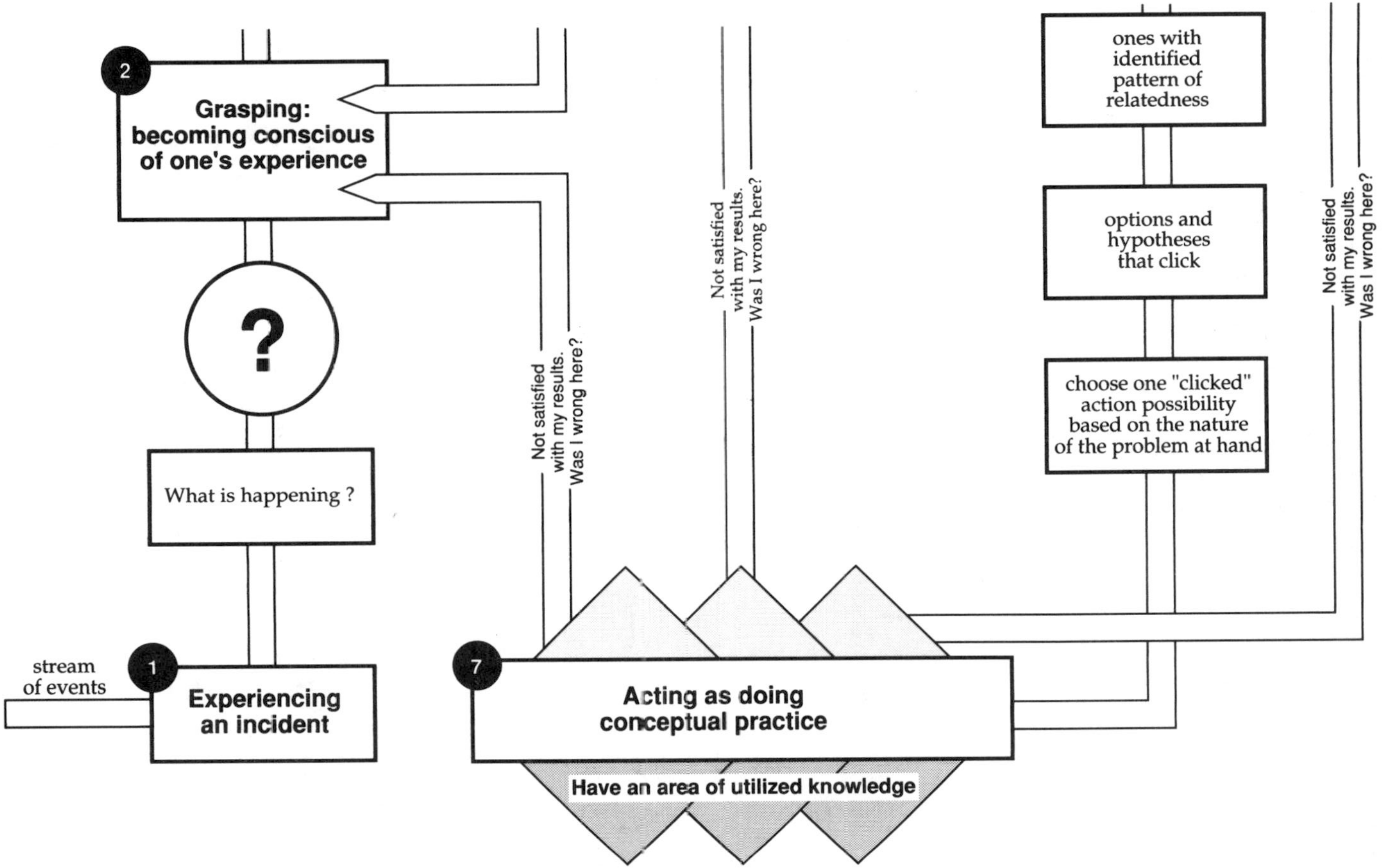

ones with
identified
pattern of
relatedness

options and
hypotheses
that click

choose one "clicked"
action possibility
based on the nature
of the problem at hand

Not satisfied
with my results.
Was I wrong here?

Not satisfied
with my results.
Was I wrong here?

**Acting as doing
conceptual practice**

Have an area of utilized knowledge

7

Not satisfied
with my results.
Was I wrong here?

**Grasping:
becoming conscious
of one's experience**

2

?

What is happening ?

**Experiencing
an incident**

1

stream
of events

Figure 2. Pathways to Knowledge Utilization.

13

are identified, together with the experience and comprehension of the event, constitute one's stock of *knowledge-at-hand*.

At this point, we are also weighing the risks and benefits involved in choosing each of the different options for action, and evaluating their probable outcomes. The assessment of action options is influenced by our previous experience and by such factors as the others who are involved; our relationship to them; who the audiences for certain kinds of actions are; the kind and degree of personal risk we are willing to take; the kinds of actions that have led to desired outcomes in similar situations in the past; the timing and quality of the action and how it accords with other activities and occurrences in the broader ecological context; the kinds of restrictions or liberties that are allowed by organizational rules and norms; the amount of action or inaction we can safely venture, given our position in the organization in which we work; and our occupational values and beliefs. The outcome of this process reflects what is often called the worker's practice wisdom.

4. Choosing a Theory

Until now, the steps presented have been experiential and inductive: that is, on the basis of concrete everyday experiences, the child and youth care worker develops abstractions that, when put into operation, become available guides to possibilities for action and their consequences. Next, the worker has to make critical decisions concerning the broader rationale for one or more of the options at hand. To do so, the worker must turn to his or her stock of abstract, theoretical knowledge. This resource is the counterpart to the knowledge-at-hand that is grounded in experience; abstract knowledge is generally grounded in empirical data or theoretical ideas and can often be linked explicitly to the overall objectives of the program involved (e.g., enhanced development, behavior change) and to the nature of the occurrence under consideration (e.g., a strange behavior, a group activity).

Within the boundaries of one's abstract, theoretical knowledge, a judgment is made concerning a specific theoretical orientation that supports one or more of the action options. This choice is guided by a process similar to that used when the options were weighed at the previous stage, but at a higher level of abstraction. The criteria for choosing a theoretical orientation may include questions such as, What are the component elements of the situation (e.g., the protagonists and germane aspects of the social system involved)? What is our occupational orientation, including values and beliefs, ethical constraints, and so forth, and what limitations, if any, are imposed by the philosophical or methodological commitments of the agency? What is the universe of actions regarded as feasible that we wish to support by our theory? As a tentative theoretical choice is made, we are ready to take the next step, generating hypotheses from theory.

5. Hypothesizing from Theory

We use the term theory here as referring to a symbolic construction or a set of propositions, arranged in a logical, deductive system or causally linked together [Wallace 1971]. Its purpose is to help us to make sense of a situation in such a way as to connect our habitual action repertoire to the situation at hand, to allow us to modify our action repertoire, or to enable us to discard it and search for new repertoires [Kaplan 1964]. To scrutinize our action repertoire, or "idea bank," and make the appropriate choice, we must first put the theory into operation by translating it into empirically testable statements (hypotheses).

The inductive part of the model ended with weighted action options or "working hypotheses" [Kaplan 1964]. These guidelines for action, based on practice wisdom, cannot be used to predict outcomes or consequences on a rational basis, particularly in terms of overall program objectives, except as the essentials of the current incident are similar to those of others that were experienced previously. The second part of the model, the deductive one, with which we are concerned now, involves developing "test hypotheses" [Kaplan 1964] from theory. These can then serve as guidelines for action, and they have the advantage of being able to predict consequences. Within the boundaries provided by the theory, a choice is made concerning the relevant hypotheses. Based on the propositions that constitute the theory, we can predict what choice will bring what outcome.

6. Confronting Options for Action with Test Hypotheses

At this point, we have grounded options for action at the inductive end of our model and test hypotheses, which can be viewed as "if" statements (if you do this, the result will be that), at the deductive end. How does the knowledge utilizer tie these two ends together?

If knowledge utilization is to occur, the inductive and deductive parts of the relevant knowledge cannot exist independently. That is, one needs inductively derived options for action to identify an appropriate theory, and one needs the theory to specify which options are likely to bring about desired outcomes. To portray how these two components of knowledge utilization co-constitute each other, let us use the well-known figure-ground illustration that appears in Figure 3 [Rubin 1958].

The picture in Figure 3 represents the relationship between the experientially derived inductive knowledge and the theoretically or empirically created abstract knowledge. When the white vase represents the one, the dark faces become the other. Thus, when experiential knowledge is the figure, abstract knowledge is the background; when abstract knowledge is the figure, experiential knowledge becomes the background. The frame of the picture is symbolic of the theoretical and experiential boundaries within which knowledge is being utilized. What is

Figure 3. Rubin's Figure-Ground Illustration: The Co-Constitution of Experiential Inductive Knowledge and Theoretical Abstract Knowledge.

significant is that effective knowledge utilization occurs on the line that co-constitutes these two illustrations, neither of which exists without the other.

It will be recalled that the worker is now confronted with options for action, on the one hand, and test hypotheses, on the other. How is he or she to utilize knowledge in action? In other words, how can the worker do conceptual practice [Bloom 1975]? From the universe of possibilities, the child and youth care worker must now attempt to bring one or several options for action and test hypotheses into a "click" relationship; that is, find a clearly identified *pattern of relatedness* among them [Kaplan 1964]. This pattern of relatedness is either logically explicit and obvious, or it is brought about by modifications and adjustments of the options and/or the hypotheses within the boundaries of the situation and the theory, respectively.

The click is observable structurally when the action option (or options) matches the content of the test hypothesis (or hypotheses). Each consists of two parts, a conditional segment (*if I do this*) and an outcome segment (*then the outcome will be that*), although the causal link between the two is far closer in the case of test hypotheses. Therefore, the click relationship may occur most readily when the conditional segments (*if I do this*) match. If the match is accompanied by too great a dissonance in anticipated outcomes of the inductive and deductive approaches, then one's choice of a theoretical premise and/or selection from his or her accumulated practice wisdom should undergo some adjustments.

If one such conceptual click (between an option and a test hypothesis) occurs, practical action [Bloom 1975] can follow directly. When several clicks between options and hypotheses are available, the worker must make a choice among them, depending on the nature of the problem at hand.

7. Acting as Doing Conceptual Practice

Once we decide on an action and perform it, we observe the outcomes. These may be as we anticipated, in which case we have developed an area of "utilized knowledge." If the observed consequences differ from the expected ones, rethinking and, possibly, also "re-acting" are likely to prove helpful. It might be that we can grasp the event differently, develop other action options, choose another theory, or form different test hypotheses. The map (Figure 2) can be used (see the cut-offs at point 7) as a guide to the points where reconsideration might be indicated. Once the point at which the process is to be restarted has been located, the remainder of the road should also be reconstructed in light of the map and the process that has been described. Repeated as necessary, this process is one of successive approximation, similar to the method of analytic induction [Cressey 1953]. The search for appropriate inductive and deductive elements continues until the finding of a click relationship that suggests action leading to outcomes congruent with our expectations in resolving the situation at hand.

The Process Applied

In this way, any practitioner can accumulate areas of utilized knowledge relating to types of occurrences that he or she encounters frequently. When a similar situation occurs, that knowledge can be utilized, and each step in the process can be undertaken in the light of pertinent knowledge already acquired. When faced with an unfamiliar event, the worker can simply follow the road map again.

This process may seem to require a great deal of effort at the beginning, but, as one continues to utilize knowledge and to do conceptual practice, his or her "data bank" grows, skill in going through the process is enhanced, and following the map becomes easier and faster as well as increasingly constructive and helpful. Eventually, the process of knowledge utilization becomes an integral component of one's daily work, which is the ideal situation. To achieve this end, however, one needs to be conscious of utilizing knowledge in as many situations as possible.

A Practice Example

A new boy who has just come into the cottage group starts pacing back and forth across the common room, shouting angrily. Apparently oblivious to the efforts of the child-care worker and the other children to determine what is wrong, he soon begins to throw things around the room and at the other youngsters. In short, he seems to be out of control. As you experience the incident, you feel a sense of urgency, that you must act fast before something else happens and things become worse. (See Chapter 4 for more on this experiential part of the process.) You may also wish you were somewhere else.

Having *experienced* the situation (point 1 in the model), you now ask yourself, "What is going on?" You draw on similar experience in your previous work and elsewhere in your life to help you understand. You recognize that the child's restlessness may relate to his being new, a stranger in the residential setting, and with the fact that the other children are watching him. (This stage is *grasping*, point 2 in the model). Considering such factors as your relationships with the other children, the amount of risk you want to take, your position in the residential setting, your beliefs, and whether other staff members are watching you, you *identify and weigh options for action* (point 3). You can, for example, put the child alone in his room, request that he be removed from the program or assigned to a different cottage, ask the other children to play with him, ask the others to leave, try to explain to the child that his behavior is disturbing, or try to strike up a friendly conversation with him.

At this stage, you can choose one option and act intuitively. If your aim is to utilize knowledge, however, you turn to your *stock of abstract knowledge* to try to make sense of the situation in theoretical terms (point 4). Knowing that (*a*) your occupational orientation is development (for example), and that (*b*) the child is a newcomer here, and keeping in mind your options for action, you may choose a "cyclic developmental" theory. One of the main arguments in this theory is that when a person is placed in a totally unfamiliar situation, he recapitulates his primary needs [Maier 1978]. From this, you *hypothesize* (point 5) that if you give the boy food and warmth, he will calm down, or that if the other children ask him to play, he will agree and then become calm.

When *confronting the options for action with the test hypotheses* (point 6), you discard the possibility of shutting the child in his room or sending him away. The idea of being warm and accepting with the child clicks with the hypothesis that giving him food and warmth will calm him down. You quietly invite him to have a bite to eat with you. This step is *doing conceptual practice* (point 7).[1]

If the child calms down, then you can conclude that you have a utilized area of knowledge. If he does not, you can examine the road map to determine where to start your next attempt. Including as "new data" your observation of what has occurred in the interim, you might grasp the situation differently. You might discover new action options, or you could choose Freudian or behavioral theory and formulate different test hypotheses. A change at any point on the map could change the nature of the conceptual practice (i.e., the intervention) to which it would lead.

Using Knowledge Utilization

Knowledge utilization is a content area and a perspective in itself, as presented in this chapter. We hope the reader will approach the following chapters, whose topics have been chosen to reflect the content of everyday life in group care settings, from this perspective as direct care personnel tend to categorize it. Our goal, however, was also to go beyond the workers' categories so as to conceptualize it more broadly. The question then becomes how we can apply one conceptualization to the field, since child and youth care work is, both by ideology and in actual practice, largely idiosyncratic or individualized. For this purpose, it must be assumed that there is a set of fundamental patterns or generic principles that underlie practice in child and youth care work. These principles cannot, due to the nature of the work, be reduced to a cut-and-dried cookbook approach, but they can help practitioners to make informed, intelligent judgments concerning their actions.

This view regards the occupation as a "craft" [Bensman and Lilienfeld 1973].[2] Its central idea is that craft practitioners generally function within similar settings or "social arrangements" and on the basis of their own idiosyncratic application of shared skills and techniques. This commonality leads to shared ways of perceiving and thinking about the world ("habits of mind"), and to the use of similar explanations of what one does and why ("ideology") [Eisikovits and Beker 1983]. From such commonalities, similar roles and task perceptions within roles arise. These often cross national and political boundaries and provide the occupation with a universalistic character. Thus, the view of child and youth care work as a craft suggests that it provides common ground as the basis for our conceptualization of what is taken for granted among colleagues, or the shared categories created by the workers in the field. It is on this basis that the authors have attempted to identify the commonalities of practice on a level that will permit and promote effective knowledge utilization on the job.

Summary

This chapter presents a conceptual framework for the material to follow. Since the book is designed to model the process of knowledge utilization in key areas of child and youth care practice, we have discussed the state of the art in utilizing knowledge and have presented a model for application in the field. The model has provided the basis for organizing the book and the chapters within it, which were selected in an effort to reflect child and youth care workers' everyday working lives. Both the method and the content have been developed to support the individuality and to enhance the competence of each worker involved in the knowledge utilization process.

NOTES

[1]In a real situation, the worker has to be aware of broader considerations as well, such as how the rest of the group will react and the implications of that reaction for his or her decisions.

[2]The craft dimension should be regarded as largely separate from the dimension of professionalization; they are not opposite ends of a continuum [Beker and Eisikovits 1983].

REFERENCES

Aichhorn, A.   1935.   *Wayward Youth.* New York: Viking.

Appelbaum, R.P.   1970.   *Theories of Social Change.* Chicago, IL: Markham.

Argyris, C., and Schon, D.A.   1974.   *Theory in Practice: Increasing Professional Effectiveness.* San Francisco, CA: Jossey-Bass.

Ashen, B.A.   1973.   *Adaptive Learning: Behavior Modification with Children.* New York: Pergamon Press.

Baizerman, M., McDonough, J.J., and Sherman, M.   1976.   *Self-Evaluation Handbook for Hotlines and Youth Crisis Centers.* St. Paul, MN: Center for Youth Development and Research, University of Minnesota.

Bandura, A.   1977.   *Social Learning Theory.* Englewood Cliffs, NJ: Prentice-Hall.

Barker, R.L., and Briggs, T.L.   1969.   *Using Teams to Deliver Social Services.* Syracuse, NY: Syracuse University Press.

Beker, J., and Eisikovits, Z.   1983.   Rejoinder. *Child Care Quarterly* 12(2): 119–120.

Bennis, W.G., Benn, K.D., and Chin, R.   1969.   *The Planning of Change.* New York: Holt, Rinehart and Winston.

Bensman, J., and Lilienfeld, R.   1973.   *Craft and Consciousness.* New York: John Wiley.

Bettelheim, B.   1950.   *Love Is Not Enough.* New York: Free Press.

Bettelheim, B.   1955.   *Truants from Life.* New York: Free Press.

Bloom, M.   1975.   *The Paradox of Helping.* New York: John Wiley.

Brill, N.I.   1976.   *Teamwork: Working Together in the Human Services.* Philadelphia, PA: Lippincott.

Caplan, N.   1975.   *The Use of Social Knowledge in Policy Decision at the National Level.* Ann Arbor, MI: Institute for Social Research, University of Michigan.

Cressey, D.R.   1953.   *Other People's Money: A Study in the Social Psychology of Embezzlement.* Glencoe, IL: Free Press.

Eisikovits, Z., and Beker, J. 1983. Beyond professionalism: The child and youth care worker as craftsman. *Child Care Quarterly* 12(2): 93–120.

Eisikovits, Z., Chambon, A., Beker, J., and Shulman, M. 1986. Toward a conceptual schema to assess and foster professionalization in child and youth care work. *Child Care Quarterly* 15: 124–137.

Erikson, E.H. 1950. *Childhood and Society*. New York: Norton.

Etzioni, A. 1975. *A Comparative Analysis of Complex Organizations*. New York: Free Press.

Feibleman, J.K. 1976. *Adaptive Knowing: Epistemology from a Realistic Standpoint*. The Hague, Netherlands: Martinus Nijhoff.

Feldman, R.A. 1980. Development, dissemination, and utilization of youth research. In Fanshel, D. (ed.), *Future of Social Work Research*. Washington, DC: National Association of Social Workers.

Flanagan, J. 1954. The critical incident technique. *Psychological Bulletin* 51: 327–358.

Foucault, M. 1972. *The Archaeology of Knowledge*. New York: Pantheon Books.

Fulcher, L.C. 1981. Team functioning in group care. In Ainsworth, F., and Fulcher, L.C. (eds.), *Group Care for Children: Concept and Issues*. London, England: Tavistock.

Garner, H. 1977. A trip through bedlam and beyond. *Child Care Quarterly* 6: 167–179.

Garner, H. 1980. Administrative behaviors and effective team functioning. *Residential Group Care* 2(5).

Garner, H. 1982. *Teamwork in Programs for Children and Youth*. Springfield, IL: Charles C. Thomas.

Glaser, B.G., and Straus, A.L. 1967. *The Discovery of Grounded Theory*. Chicago, IL: Aldine.

Goffman, E. 1974. *Frame Analysis: An Essay on the Organization of Experience*. Cambridge, MA: Harvard University Press.

Goodrich, D.W., and Boomer, D.S. 1958. Some concepts about therapeutic intervention with hyperaggressive children, I and II. *Social Casework* 39: 207–213, 286–292.

Guba, E.G. 1968. Development, diffusion, and evaluation. In Eidell, T.L., and Kitchel, J.M. (eds.), *Knowledge Production and Utilization in Educational Administration*. Eugene, OR: Center for the Advanced Study of Educational Administration, University of Oregon.

Hage, J. 1965. An axiomatic theory of organizations. *Administrative Science Quarterly* 10: 289–320.

Hall, H.R. 1977. *Organizations: Structure and Process*. Englewood Cliffs, NJ: Prentice-Hall.

Hasenfeld, Y., and English, R.A. 1974. *Human Service Organizations*. Ann Arbor, MI: University of Michigan Press.

Havelock, R.G. 1971. *Planning for Innovation Through Dissemination and Utilization of Knowledge*. Ann Arbor, MI: Center for Research on Utilization of Scientific Knowledge, University of Michigan.

Havelock, R.G., and Havelock, M.C. 1973. *Training for Change Agents: A Guide to the Design of Training Programs in Education and Other Fields*. Ann Arbor, MI: Center for Research on Utilization of Scientific Knowledge, University of Michigan.

Heidigger, M. 1962. *Being and Time*. Translated by J. Macquarrie and E.S. Robinson. New York: Harper and Row.

Hobbs, N. 1974. Helping disturbed children: Psychological and ecological strategies. In Wolins, M. (ed.), *Successful Group Care: Explorations in the Powerful Environment*. Chicago, IL: Aldine.

Hume, D. 1928. *A Treatise of Human Nature*. London, England: J.M. Dent and Sons.

Kaplan, A. 1964. *The Conduct of Inquiry*. San Francisco, CA: Chandler.

Kilmann, R.H. 1981. Organization design for knowledge utilization. *Knowledge* 3(2): 211–231.

Kohlberg, L. 1969. Stage and sequence: The cognitive developmental approach to socialization. In Goslin, D. (ed.), *Handbook of Socialization Theory and Research*. Chicago, IL: Rand McNally.

LaPiere, R.T. 1965. *Social Change*. New York: McGraw-Hill.

Larsen, J.K. 1980. Knowledge utilization—What is it? *Knowledge* 1(3): 421–442.

Lazarus, A.A. 1976. *Multimodal Behavior Therapy*. New York: Springer.

Lewis, W.W. 1971. Project Re-ED: The program and a preliminary evaluation. In Rickard, H.C. (ed.), *Behavioral Intervention in Human Problems*. New York: Pergamon Press: pp 79–100.

Lindblom, C.E., and Cohen, D.K. 1979. *Usable Knowledge: Social Science and Social Problem Solving*. New Haven, CT: Yale University Press.

Linton, T.E. 1971. The educateur model: A theoretical monograph. *Journal of Special Education* 5(2): 155–190.

Linton, T.E. (ed.). 1973. The educateur: A European model for the care of problem children. *International Journal of Mental Health* 2(1): 1–88 (Special issue).

Locke, J. 1964. *An Essay Concerning Human Understanding*. London, England: J.M. Dent and Sons.

Maier, H.W. 1978. *Three Theories of Child Development*. New York: Harper & Row.

Piaget, J., and Inhelder, B. 1958. *The Growth of Logical Thinking*. New York: Basic Books.

Polanyi, M. 1967. *The Tacit Dimension*. New York: Doubleday.

Redl, F. 1966. *When We Deal with Children*. New York: Free Press.

Redl, F., and Wineman, D. 1957. *The Aggressive Child*. New York: Free Press.

Rich, R.F. 1981. *The Knowledge Cycle*. Beverley Hills, CA: Sage.

Ritzer, G. 1972. *Man and His Work: Conflict and Change*. New York: Meredith Corporation.

Rubin, E.D. 1958. Figure and ground. In Beardslee, D.C., and Wertheimer, M. (eds.), *Readings in Perception*. New York: D. Van Nostrand.

Schein, E.H. 1971. The individual, the organization and the career: A conceptual scheme. *The Journal of Applied Behavioral Science* 7(4): 401–425.

Schlick, M. 1974. *General Theory of Knowledge*. Translated by A.E. Blumberg. New York: Springer Verlag.

Schlick, M. 1979. *Philosophical Papers* (Vol. 1). Translated by P. Heath. Dordrecht, Netherlands: Reidel.

Schutz, A. 1967. *Collected Papers* (Vols. 1, 2). The Hague, Netherlands: Martinus Nijhoff.

Schutz, A., and Luckmann, T. 1973. *The Structures of Life World*. Translated by R.M. Zaner and H.T. Engelhardt. Evanston, IL: Northwestern University Press.

Thomas, E.J. 1964. Selecting knowledge from behavioral science. In *Building Social Work Knowledge—Report of a Conference*. New York: National Association of Social Workers.

Thomas, E.J.   1980.   Beyond knowledge utilization in generating human service technology. In
    Fanshel, D. (ed.), *Future of Social Work Research.* Washington, DC: National Association of
    Social Workers.

Tripodi, T., and Epstein, I.   1978.   Incorporating knowledge of research methodology into social
    work practice. *Journal of Social Service Research* 2(1): 65–78.

Vander Ven, K.D.   1979.   Towards maximum effectiveness of the unit team approach in residential
    care. *Residential and Community Child Care Administration* 1: 287–298.

Wallace, W.   1971.   *The Logic of Science in Sociology.* Chicago, IL: Aldine and Atherton.

Weiss, C.H.   1977.   *Using Social Research for Public Policy Making.* Lexington, MA: Heath and Co.

Yin, R.K.   1976.   *R & D Utilization by Local Services: Problems and Proposals for Further Research.* Santa
    Monica, CA: Rand Corporation.

Zaltman, G.   1977.   A discussion of the research utilization process. In Zaltman, G., and Duncan,
    R. (eds.), *Strategies for Planned Change.* New York: John Wiley and Sons.

Zaltman, G., Duncan, R., and Holbek, J.   1973.   *Innovations and Organizations.* New York: John
    Wiley and Sons.

2

Developmental Foundations of Child

and Youth Care Work

HENRY W. MAIER[1]

In what way can group care, that is, nonfamilial living, assure children a development progress similar to that of children growing up within regular family care settings? The following conversation illustrates the kind of issues to be encountered wherever young people spend their daily lives.

On returning home from school, the author's nine-year-old son, Peter, was overheard questioning his mother:

> Mom, how come you don't go to work like other mothers? . . . I was just wondering. I guess it's okay that you don't work. But why did I have to come home to change my clothes? I like it when you make me my crackers and jelly. How do other kids get their snacks?

What Peter is really wondering is how children receive care in the absence of their central caregivers. That issue is reviewed throughout this chapter: How children and adolescents have their primary developmental care requirements fulfilled when care has to take place temporarily or for extended periods away from familial settings.

Peter's questions allude to four important aspects of caregiving. First, the judgment about who is a proper caregiver is *culturally* determined. One likes to live one's life in a way that is similar to others in one's own sociocultural group (Mom, why are you at home when other parents are not?). Second, care as a *personalized* experience is a basic human desire. (Peter likes personally prepared crackers and jelly.) Third, personal care emerges from *give-and-take interaction*. (Peter's response to his mother's giving enlivens her giving; he also assures his mother that she is okay even if she is not at work like other mothers.) And fourth, *a questioning of the care received* is part of the process of accepting that care (Why do I still have to come home and change after school?).

Peter's first question: "Mom, how come you don't go to work like other mothers?" articulates his concern that his life is different from that of other children. The notion is central to this chapter. A nine-year-old "is able to conceptualize the quality of his or her rearing and is sensitive to the differences in the environment between self and other children" [Kagan 1974]. Children are apt to evaluate differences as negative and may conclude that something is wrong. As Kagan states:

> Thus, the child's conclusion that he or she is not valued by adults depends in part whether the form of rearing is different from that of the majority. If the vast majority of children in a society were raised by surrogates . . . . there would be no reason to worry about the consequences of that practice, for the culture would accommodate to whatever special traits were associated with universal rearing.

We shall deal with those developmental issues to find ways to assure keen sensitivity to differences and to explore ways to assure full developmental life experiences for children and youths in nonfamilial living.

The reader is first introduced to a major developmental premise about the interdependence of human beings and their needs for basic attachments. Care workers are then defined as the most likely attachment objects in group care in light of contemporary research findings on attachment formation and human development, which is followed by examination of the developmental perspective, a singularly emerging perspective in psychology, social work, and child care [Maier 1987b]. The direct implications of this knowledge for the practice of group care [Maier 1987c] are explicated in this chapter, with the latter sections of it leading the reader into "steps" of practice, based on interpretation of the developmental stance. This orientation has much direct applicability to beginnings such as placement, starting counseling or group sessions, and the fostering of attachment formations. Separate segments on grouping residents developmentally, dealing with questions of consistency, and appropriate program activities for children and adolescents are detailed at the end of the chapter. Throughout, current knowledge is cited as the basis for guidelines and interventive techniques for direct care workers in conceptualizing and implementing effective practice.

Development and Care

Children and youths, whether in their own homes, day care, or around-the-clock group care settings, have the same basic life requirements for personal care, social and intellectual stimulation, leeway for creativity, and, above all, a sense of rootedness. Thus, the application of knowledge about human development as it applies to the major caregiving activities with a child or youth is particularly pertinent. Consequently, the focus in what follows is not on existing practice in group care [e.g., Arieli et al. 1983; Whittaker 1979]; instead it is on what could be accomplished in group care on the basis of contemporary knowledge of human development.

Nurturing care experiences are essential for the healthy development of all children [Ainsworth 1972; Bronfenbrenner 1979], but these experiences are even more urgently needed by children and youths lacking secure and permanent roots. Being placed in day or residential care, or even going away to school or camp, may weaken a child's previous linkages and cause a search for new attachments. We are reminded of instances where, in the absence of a valid caregiver, individuals create substitutes. For example, children in concentration camps became caregivers for one another when alternatives were absent [Freud and Dann 1951]. Rhesus monkeys attached themselves to wire mesh "mothers" in the absence of their mothers [Harlow and Mears 1977]. It is in providing such nurturing care that care workers, frequently perceived as generalists, are actually (or should be) specialists [Barnes and Kelman 1977]. They are the "social engineers" for nurturing care experiences. Other services, such as education, recreation, counseling, and health care, are supplements to this kind of fundamental caring.

Interpersonal Dependence as a Major Life Spring

Interpersonal dependence is a continuing force in human existence. Throughout our lives we depend on one or several central persons—a parent or an alternate caregiver, a partner, or friends—for intimate, mutual care experiences. Dependence on personal nurturance is as essential as our dependence upon food and shelter. Thus, we do not develop from a state of dependence to one of independence; development is a continuous process, and movement occurs from one level of dependence to another [Maier 1987a]. Certain caring persons—for example, parent, elder, or significant friend—remain an ongoing part of our lives whether or not they are in close proximity.

In nonfamilial living situations, child-care workers provide the main source and substance of care experience and are the pivotal people in the residents' daily lives [Pecora and Gingerich 1981]. They are the people most accessible and instrumental in providing care; they are Peter's care persons with "jelly on crackers." The child-care worker, as the target of the residents' demands, is taken for granted, criticized, and cherished all at the same time. For the child, the care worker provides the essential experience of being cared for, of learning how to respond and to interact, and, finally, of developing the capacity for extending caring to others.

The Direct Care Worker as the Pivot of a Caring System

In nonfamilial settings, many persons share in children's lives and progress; however, only the designated primary caregivers, the direct care workers, carry the full obligation for and personal involvement in providing "caring care." These institutionalized caregivers, like the parents or foster parents in a home setting, are the nurturers who provide life's necessities, sustained presence, and intimate care. This nurturance has considerable significance in that the caregivers are the immediate representatives of societal norms and are a child's personal backup in the residential living unit or family and in the world outside. In part, this relationship is so central because "individuals do not learn their coping behaviors or their mores, social drives, or values from the larger society. Children learn a particular culture and a particular moral system only from those people with whom they have close contact and who exhibit that culture in frequent relationship with them" [Washington 1982].

Thus the core care person comprises three basic structural components: the central person for caring and attachment formation, the major norm conductor for primary group life, and the legitimate representative of the norms of the larger context, including those of the immediate setting. Consequently, the care worker is always occupied in building a relationship, setting norms, and maintaining a linkage with society.

While focusing on the role of caregivers, one must emphasize the experience as such, because care has not only to be delivered but to be received; it is not enough simply to deliver the elements of caring without the message of being cared for. Hearing such messages, or experiencing the care offered to them, is particularly difficult for many of the youngsters in group care. They may want it and reject it at the same time, and this push-pull is what makes direct care work so complex.

In addition, care workers are constantly faced with a particular challenge—to provide children or youths with the experience of being cared for in the course of the daily activities—in the face of limited time, energy, and skills. Something as routine as requesting a child to put on fresh socks can be expressed as an act of caring; inquiring about a day in school can be experienced as genuine interest rather than as intrusion. Perseverance in the face of repeated rebuffs, and tolerance of one's own less than perfect approaches in expressing concern (with the hope that the message is picked up), lie at the heart of child-care work and constitute one of the human service discipline's most difficult challenges.

That the caring activities of residential workers have not received the degree of scrutiny and support they deserve is not surprising, for such fundamental personal involvement tends to impede organizational requirements [Maier 1985; Parsons 1964; Resnick 1980]. For instance, allowances made for a child's tardiness in being ready for school because the child is temporarily overwhelmed raise concern about the orderliness, uniformity, and managerial efficiency of the institution. Actually, care and control are interconnected and cannot be divided into separate functions [Harris 1980]. Therefore, the child's tardiness may be viewed as an essential personal variation that will lead eventually to a greater measure of punctuality for this child, but which may also create apparent disorder in the observable scheme of group management, as schedules are disrupted and other residents seek similar exceptions for themselves or attack the beneficiary of this exception. Such conflicting strains need to be understood as a natural part of residential child and youth care work [Maier 1985], in which constant attention must be given to ways of establishing and maintaining a balance between the requirements of nurturing care and what is needed to keep the system functioning. Experience suggests that, in the absence of such attention, system-maintenance priorities tend to become dominant.

A Developmental Perspective

Child and youth care workers will do well to anchor their work in developmental psychology [Beker and Maier 1981; Bronfenbrenner 1979; Vander Ven et al. 1982]. To emphasize a developmental approach represents a break from previous attempts by child-care workers to adopt behavioral, psychodynamic, or experiential theoretical stances of other professions. It means taking the lead in an emerging trend that moves away from personality and behavioral formulations toward a developmental perspective [Maier 1987b; Whittaker 1979].

This body of knowledge establishes a discernable progression of development [Maier 1978; Jones et al. 1985; Smart and Smart 1977]. The actual timing and rate of steps of developmental progress vary from child to child as the nature of life experiences differs from one sociocultural context to another. Nevertheless, developmental knowledge can serve as a guiding foundation in the pursuit of effective child-care work. From this perspective, a child with unusual (that is, untimely) behavior is viewed in terms of how this behavior fits into his or her developmental progression rather than as "deviant" [Bronfenbrenner 1979; Kagan 1978; Segal and Yahraes 1978]. The emphasis on "ordinary" development is important, for it demands from us an astute appraisal of the child's behavior, or how this person manages particular life situations. The worker thus gains an understanding of the individual's pattern of coping—an invaluable basis for discerning what the next developmental task should be. Caring work means helping to meet an individual's developmental requirements rather than a focus on working to undo or to correct unwanted behaviors.

For example, big, boisterous Steven, 13, demands continuous adult approval as if he were a mere four-year-old; he goes to pieces when he feels slighted. A developmental point of view looks at what Steven *is* doing rather than what he is not doing (i.e., not acting like a 13-year-old or not "fitting in"). His demands for continuous adult approval and his temper tantrums when things don't go his way are not "deviant" behaviors as much as efforts to reach out to adults and to get continuous assurance that he is succeeding in his efforts. When Steven is confident of his ability to make contact with adults, when he has "practiced" doing it and succeeded over and over again, this aspect of his development will be part of him and he will be off and running with another developmental task. "Promotion of competence and normal growth and development" as a treatment objective is discussed by Denholm et al. [1983], who state that this goal "can provide a consensus necessary for a collaborative effort of staff, the child in care, and parents, which [otherwise] often creates an adversary relationship between parent and child, and brings out decisive differences in staff."

Working from a developmental perspective demands not only that a practitioner have a background knowledge of human development, but also that he or she be able to observe and verify what residents are doing and to ascertain their ongoing competencies—how each is actually managing his or her life. Such attention to what a child or youth is doing might sound self-evident. Yet in everyday accounts of children's behavior, it is a common practice to report what youngsters are *not* doing. For example: "She doesn't pay attention to what I tell her!" The latter reveals only the caregiver's expectation, but not the child's way of handling her situation. In this illustration, the child kept on doing what she was absorbed in, and this behavior may provide a clue to the situation. It may be necessary for the worker to gain the child's momentary attention before dealing with a secondary message. Moreover, to ascertain fully a child's progression in managing life events, the concern should be with the "how" rather than the "why." An explanation, whether real or assumed, may satisfy a worker's puzzlement, but it will rarely mobilize a sense of what action to take next. The "how" will open a path for the next steps of interaction; the "why" leads to an interpretation, possibly empathic understanding, and an explanation for action, but little specificity regarding what should actually be done.

Developmental Work: Building on Small Increments of Change

Development occurs by small steps through the minutiae of ordinary human interactions, and within the context of events [Elkind and Weiner 1978]. An understanding of development in this way can mobilize residential care personnel to utilize activities that—however insignificant they may appear—have powerful potential for change. Such interactions as the wink of an eye, a clear and honest expression of disagreement, or a hand on the shoulder can represent most significant work with a child. It is important to keep in mind that concrete care involves flexibility, adapting personal care and management to the situation at hand. Consequently, care work interactions should be situational rather than behaviorally specific. A momentary backrub, for example, may at one time create instantaneous closeness, but at another time result in an explosive, "Bug off!" The reaction will depend upon the situational timing.

In many ways, the care worker is like a street worker[2] with a roof overhead. The worker is *there*. Workers are present not only for order or personal emergencies; they are there as agents of growth and change. They enter situations directly, as requested by the youngsters or as the workers deem advisable, just as street workers do. While life proceeds smoothly, resident workers may join the children's or youths' activities to share in their lives, their fun, and their joint opportunities to widen their experience. At rough spots, in anticipation of difficulties or in an actual crisis, workers also become directly involved in order to assist the youngsters in "reaching the shores safely through troubled waters." Most important is the fact that residential group care workers, like street workers, must be where the youngsters are and do their work where the action is.

The understanding of human development and its progression by minute but discernible steps has important implications for intervention (treatment) planning. The work emphasis is on operational steps (process work) for fostering change rather than outcome objectives or treatment goals per se. The focus is on what to do right now, in the next minute or hour, rather than what is to be accomplished eventually. The latter is an important consideration for overall planning, of course, but it falls short of operationalizing the actual task. For example, the important intervention for a distressed 13-year-old is what she and the worker can do immediately to ease her situation, such as discussing her worries and working together to identify and initiate a first step that will begin a change in her problematic situation. The long-range goal of assisting her to become a "more spontaneous" teenager, while not negated, is in the background at this time.

First- and Second-Order Change

Child and youth care practitioners may find it useful to clarify for themselves whether they deal with developmental change of first- or second-order [Maier 1986; Watzlawick et al. 1974]. An analogy would be water becoming warmer or colder: a first-order change. (Water turning into ice or steam constitutes a second-order change.) First-order change is incremental, a linear progression to do more or less, better, faster, or with greater accuracy. Practice, reinforcement, and time will be the most likely approaches for facilitating sound developmental change of this kind. Activities are tangible, usually verbal, involvements between the caregiver and the young person involved.

Second-order change, however, involves a nonlinear progression, a transformation from one state to another. The aim would be to enable the individual to behave, think, or feel differently. Within the second-order change approach, applicable practice tools might be modeling, confrontation, conflict work, reframing, and, most important, the introduction of decisively different personal experience over time. Second-order change requires greater creativity and prolonged investment of time and contact by caregiver and receiver [Maier 1986]. A crucial task of care workers is to be clear as to which order of change they are striving to create. Typically, residential care and treatment work calls for second-order change, since it demands substantial intervention and leads to transformational new learning.

Specific Enhancement of Change

Strategies for change are most effective when they are matched with the child's level of operation. The objective is to enhance the child's development along its ordinary path. For instance, fear of being overlooked or left out tells us about a child's current operating level. Caregivers need to understand that a child will be able to wait longer when he or she has a broader notion of time. One potentially effective change strategy in assisting a child to move developmentally forward is for the caregiver to act *as if* the caregiver expects a desirable event or behavior to take place [Vygotsky 1978]; that is, to respond to a child *as if* the child were moving intentionally toward a desired goal. Thus, in working with a teenager who has difficulty speaking up to authority figures, the caregiver might suggest spontaneously, "Let me know what your teacher arranges with you when you ask her to be excused from school to check out your job possibility." This method is a time-honored approach that has been employed by parents and other caring adults; it can serve the same purpose in child-care work.

Nonlinear Approach to Child-Care Work

In applying a developmental perspective, it is essential to think of human development as nonlinear. Practice experience has made us aware of many ups and downs in a child's life, as growth and progress proceed over a zigzag course. Basic to residential care are the variations in the course of the day when children require greater latitude in time or space or contact. Starting the day, waiting for meals, mail time, and going to sleep are all important moments for children and require extra staff involvement and time [Trieschman et al. 1969]. At these moments, children may function on a more fundamental level. These fluctuations and variations in self-management are a natural part of the cycle of growth and not a breakdown in self-control, and child-care staff members sometimes need to create interventions that are in tune with the children's earlier basic levels of functioning.

With so much emphasis placed on growth and improvement in many child-care settings, it is particularly important to remember that ordinary development proceeds in nonlinear patterns. There are periods in everyone's life when old issues reemerge. In infancy, during preschool development, and in early adolescence, building relationships and reaching out to a larger world are the main focus. At each stage, the theme is similar—risking, exploring, bonding. Similarly, children's sense of order and their attitude toward details vary cyclically. All of these factors have direct implications for how we relate to them—for instance, how we implement demands for the maintenance of their belongings. Before intervening, it is important that we assess whether we are dealing with fundamental issues or merely temporary phases.

As another example of nonlinear variation, recent research findings strongly suggest that there is a "vulnerable age phenomenon" for youngsters in geographical transition [Inbar 1976]. Children around the age periods of five to seven and 13 to 15 whose primary living arrangements had been relocated and who also had had to adapt to a culturally different secondary setting (e.g., a different school) were less successful in their educational and vocational pursuits than those who either relocated at a different age or did not relocate at all.[3] These tentative findings remind us to explore sensitively the children's experiences of transitions when they must move into culturally different systems through being placed in residential programs at these ages of apparent high vulnerability.

Thus, the recognition of a nonlinear, cyclical pattern of human development is more than an intellectual exercise. It is a very practical stance. Each event in the constellation of behavior needs to be viewed *contextually* for what it means in terms of each individual's progression. As frustrating as it may be for the worker, a messy room is not just a messy room! In Michael Cole's [1979] words: "It all depends!"

"Beginnings" in Residential Work

Beginnings particularly reflect the cyclical nature of development. In the beginning of life, infancy, in the formation of new interpersonal relationships, in the management of new situations, and in moments of crisis, we find that a predictable progression is reenacted. This understanding of beginnings can serve as a profound resource in our approach to beginnings in children's placement.

Beginnings in early life as well as later are essentially *body* experiences. Thus, it is important to provide a newcomer with a welcome that has physical as well as verbal components. This task involves assisting the newcomer with the physical process of settling in by encouraging relaxation and providing opportunities for establishing private space.[4] Guarantee of, and active support for, private space, providing "ownership" of a bed, personal box, or corner—all these are fundamental to new beginnings [Bakker and Bakker-Rabdau 1973; Maier 1981].

Next, "action space" takes on importance. Newcomers want to *do* things and to show what they can do rather than to be pressed to do what they cannot do. Simultaneously, they become concerned over who is going to be with them, who will be taking care of them. Once assured that there is an array of caregivers, they become concerned with what these workers do. Awareness of this progression may help care workers to increase their effectiveness. Although we all have a natural eagerness to explain our roles to a newcomer, we need to save this account for the time when a new person can really hear it. Again, the worker's spontaneity and timing are crucial.

Transitional Objects

At moments of dislocation and relocation, transitional objects serve as linkages between old and new and assist in making the unfamiliar familiar [Winnicott 1965], as they do in early childhood. Before admission, young people should be encouraged to bring along transitional objects—a blanket, a teddy bear, an old sweater, an old hat, or other cherished and seasoned object. (Linus with his blanket comes instantly to mind!) Child and youth care workers can themselves be transitional objects, as it were, when they help with a child's moves from one life situation to another, eventually from residential placement to the outside community [Maier 1981].

Transformational Objects

Like transitional objects, transformational objects are reminders of a previous time but have the added significance of being reminders of earlier "monumental" achievement and growth. Such symbols or "trophies" might be a driver's license, a ticket from a dance, a team or club (or gang) jacket, a poster from a rock concert, a funky T-shirt, or other memorabilia from home. Transformational objects are based entirely upon a youngster's choice. Most likely, they are more treasured than anyone without analogous needs and experiences can possibly imagine.

The Dependence Cycle

As previously discussed, all children and youths require secure dependence upon reliable adults in order to develop into dependable adults themselves. Research findings in the past decade clearly establish that a dependent and nurturing attachment leads to greater readiness to branch out and proceed on one's own [Sroufe 1978]. In fact, children whose highly responsive parents have "pampered" their dependency are the ones who are least fretful. These children ultimately achieve secure independence in the same behaviors where they earlier had clamored for support [Ainsworth et al. 1974; Brunner 1970]. Interestingly, dependence begets independence. In child-care work, dependence, support, and nurturance are fundamental ingredients of care.

To permit such knowledge to be applied, group care programs must be structured so that staff members have as one of their central and continuing tasks to provide not only immediate support but nurturance of the dependency of those in their care [Maier 1981]. We need to be mindful that, at the beginning of new experiences or at points of crisis, a child's dependence upon physical support and nurturance is primary. To be able to depend on dependence feels good and helps to promote development. Effective care work necessitates a program that provides countless opportunities and resources for rendering concrete caregiving.

Once a person feels assured that dependency needs will be met, self-mastery ("me-do-it") becomes alive as a developmental issue. In residential care situations, this frequently occurs after the individual has seemingly "fit in so well." Youngsters will suddenly rebel, such as by rejecting well-meant suggestions that had earlier been accepted. They act not unlike the two-year-old who insists on self-feeding. As in the case of the two-year-old, this rebellion is an indication of a growth spurt rather than a slight to the institution. It does provide a delicate challenge in group care settings, however—how to support self-mastery while maintaining a sense of values and order. For example, the balance may entail supporting a child's determination to dress as he or she chooses, while making clear the expected dress code on the unit. Again, as this new phase is supported, the struggle over self-mastery becomes less of an issue (e.g., a youngster will no longer view staff involvement as a personal affront but as potential assistance).

Getting support when trying something new and reaching beyond previous mastery into new areas of experience are, for many residents, basic and ongoing developmental issues. In residential programming this means that a range of activities in play and work, variations in routines, contacts with peers and adults, and events within and outside the institution need to be arranged and supported. It is hoped that the worker can understand and evaluate the *trying* rather than expecting success with each new venture. Eventually the trying will become doing, and doing will become succeeding. It is the process along the way that needs support [Maier 1982].

Attachment Development and Attachment Behavior

Attachment is as basic a life requirement as the more traditionally cited food, shelter, and clothing. Attachment involves a state of mutual dependence felt by individuals, experienced but not necessarily manifested behaviorally; attachment provides a sense of rootedness. Genuine attachment experiences are vital for sound development; in fact, for mental health and life anywhere [Brazelton 1981; Bronfenbrenner 1979; Rutter 1979].

Attachment behaviors, as contrasted to feelings of attachment, are really frantic efforts to obtain close attachment. They are at times appropriate, and other times awkward or even unpleasant; nevertheless, they are neither deviant nor totally undesirable because, in essence, they reflect urgent relationship-enhancement efforts. They represent an investment of energy to build or rebuild processes of attachment when a person experiences these to be absent or in a state of flux. Attachment behaviors may be seen in such proximity-seeking or attention-getting acts as clinging or running away, asking self-evident questions, or demonstrably ignoring a person. Attachment development proceeds in a cyclical (nonlinear) way. After an apparent linear progression, when attachment between individuals seems to be in the process of forming, the attachment experience is particularly vulnerable to any variation in the relationship [Maccoby and Masters 1970].

At such points, attachment behaviors are not only more pronounced, but also strong indicators of fear that the attachment will be interrupted. For child care, this means that the relationship between the worker and the child or youth becomes even more sensitive and important *after* the young person has been with the worker for some time and at a point when things seem to be "going well between them" [Rodriguez and Hignett 1981]. It is at this point that a youngster may place unusual demands on the caregiver and act as if trust is absent. Relationship formation cannot be gauged on a timetable basis nor can availability be scheduled in a linear way. Much staff time and energy needs to be available for cyclic and spontaneous "renewing."

For residential programming, these observations may require revamping institution policies and training residential workers in such a way that attachment-seeking behaviors can more easily be dealt with for what they are: a desperate striving for more human contact and closeness. Child-care work could then focus upon enriching children's attachment experiences rather than merely struggling with their attachment behaviors [Maier 1981; Rutter 1979].

Grouping Residents Developmentally

The stress upon developmental progression might appear to suggest that it is advisable to group children according to developmental readiness rather than by age. In fact, if we are thinking in a nonlinear way, programming cannot rest upon any one fixed index of a youngster's development. We know from experience, for example, that some children temporarily need to live as if they were much younger—in fact, they may demonstrate this need by preferring the company of much younger children. The progress of others in the unit would be hampered if the unit's programming were fully adapted to that younger level. We must also remain mindful of the fact that some children tend to progress more readily when their learning is modeled and supported by highly respected peers who are at a slightly more advanced level of development [Elkind and Weiner 1978].

Research findings, it is useful to point out, indicate that stronger and more capable children are apt to be able to get more attention on their own. Programming of all kinds tends to be adjusted to meet their interests and requirements, while those who are less able to influence their surroundings tend to be controlled and ignored [Rutter 1979]. We need to keep this fact in mind so that we continually reappraise and restructure activities on the unit to involve all children, regardless of their current development stages and tasks. When children's capabilities present a strong divergence between developmental and chronological age, it becomes of particular importance to reconstitute programming within a normalization perspective [Horejsi 1979; Maier 1981], as is discussed elsewhere in this volume.

Consistency and the Provision of Care

Consistency in child care is advocated in all child psychologies. Choices occur in the conception of what constitutes consistency, however, and how consistency is achieved. Do we mean consistency in values, affect, or behaviors of the caregivers? Do expectations apply to both caregivers and care receivers? Or does consistency apply, as advocated here, to the child's experience of pre- dictability based on the efficacy of his or her own actions? This latter conception shifts the emphasis from behaviors and values to the child's perceptions of be- haviors and their meanings. In other words, consistency is most useful when viewed from the child's frame of reference. Thus, consistency means a predictable environment in terms of the child's capacity to assess it. A residential setting provides a consistent environment where residents can predict the outcomes of their actions. For them, the conception of the situation as consistent depends upon a meshing or congruence in the definition of events and in expectations between the staff members and the young people involved [Division of Youth . . . 1978].[5]

Consistency Applied to Child-Care Practices

Children view their workers as consistent when, for example, bedtime is specified within the youngsters' own time framework. For young children, this may be "after snacks" or "when the big hand of the clock is at—," for example. For developmentally older, school-age children, consistent bedtime may be dic- tated by rules that have been discussed by the workers and the youngsters. For adolescents, consistency is experienced through the workers' capacity to be flexible in meeting the demands of each situation rather than through adherence to a fixed schedule. A ten-o'clock bedtime might not, for example, be perceived as consistent if applied equally on a school night, on the night before vacation, and when other contextual variables make the established bedtime a difficult factor.

If we were to study current residential care practices, adaptability to the demands of the situation seems likely to be a more common practice than consistent adherence to schedules. That is, when workers are busy, when tempers are high, or when youngsters are happily engaged in activities, established bedtimes may frequently be superseded; a similar situation applies in most spheres of life in group care and in the world outside. Irregularity of the rules might be questioned by youngsters in any of these situations. Their appreciation of their workers as predictable and dependable persons, however, will be directly related to their workers' readiness to disregard a legalistic interpretation of consistency and to follow developmental and contextual demands instead. Thus, it is suggested here that effective child and youth care work requires consistency that is in keeping with a child's developmental understanding and individual requirements rather than through steadfast, generalized rules.

Developmental Programming

Programming Developmentally for School-Age Children[6]

School-age children are at a developmental stage where they push forth simultaneously on three fronts: personal competence development; the development of close peer associations; and the development of encounters with the outside world, including business, transportation, entertainment, the arts, sports, youth movements, and, of course, education, as well as others.

Competence Development

For program planning on a developmental basis, it is important to create continual opportunities for *doing*, both individually and with others. Children at this stage require support, time, space, and equipment for developing body coordination such as running, dancing, throwing, and tumbling. They are also ready to expand their knowledge in all directions. Learning through experimentation is important at this point and should take place in such developmentally appropriate spaces as workshops, laboratories, gyms, or backstage. Less appropriate to their developmental requirements are study halls and formal settings.

Most important in care work, the children's concerns and energies tend to be vested in proving their competence to themselves and to others. They are bent on doing better than before. We may mistakenly interpret the competitiveness of this period as the child's negation of others [White 1972], but it actually represents a desire to improve and stretch oneself. Workers' sensitivity to this personal striving can help to create new avenues for planning and pursuing play, study, and work situations that are developmentally appropriate and allow children to experience their own improvement.

Close Peer Association

Also of concern to children at this period in their development is the building of peer associations so as to deepen their social worlds. Peer relationships and interests fluctuate at this point, creating a curious dilemma in group care. Residential mates (as with siblings in a family) are not necessarily the ones whom a child considers to be peers or playmates. Frequently, the familiarity and self-protection inherent in intense group living make it difficult for residential peers to become personal pals. Contacts with peers beyond the residential living group become a necessity. Daily interactions among children, whether in the group living unit or outside it—hassling; testing; building bravado skills; uniting; separating; clustering; or isolating—may be crucial to a child's development, even though the manifestation of these activities may not always be in harmony with the orderly life of a unit.

Children not only need love and care, but they also want and need to be responsible for others, to learn to love and to care [Kobak 1979; Maas 1980]. This learning appears earlier in development as well, but it is confirmed socially at this stage when the child is no longer limited to the home base. Consequently, expanding friendships away from the living group and greater generosity and helpfulness toward others outside the family are natural indicators of growing up rather than evidence of a child's lack of appreciation or loyalty for the home front. Residential workers, as well as parents, need to remind themselves that a helping hand is usually first truly exercised away from home. (Charity actually begins away from home.)

Care workers with this school-age group are challenged to pursue a dual course: to be a child's own special worker and, simultaneously, to be the children's group leader. Although this dual task may appear to be overwhelming, it can also offer a rich and potent program resource. In fact, these dual responsibilities can be well integrated within a developmental perspective, where an individual's gains and adaptations are always envisaged within a social context. In group care, a child's requirements have to be met within the context of the group; conversely, a group can progress only as the members flourish within it.

Ordering, organizing, and establishing rules that can be generalized are of great concern to children in this developmental period [Piaget 1951]. Much of their interest in setting up collections or charts of one form or another, their play, and their conversations with one another involve the dynamics of sorting, ordering, and organizing their collections, interactions, or ideas into hierarchical wholes. Their interest in such complicated games as Dungeons and Dragons and in charting the progression of favorite athletic teams and players, or of friends within friendship cliques, illustrate these trends. Thus, many of the peer inter-actions of school-age children involve elaborations of rules and procedures. They seem to need to experiment with rules, require many opportunities to try them out, and to work on interpersonal dilemmas. Thus, much of a care worker's effort may go into finding an elusive fit between predictable and extraordinary ways of doing things.

Encounters with the Outside World

Children of school age are also in transition developmentally, between managing in their primary systems (home or residential unit and primary school) and being able to find their ways within secondary systems (businesses, recreation and entertainment, transportation, secondary school, and other community systems). They are absorbed in mastering new situations and environments, in entering the world. Caregivers are challenged to become involved and to show interest in a child's secondary systems [Garbarino 1982; Garbarino and Stocking 1980].

It is also essential for school-age residents to have full, individual experiences in shopping, traveling, and in other settings beyond the residential confines. Encouraging children and actively participating with them in such branching-out endeavors should be viewed as part of the caregivers' regular work. Research suggests that a child's comfort in the use of secondary settings is severely diminished when these settings are not shared with that child's caregiver [Inbar 1976]. We should be mindful of the fact that the quality of care in residential work is enhanced, therefore, when a child experiences a worker's concerns and care in a variety of settings—at the residence, in the park, at school, downtown, and in other settings [Garbarino 1982]. It appears that the ultimate effect of such shared experiences remains with the child after he or she leaves the group care setting.

The life of the school-age child has thus far been pictured as primarily a life of activities and events. True. The worker-child relationship continues, however, to be most important. When hungry or tired, in moments of crisis or boredom, when happy or distressed, children, like Lassie on television, will consistently return to the care of "home." Even if it appears that children have little use for their caregivers when they hurriedly dash off after a meal or abruptly end a conversation, they do want and need their caregivers to be at hand. Workers must be provided with enough institutionally acknowledged time so that they can be part of children's lives in ways that extend beyond residential boundaries [Garbarino and Stocking 1980].

Programming Developmentally with Adolescents

Time, Space, and Structure for Searching and Questioning

Development can be characterized as a progression of doing more with more people, doing more with more people in more places, and doing more with more people in more places at varied times. This expanding progression certainly holds true for adolescent development. Many experienced youth workers may wisely add that, for adolescents, the "doing more" often leads to a kind of bottomless pit, as if there were no end to their requests, wishes, and, at times, their involvements in manifold activities. Actually, as continuing growth and confrontation with reality make clear, there is an end, because everyday events will never fully allow these plans and wishes to be carried out.

Programming developmentally with youths presents a strange paradox: adolescents want a life full of happenings, yet planning and preparing "is such a drag!" The worker must constantly decide whether to program (to plan for them and to be prepared) or not to program (to let things happen and allow the consequences to be a learning experience). Who should carry out the major responsibilities for activities is an additional struggle. Formal or informal deliberations at this stage often end as discussion about whether or not to talk, whether or not to plan, and whether or not certain people ought to "mind their own business!" Such behavior is developmentally on target for this group, even if the planning leads no further than a preliminary "let's think about it."

In the youngster's pre-adolescent years, similar tumultuous planning sessions centered on the establishment of rules and procedures for getting things done, but for adolescents the central issues are the discovery and exploration of alternatives. The apparent negativism, the ridiculing, and the preoccupation with what *not* to do are also adolescents' constructive efforts at developing new boundaries and directions for themselves. Caustic inquiries and sarcasm are less an evaluation of the world around them than an indication of their uneasiness about their place in it. Because they feel some discomfort in this world, a place created and delegated as their own is a basic requirement of this age group.

We note also that adolescent residents in particular need the freedom, support, and materials to create private spaces in bedrooms [Maier 1981]. Youth care workers can convey an active interest in adolescents by noticing their ways of decorating their private space. A sense of rootedness is also experienced by residents when they are involved in the management, daily procedures, outfitting, and decorating of their unit. Life beyond the residence becomes equally important in establishing a sense of rootedness. The world of adolescents also includes school, shopping, community, and special activities such as sports or popular music. A worker will often need to help teen residents to expand their experiences in these spheres.

Youth workers need time to be involved in much discussion and attentive listening to understand adolescents' thoughts and questions and to engage with them in a search for solutions. "Rapping" helps the adolescents develop and provides a major avenue for them to test and build peer relations. They consequently require ample time, space, and sanction for sporadic rapping, sometimes with and sometimes without adult involvement. Rapping, we know well, proceeds more readily when the participants are comfortable, sustained with snacks, and able to interact informally. We also need to remember that sharing a youngster's account of events in school or listening to a new record can be at least as urgent and significant as a case worker's managerial tasks or as completing reports.

The outside world can be partly brought into the unit by posters, catalogs, visitors, television viewing, and verbal accounts. Outside experiences, moreover, require continual rehearsals within the unit. Practicing dance steps, discussing potential purchases, conversations about dates, appointments with a principal or prospective employer—these are all outside experiences that may require rehearsing in the safe harbor of the unit. Rehearsals may be verbal or through some form of role playing. Much of a caregiver's energies need to be invested in rehearsing with adolescents a variety of life experiences that are apt to be encountered away from unit supervision. Thoughts, feelings, moral values, and various behaviors all need to be weighed and practiced.

In addition, caregivers need to bring some of their personal experiences to work in order to share them with adolescents. This sharing is important because adolescents need to experience an adult as a whole person. It also brings added experience repertoires to the unit and provides bridges between adolescent and adult worlds and between the work outside and that of the residential unit.

Personal Relationship Encounters

A second guiding principle in programming developmentally with adolescents is to provide an arena for helping them with primary relationship skills [Maier 1965]. Group life serves as a rich laboratory for helping adolescents establish effective relationships, deal with conflict, and survive disagreeable interpersonal situations. A conflict over who sits where, or the realization that several group members cannot stand each other, may cause institutional tension, but such situations can serve as opportunities for learning how to deal with such problems in the future. Good programming means spontaneously exploiting the developmental features of ongoing group life situations. Spontaneity in care is "one of the most 'therapeutic' characteristics of residential 'care' " [Carlebach 1983].

To be able to accomplish tasks through their own labor and to be able to see visibly their contributions to others are important life experiences for adolescents. Tasks within the residential unit can provide such opportunities, as long as they are special tasks, tailored to the youth's own level of readiness, rather than routine daily chores. Attending to a long-awaited repair or improvement in the unit, raising vegetables, or taking care of a pet or special unit machinery are examples of challenging work opportunities. Moreover, effective programming also requires attention to the inclusion of work opportunities outside the residence. Gardening jobs, shopping, newspaper delivery, baby-sitting, dog-walking, or other odd jobs in the neighborhood are a few possibilities. Volunteer work in the form of giving a hand to the physically disabled at a senior citizen center, or in work and play with younger children also reflects the important ingredient of giving to others. Work or volunteer service tasks are to be envisaged as developmental opportunities when young people are ready to progress in that direction rather than purely as rewards for developmental achievements. These considerations and their programmatic implications are detailed elsewhere in this volume.

Adolescents' interactions with their direct care workers, like those of younger children, involve struggles about dependency/independency and authority issues. The challenge for care workers is to present themselves in different roles and to provide youths with a variety of interpersonal encounters so that the workers relate in different ways—sometimes as pals, sometimes as partners in mutual undertakings, but most of the time as guiding, committed elders.

Growing into new relationship systems and augmenting old ones takes place not only on the unit, but in the adolescents' relationships with their families as well. These changes require more than periodic contacts by mail, phone, or occasional get-togethers.[7] Regular contacts and involvements with youths' families and other important adults and peers from home are needed so as to draw them into residents' daily lives. Residential care should be conceived as an extension rather than a replacement of the family.[8]

Family members or friends from "back home" may be asked to join in for meals, work parties, recreational activities, and serious deliberations. These involvements not only help families stay in touch, but provide opportunities for relationship patterns to change over time. Most relevant is the fact that adolescents tend to evaluate events and people through the eyes of peers. The discovery of parents as ordinary, struggling human beings (and for parents to see their children as not too different from others) can occur more easily through observation. A joint outing, a residential all-fun evening, a picnic, a painting or fix-up work party can provide growth (therapeutic) experience.

In summary, adolescent development occurs through a variety of intimate and communal experiences, through regular life encounters, and through continual exposure to new life situations. Adolescents learn a particular culture and the awareness of other cultures and basic values only from those persons with whom they have vital interactions and meaningful relationships [Washington 1982].

Closing Comments

This chapter poses a challenge for child and youth care workers, in many ways the same challenge faced by every parent, grandparent, foster parent, and baby-sitter. Children's issues are the same regardless of where they reside. For children and youths in socially engineered, nonfamilial settings, child and youth care workers provide life's essentials and more. They are the ones who are always available until children don't need them any more. Workers are keenly aware, as well as uncertain, of how important they are in the children's growing-up struggles and must always work toward the bittersweet eventuality of letting them move on, while starting anew with "fresh" arrivals [adapted from Furman 1982].

Child and youth care workers are pivotal in nonfamilial care, yet their roles as societal caregivers remain essentially unrecognized. Ultimately it will be necessary to provide for them the same societal recognition that has been accorded to other professionals involved with the complexities of human health and safety, such as air traffic controllers and surgeons. Child and youth care workers require full societal and organizational support through well-circumscribed on-duty hours and an income that can assure them a reasonable personal life. Moreover, experience suggests that child and youth care workers themselves must actively pursue these essentials, thus modeling the kind of personal and group development and interpersonal competence required to enhance the lives of the young people in their care. Only then can they fully invest their energies in serving the developmental demands of those children and youths for whom society has given them such major responsibilities.

NOTES

[1] This chapter has been previously published in Maier, Henry W. *Developmental Group Care of Children and Youth.* New York: The Haworth Press, Inc., 1987, pp. 9–33. That chapter was footnoted: "An earlier version of this article was presented at the Study Group in Residential Care, Haifa, Israel, 1982. The article here appears with permission of the study group sponsors." (Maier 1987:9)

[2] Street gang work by social group workers and other service workers has been effectively utilized in helping adolescents and youths to find more purposeful adventures [Spergel 1971]. The perspective suggested here was once defined as "marginal or life space interviews" [Long et al. 1972; Wineman 1972].

[3] Success or lack of success was evaluated longitudinally as compared with that of siblings who faced the same transitions at a different point of their development [Inbar and Adler 1977].

[4] The same factors apply in assisting individuals at moments of crisis. The requirements for bodily comfort vary considerably for children, adolescents, and adults, but, regardless of age, beginnings are fundamentally body experiences. The opposite is also true: the message that persons are *not* welcome is quickly conveyed by denying comfort to their bodies through denial of seating opportunities, crowding, and obliteration of private space. Police stations, prisons, and some of the welfare service waiting rooms in the United States are cases in point.

[5] It is noteworthy to add here the findings of a recent Oregon study where, in a secure treatment center, residents who were found to be most receptive and compliant to a consistently managed program ended up more frequently in the failure group, while those with more demanding behavior, if they found staff members who were responsive to their provocations, ended up more frequently in the success group [Benning 1981].

[6] Programming for preschool-age children and children developmentally akin to them is not discussed here because the subject is well covered in the literature on day care, nursery school work, kibbutzim, and residential treatment of severely disturbed as well as autistic children.

[7]We deliberately use the term get-togethers in place of visits at the home or parental visits at the residence (or school) because it is misleading to speak of a child's visit home or to a parent, or of a family visiting a child.

[8]A similar approach and activities also apply in work with younger children.

REFERENCES

Ainsworth, M.D.   1972.   Attachment and dependency: A comparison. In Geriwitz, J.S. (ed.), *Attachment and Dependency*. Washington, DC: Winston: pp 97–136.

Ainsworth, M.D., Bell, B.M., and Stayton, D.   1974.   Infant-mother attachment and social development: Socialization as a product of reciprocal responsiveness to signals. In Richard, M.P. (ed.), *The Integration of the Child into a Social World*. Cambridge, England: Cambridge University Press: pp 99–135.

Arieli, M., Kashti, Y., and Shlasky, S.   1983.   *Living at School: Israeli Residential Schools as People-Processing Organizations*. Tel Aviv, Israel: Ramot.

Bakker, C., and Bakker-Rabdau, M.K.   1973.   *No Trespassing: Explorations in Human Territoriality*. San Francisco, CA: Chandler and Sharp.

Barnes, F., and Kelman, S.H.   1974.   From slogan to concepts: A basis for change in child care work. *Child Care Quarterly* 3(1): 7–23.

Beker, J., and Maier, H.W.   1981.   Emerging issues in child and youth care education: A platform for planning. *Child Care Quarterly* 10(3): 200–209.

Benning, R.J.   1981.   *Secure Treatment: An Analysis and Outcome*. Salem, OR: Oregon State Publications (Unpublished report).

Brazelton, T.   1981.   *On Becoming a Family*. New York: Delacorte Press.

Bronfenbrenner, U.   1979.   *The Ecology of Human Development*. Cambridge, MA: Harvard University Press.

Brunner, J.S.   1970.   *Poverty and Childhood*. Detroit, MI: Merrill Palmer Publications.

Carlebach, J.   1983.   Foreword. In Arieli, M., Kashti, Y., and Shlasky, S., *Living at School: Israeli Residential Schools as People-Processing Organizations*. Tel Aviv, Israel: Ramot: pp 7–8.

Cole, M.   1979.   Introduction. In Bronfenbrenner, U., *The Ecology of Human Development*. Cambridge, MA: Harvard University Press: pp vii–x.

Denholm, C.J., Pence, A., and Ferguson, R.V.   1983.   *The Scope of Professional Child Care in British Columbia*. Victoria, BC: School of Child Care, University of British Columbia.

Division of Youth and Family Service of the State of New Jersey.   1978.   *The Impact of Residential Treatment*. New Brunswick, NJ: Institute for Criminological Research, Rutgers University.

Elkind, D., and Weiner, I.B.   1978.   *Development of a Child*. New York: John Wiley.

Freud, A., and Dann, S.   1951.   An experiment in group upbringing. In Eisler, R.S., and Freud, A. (eds.), *The Psychoanalytic Study of the Child* (Vol. 6). New York: International Universities Press: pp 127–168.

Furman, E.   1982.   Mothers are there to be left. In Solnit, A.J., and Eisler, R.S. (eds.), *The Psychoanalytic Study of the Child* (Vol. 37). New Haven, CT: Yale University Press: pp 15–28.

Garbarino, J. (ed.).   1982.   *Children and Families in the Social Environment*. New York: Aldine.

Garbarino, J., and Stocking, S.H.   1980.   *Protecting Children from Abuse and Neglect*. San Francisco, CA: Jossey-Bass.

Harlow, H., and Mears, C.   1977.   The power of passion of play. *New Scientist* 73(1038): 335–338.

Harris, R.J.   1980.   A changing service: The case for separating "care" and "control" in probation practice. *The British Journal of Social Work* 10(2): 163–184.

Horejsi, C.   1979.   Applications of the normalization principle in the human services: Implications for social work education. *Journal of Education for Social Work* 15(1): 44–50.

Inbar, M.   1976.   *The Vulnerable Age Phenomenon*. New York: Russell Sage Foundation.

Inbar, M., and Adler, C.   1977.   *Ethnic Integration in Israel*. New Brunswick, NJ: Transaction Books.

Jones, F.R., Garrison, K.C., and Morgan, R.F.   1985.   *The Psychology of Human Development*. New York: Harper and Row.

Kagan, J.   1974.   Family experience and the child's development. *American Psychologist* 34(10): 886–891.

Kagan, J.   1978.   *The Growth of the Child*. New York: Norton.

Kobak, D.   1979.   Teaching children to care. *Children Today* 8(2): 6–7.

Long, N., Stoeffler, V., Krause, U., and Jung, C.   1972.   Life-space management of behavioral crises. In Whittaker, J.K., and Trieschman, A.E., *Children Away From Home*. Chicago, IL: Aldine: pp 256–266.

Maas, H.S.   1980.   The child's responsibility to society. In Freeman, D.S. (ed.), *Perspectives on Family Therapy*. Vancouver, BC, Canada: Butterworth: pp 201–214.

Maccoby, E.E., and Masters, J.C.   1970.   Attachment and dependency. In Mussen, P.H. (ed.), *Carmichael's Manual of Child Psychiatry* (Vol. 2). New York: John Wiley: pp 73–157.

Maier, H.W.   1965.   The social group work method and residential treatment. In Maier, H.W. (ed.), *Group Work as Part of Residential Treatment*. New York: National Association of Social Workers: pp 26–42.

Maier, H.W.   1978.   *Three Theories of Child Development* (3rd revised edition). New York: Harper and Row.

Maier, H.W.   1981.   Essential components in care and treatment environments for children and youth. In Ainsworth, F., and Fulcher, L.C. (eds.), *Group Care for Children: Concept and Issues*. New York: Methuen: pp 19–70.

Maier, H.W.   1982.   To be attached and free: The challenge of child development. *CHILD WELFARE LXI*(2): 67–76.

Maier, H.W.   1985.   Personal care within an organizational service context. In Fulcher, L., and Ainsworth, F. (eds.), *Group Care Practice with Children*. New York: Methuen: pp 21–47.

Maier, H.W.   1986.   First- and second-order change: Powerful concepts for preparing child care practitioners. In Vander Ven, K., and Tittnich, E. (eds.), *Competent Caregivers—Competent Children*. New York: Haworth Press: pp 37–45.

Maier, H.W. 1987a. *Dependence and Independence Development Throughout the Human Life Cycle: Implications for the Helping Professions*. Seattle, WA: University of Washington (Manuscript submitted for publication).

Maier, H.W. 1987b. Human development: Psychological basis. In Minahan, A. (ed.), *Encyclopedia of Social Work* (18th edition). New York: National Association of Social Workers: pp 850–856.

Maier, H.W. 1987c. Introduction. In *Developmental Group Care for Children and Youth: Developmental Concepts for Practice*. New York: Haworth Press: pp 1–8.

Parsons, T. 1964. *The Social System*. New York: The Free Press.

Pecora, P.J., and Gingerich, W.J. 1981. Worker tasks and knowledge utilization in group care: First findings. *Child Welfare* 60(4): 221–231.

Piaget, J. 1951. *Play, Dreams and Imitation in Childhood*. London, England: Heineman.

Resnick, H. 1980. A social system view of strain. In Resnick, H., and Patti, R., *Change from Within*. Philadelphia, PA: Temple University Press: pp 28–45.

Rodriguez, D.T., and Hignett, W.F. 1981. Infant day care: How very young children adapt. *Children Today* 10(6): 2–6.

Rutter, M. 1979. Review: Maternal deprivation, 1972–1978: New findings, new concepts, new approaches. *Child Development* 50: 283–305.

Segal, J., and Yahraes, H. 1978. *A Child's Journey*. New York: McGraw-Hill.

Smart, M.S., and Smart, R.C. 1977. *Children: Development and Relationships*. New York: Macmillan.

Spergel, I.A. 1971. Street gang work. In Morris, R. (ed.), *Encyclopedia of Social Work*. New York: National Association of Social Workers: pp 1486–1494.

Sroufe, L.A. 1978. Attachment and the roots of competence. *Human Nature 1* (October): 50–57.

Trieschman, A.E., Whittaker, J.K., and Brendtro, L.K. 1969. *The Other 23 Hours*. Chicago, IL: Aldine.

Vander Ven, K., Mattingly, M.A., and Morris, M.G. 1982. Principles and guidelines for child care personnel preparation programs. *Child Care Quarterly* 11(3): 221–244.

Vygotsky, L. 1978. *Mind in Society*. Cambridge, MA: Harvard University Press.

Washington, R.D. 1982. Social development: A focus for practice and education. *Social Work* 27(1): 104–109.

Watzlawick, P., Weakland, J.W., and Rish, R. 1974. *Change*. New York: Norton.

White, R.W. 1972. *The Enterprise of Living: Growing and Organization of Personality*. New York: Holt, Rinehart and Winston.

Whittaker, J.K. 1979. *Caring for Troubled Children*. San Francisco, CA: Jossey-Bass.

Wineman, D. 1972. The life-space interview. In Whittaker, J.K., and Trieschman, A.E., *Children Away from Home*. Chicago, IL: Aldine: pp 236–255.

Winnicott, D.W. 1965. *The Family and Individual Development*. London, England: Tavistock.

3

Interpersonal and Group Life

in Residential Care:

A Competence-Centered, Ecological Perspective

ANTHONY N. MALUCCIO

Everyday life in a residential care setting is marked by a myriad of events or experiences as young people and the members of the staff go about living together. Some of these are dramatic or attention-getting events, but most are routine or ordinary occurrences. Some typical examples might include the following:

> A recently arrived youth runs away.
>
> A nine-year-old boy cries uncontrollably as he realizes that his father has again failed to visit him.
>
> Two youths are fighting as everyone else is trying to get ready to go to school.
>
> A 12-year-old boy has just learned that he is failing in school.

A ten-year-old girl refuses to participate in her group's activities.

Mass confusion reigns at the dinner table.

A 14-year-old girl, about to go for a visit with her family, is acting up in her cottage.

An angry adolescent is destructively dominating a group of boys intent on completing a difficult climb.

As staff members who provide a major portion of round-the-clock care, supervision, and resources for children and youths in group care [Maier 1977], direct care workers usually find themselves in the midst of these and countless similar incidents. How do they react? How should they react? How can they use these experiences to promote each child's or youth's best interests? Such questions constantly confront child and youth care workers. Their greatest challenge is to use life events—the ordinary as well as the dramatic ones—as extraordinary opportunities to enhance the growth and development of young people in their care.

This task is a crucial challenge since, by virtue of their close involvement, direct care workers play a powerful role in the lives of children and youths who are placed in residential settings. The thesis of this chapter is that the positive influence of this role can be maximized if, in their relationships with individuals and groups, child-care workers use a *competence-centered, ecological perspective*, regarding the promotion of competence in children and youths as one of their most important functions. The essence of this perspective is that, rather than being preoccupied with pathology, workers recognize each person's natural strivings toward growth and promote effective functioning by focusing on his or her unique coping and adaptive patterns, mobilizing his or her actual and potential strengths, removing obstacles, and providing supports in the person's environment [Maluccio 1981a, 1981b, 1983].

Following an overview of the concept of competence and its philosophical and theoretical foundations, this chapter explores the significance of a competence orientation for child-care practice. The focus is on how direct care workers can develop and utilize competence-oriented relationships with children and youths, both individually and on a group basis.

Competence: An Overview

Competence is generally defined as the network of skills, knowledge, and talents that enable a person to interact effectively with the environment [White 1963]. As outlined below, theorists and researchers from various disciplines have contributed much to its study.[1]

[1]This section is adapted from Maluccio [1981a].

On the basis of evidence from research on animal and early childhood behavior that cannot be adequately explained by traditional motivational theories rooted in instinctual drives and tension reduction, White [1963] postulates that an autonomous drive toward competence motivates the human being to keep trying out the effectiveness of his or her ripening capacities for action. Gladwin [1967] emphasizes the role of social processes and interactions in personality development. He believes that competence develops along three principal and interrelated axes: *(1)* "the ability to learn or to use a variety of alternative pathways or behavioral responses in order to reach a given goal"; *(2)* the ability to comprehend a variety of social systems within society and in particular to use the resources that they offer; and *(3)* effective reality testing, involving not only "lack of psychopathological impairment but also a positive broad and sophisticated understanding of the world."

Smith [1968] points out that competence involves intrinsic as well as extrinsic motivation, social skills as well as personal abilities, and effective performance for self as well as society in one's social roles. He indicates that competent functioning is affected by key factors in the personal system of the organism as well as by strategic components in the social structure. The key factors in the personal system include the sense of efficacy or potency in controlling one's destiny, the attitude of hope, and a favorable level of self-respect or self-acceptance. Corresponding features in the social system are opportunity (e g , supports or resources), which stimulates and reinforces the sense of hope; respect by others, which provides the social ground for respect of self; and power, which guarantees access to opportunity.

These varying formulations contribute to a comprehensive idea of competence in its multiple biological, psychological, social, and cultural aspects. The notion of the human organism's drive toward dealing effectively with the environment is uniformly emphasized, with agreement also that personality growth takes place in the dynamic interplay between the qualities of the organism and the characteristics of the impinging environment. Traditional formulations frequently place the burden on the human organism, because competence is viewed simplistically as a property or trait of the person. It seems more accurate, however, to regard it as a transactional concept, an attribute of the interplay between the person and the environment.

This view is emphasized in particular by Sundberg et al. [1978], who propose the notion of ecological competence. These authors point out that an adequate consideration of competence should take into account all appropriate personal dimensions, such as one's skills, qualities, and expectations. In other words, competence is not a fixed attribute of the person. It is the outcome of the transactions between *(1)* the person's capacities, skills, and motivation, and *(2)* environmental qualities such as social networks, social supports, and demands or obstacles in one's ecological context. For example, how competent a child might become in various academic subjects depends not only on his or her native ability and motivation, but also on the quality and quantity of opportunities available in the school setting. This view is further supported and elaborated by writers on the ecology of human development, notably Bronfenbrenner [1979] and Garbarino [1982].

Components of Ecological Competence

Drawing from the formulation of Sundberg et al. [1978] as well as related theoretical perspectives, I regard the major components of ecological competence as *(1)* capacities and skills, *(2)* motivational aspects, and *(3)* environmental qualities [Maluccio 1981a].

Capacities and Skills

This dimension includes the capacities of an individual in cognition, perception, intelligence, language, and physical health. It also encompasses the person's qualities in, for example, flexibility, tolerance for diversity, initiative or self-direction, reality testing, judgment, and tolerance for anxiety. In addition, it refers to proficiencies of an individual in such areas as athletics or interpersonal skills.

Motivational Aspects

This category comprises the person's interests, hopes, aspirations—in short, the set of drives or energies variously described as competence motivation [White 1963], intrinsic motivation [Deci 1975], or self-actualization [Maslow 1954]. These terms in essence refer to the human being's drive to deal with the environment, to seek stimulation, to cope with challenges, to accomplish, and to master.

Environmental Qualities

The other principal component of competence consists of the significant environmental resources and demands that impinge on one's functioning at any given point. Examples include social networks and institutional pressures and supports. Effective behavior requires a goodness of fit between personal factors and environmental ones [Germain and Gitterman 1980]. The complementarity between people's needs and qualities, on the one hand, and environmental demands and characteristics, on the other, strongly influences adaptation and competence development.

Significance of a Competence-Centered,
Ecological Perspective

What does an ecological competence orientation offer to the field of human services in general, and to residential care in particular? More specifically, what is the utility of the ecological concept of competence for child and youth care practice? These are valid questions, not only because the notion of competence seems to be so all-encompassing, but also because it overlaps with other concepts such as self-image, ego strength, and coping and adaptation. Moreover, the competence orientation has much in common with the interactionist and developmental perspectives [Maier 1981] (see also Chapter 2 in this book), the ecological or life model of practice in social work [Germain and Gitterman 1980], and other approaches to understanding and helping human beings. Each of these approaches has something to offer to the study of human behavior and development. And each of us finds, perhaps for complex reasons, the particular perspective or blending of perspectives that is most attractive.

I view the competence orientation as having a number of advantages. There is, first of all, its heuristic value: by emphasizing the dynamic transaction between people and their environments, the concept of ecological competence helps to sensitize practitioners to the effect that environmental demands and properties have on the personal, interpersonal, and social competence of human beings. Furthermore, the view of competence as a transactional concept rather than as a fixed property or trait of the individual can help practitioners to appreciate more deeply the significance of the context of human behavior and guide them in identifying, understanding, and manipulating the environmental obstacles and supports that affect a client's competence in one way or another.

From the ecological perspective, human beings are regarded as engaged in dynamic transactions with their environment, and specifically in a continuing struggle to maintain a moving equilibrium while faced with a complex and ever-changing array of environmental challenges. Similarly, biology emphasizes the interplay between the organism and the environment—a process of mutual adaptation in which each human being responds both personally and creatively. From general systems theory comes the notion of the human organism as an open system constituting one component in an interconnected, interdependent, and complementary set of parts. As with any other living organism, the human being is constantly influenced by—and, in turn, exerts influence upon—other systems at varying levels, including family, school, community, work, or culture.

The integration of insights from general systems theory, ecology, developmental theory, and biology in the form of an ecological perspective on competence suggests several interrelated themes that can guide child-care practice:

The view of children and youths as engaged in continual, dynamic transactions with their environment and in a continual process of growth and adaptation

The concept of children and youths as open systems that are spontaneously active and motivated to achieve competence in their coping with life's demands and with environmental challenges

The premise that varied environmental opportunities and social supports are necessary to sustain and promote each child's or youth's efforts to grow, achieve self-fulfillment, and contribute to others

The conviction that environmental challenges and supports should be matched to the child's or youth's changing qualities and needs in order to maximize the development of his or her competence, identity, autonomy, and self-fulfillment

The shift away from *treating* children and youths toward *teaching* them social skills, coping, and mastery [Eisikovits and Guttmann 1985]

Above all, as Maier [1981] observes in his discussion of the developmental conception of human functioning:

Life is conceived as a process in which the human being is in a continuous search for stimulation, variation, and new experience rather than a homeostatic, balanced, stimuli-free existence . . . . Most important, a nonhomeostatic conception challenges us to value people for their capacity to reach out and to develop more fully rather than for their low-risk striking for balance.

It should be evident that the competence orientation embodies a humanistic world view. Human beings are regarded as striving, active organisms capable of organizing their lives and developing their potentialities as long as they have appropriate environmental supports. This view reflects the ideas of various humanistic thinkers, especially Angyal [1941], with his concepts of autonomy, self-determination, and human strivings toward active mastery of the environment, and Maslow [1954], with his emphasis on positive personality growth and human motivation toward self-actualization. Through its emphasis on growth and adaptation, the humanistic perspective leads naturally to de-emphasis of pathology, particularly psychopathology, and to recognition of each person's multiple potentialities, including latent as well as currently evident resources, strengths, and creativity.

In residential child and youth care practice, a competence-centered approach can help workers to avoid the "sick-role" model and its dysfunctional consequences in the treatment process [Eisikovits 1983], and can facilitate their efforts to follow normalization principles in working with young people [Mesibov and LaGreca 1980; Walsh 1985].

Fostering Competence in Interpersonal and Group Life

As the staff members who, in nearly all residential settings, are those most intensely involved in the children's lives, direct care workers "become the extension of the children's parents, by assuming immediate responsibility for nurturing care, socialization, and specific therapeutic requirements" [Maier 1977]. This difficult, multifaceted challenge demands unique personal qualities, extensive knowledge, and refined skills.

The rest of this chapter deals with selected principles flowing from a competence-centered perspective that may guide direct care workers in their relationships with children and youths in such a way as to foster competence through the skillful use of interpersonal and group life. Some of the specifics are further elaborated, and additional important relationships, particularly with parents and other staff members, are treated in other chapters. It should also be noted that implementing such a perspective requires environmental supports for staff members as well as for young people, as considered briefly later in this chapter and more extensively elsewhere in this book.

Developing Close Relationships

Perhaps the most basic principle in residential child-care practice, as in the human services in general, is to develop a close, trusting relationship with each child or youth. To be effective in promoting competence, the child-worker relationship should be one in which openness, authenticity, and human caring flourish. The qualities of warmth, empathy, and genuineness are especially important, since these may have been missing or inadequate in the child's relationships with previous parental figures [Pierce and Pierce 1982]. Above all, the direct care worker must offer consistent nurturing and meet the young person's dependency needs while encouraging his or her strivings toward independence and autonomy.

The girl who acts out in preparation for a visit home, for instance, may be expressing her ambivalence about her parents, her confusion about where she belongs, or her uncertainty about how she will be received. Her acting out may reflect her regression and her unmet dependency needs. The worker can respond supportively by allowing her to share her feelings and by appreciating her ambivalence and confusion. At the same time, the worker can relate to the girl's positive strivings by showing conviction about her ability to cope with a realistically difficult life event. The worker can also redefine the acting-out behavior as evidence of the girl's struggle to achieve autonomy, rather than as an indication of her "nasty" or "childish" disposition or her rejection of the worker's attention and caring.

As children and youths elicit responses such as that just described in their relationships with child-care workers, they experience what Maier [1979] describes as the "core of care":

> The core of care in and away from home has to be experienced in a series of meaningful activities as children mature. While engaged with their caring adults, children will periodically dip into emotional dependency upon those caring persons, and this linkage will be both fundamental and freeing. In other words, fostering self-management and enriching children's behavioral repertoires are intimately linked with the formation of close relationship with the care givers.

While seeking to develop close relationships, workers should approach young persons carefully, respecting their particular tolerance for closeness, accepting their hesitation or ambivalence in forming close relationships, and allowing them to control the pace and intensity of emerging relationships. At the same time, workers must be aware of their own feelings and needs in this area and be prepared for rejection by the youngsters. This preparation involves, among other aspects, understanding the reasons for the child's or youth's reactions and avoiding taking the rejection personally.

Individualizing the Children

By virtue of their different needs, qualities, and temperaments, children respond differently to the same phenomena. In residential care, one frequently sees different responses in relation to major upheavals, such as separation from one's biological family, as well as routine events such as bedtime, mealtimes, or preparation for going to school each day. Individualizing the child or youth is therefore another guideline for promoting competence.

Workers' skills in individualizing are essential, because young people cope differently with similar life challenges or crises. In residential care, for example, residents' visits with members of their families tend to reactivate similar anxieties about separation, but individual responses vary greatly, from withdrawal to crying to acting-out behavior. Other family members participating in the visits are also likely to be under stress and will respond differently as well.

As child and youth care workers begin to understand each person's unique ways of coping and adapting, they will be better able to perceive opportunities for helping each individual in his or her struggle toward mastery:

> A child welfare practitioner described a pertinent experience with Jean, a blind 12-year-old girl placed in foster care following the death of her parents. When Jean was confronted with the impending demolition of her

biological family's home owing to urban renewal, she urged the worker to take her on a final tour of the house. During this visit, Jean methodically touched everything in each room, climbed into the attic, played the piano, and ran repeatedly around the back yard. While alternately crying, laughing, talking, and pausing in silence, Jean recalled innumerable family experiences and vividly traced her family's history and her own development. In reliving the past in a spontaneous and active manner at a crucial point in her life, Jean was courageously bracing herself for the future [Maluccio 1974].

As direct care workers look at and understand every child and youth differently, they are more likely to respond in ways that are geared to each one's particular needs and qualities. For example, children who cannot tolerate waiting for an activity to begin can be assigned some role or given some task to perform; children who tend to withdraw from group activity can be given special encouragement or individual attention; the angry adolescent boy who dominates the group in a negative fashion can be confronted with his destructive behavior, helped to find alternate ways of behaving, and encouraged to channel his energies into a leadership role within the group.

As these brief illustrations suggest, the competency-oriented worker is sensitive to each young person's needs, identifies his or her latent potentialities and creative strivings, and creates opportunities for the child to use and develop them further. Especially crucial in this context is the skill of "tuning in," that is, "putting oneself in the client's shoes and trying to view the world through the client's eyes" [Shulman 1984]. For example, workers can be tuned in to the feelings and needs of youngsters in their care, as well as to varied possibilities for teaching them skills in areas such as social interaction and solving problems. As discussed by Reiter and Bryen elsewhere in this book and by Small and Fulcher (1985), there are many techniques for promoting skill development in young people in residential care, particularly within a social learning perspective.

Group life generates unending opportunities in this regard, as youngsters and staff members interact in the activities of living on a daily basis. In light of young people's different learning styles and coping patterns, however, it is necessary that direct care workers consciously seek to provide diverse opportunities for children and youths to learn, to work through their conflicts, to practice interpersonal skills, and thus to build competence.

Using Life Experiences

In the competence-centered approach, "life itself is viewed as the arena of change: life experiences, events, and processes can be exploited for their 'therapeutic value' as a means of providing effective help" [Maluccio 1979]. In light of their intimate involvement in the children's lives, direct care workers have an unparalleled opportunity to use life experiences actively and purposefully, so as to enhance the young person's self-image, release latent potentiality and innate creativity, and promote competence [Maluccio 1983].

To do so, child-care workers must regard each event, dramatic or ordinary, as a potentially therapeutic experience and consciously exploit it in behalf of the youngster as much as possible. Toward this purpose, workers need sharp skills in selecting situations that arise in the natural course of interpersonal and group life and using them to generate opportunities for promoting growth.

Especially valuable in this regard is the life space interview, a technique that was pioneered by Redl [1959] in his work with young people. As defined by Redl, the life space interview consists of the clinical exploitation of life events or on-the-spot provision of emotional first aid. The worker responds quickly, while the particular episode is still fresh and immediate, and deliberately uses his or her responses to teach something to the children or youths involved or to meet some need that they have. For example, as children cry or throw a temper tantrum or fight with each other in the cottage, the worker can, as appropriate, use these experiences as opportunities to encourage the expression of feelings, provide support, set limits, clarify rules, or take disciplinary action.

In addition, opportunities for growth and the development of competence can be created through the use of individual and group activities, as discussed by Barnes elsewhere in this book. As suggested by White [1963] and other theorists, the child or youth can change and grow "through involvement in activities providing opportunities for need satisfaction, task fulfillment, crisis resolution, and learning of social skills" [Maluccio 1974]. Informal group activities, such as a family day picnic, can be effectively used as integral components of a residential facility's therapeutic program [Matsushima 1982]. Fun activities are especially important, since "a child should know some joy in each day and look forward to some joyous event for the morrow" [Hobbs 1982].

Several of the examples of residential life briefly outlined at the beginning of this chapter can be examined in light of the principle of using life experiences, thus suggesting various techniques and skills that workers can employ. The running away of the newly admitted youth can be redefined as reflecting his struggle to adapt to a new environment, rather than as an indication of his immaturity. The experience of the nine-year-old whose father again fails to visit him can be seen as an opportunity to help the child express his pent-up feelings and begin to accept the reality of his father's inability to care for him; the angry youth who destructively dominates group life can be seen as someone who is struggling to find acceptance and a meaningful role in the group; and mass confusion at the dinner table can be regarded as an opportunity to teach group members the importance of interdependence and mutual responsibility.

As is shown in these examples, reframing is a pertinent technique; it is commonly used in family therapy [Hartman and Laird 1983]. Reframing refers to the restatement of a problem, behavior, or situation in positive terms, so as to stimulate increased understanding, consideration of new options, and development of altered responses. By using an ecological competence orientation and building on techniques such as reframing, the direct care worker can translate personal or interpersonal problems, needs, and conflicts into adaptive tasks providing opportunities to promote growth and competence. Doing so calls for a great deal of energy on the part of workers as they face the challenge of responding to multiple pressures and demands emerging from everyday life. The challenge can seem overwhelming, but it may ultimately be much more rewarding than putting one's energies into such frustrating activities as trying angrily (and perhaps fruitlessly) to control a group or to punish a child.

For coping with this challenge, Guttman, in her chapter on immediacy in residential work elsewhere in this book, offers a comprehensive set of principles and techniques for using life experiences. She shows in particular how workers can examine events in their daily interaction with young people, reflect upon their experience with, and handling of, each event, and consider alternative possibilities for action when experiencing similar events in the future.

Mobilizing Motivation

Mobilizing the young person's motivation toward growth and mastery is another key principle, one that flows from the conviction that human beings are essentially motivated to achieve competence in coping with life's demands and with environmental challenges. Motivation is a complex human phenomenon that can be manifested through diverse behaviors. Some youngsters openly express their motivation for change and growth verbally. Others show it indirectly through anxiety, acting out, or other manifestations. A child's crying over a poor grade in an exam, a youth's refusal to participate in a game, or another youth's belligerent response to a worker may signal a need for understanding, a painful underlying concern, and, thus, a plea for help.

Direct care workers can be alert to these signals from young people in their care. Furthermore, they can identify and mobilize each child's motivation toward competence by following guidelines such as those that follow.

Recognize Signs of Anxiety

Young people may not verbalize their anxiety, but in one way or another they do signal their discomfort or dissatisfaction with themselves or their situations. They often do so indirectly, by crying, reacting with guilt, withdrawing to their rooms, or displaying outbursts of anger. By relying on their own sensitivity and empathy, workers seek to understand what triggers these behaviors, reframe them as signals of anxiety, and tap the young person's underlying motivation to deal with his or her pain and make things better.

Provide a Sense of Hope

To be engaged in the painful process of growth and change, a child, as do all human beings, needs to have some conviction that things can be better. This need is particularly true of young people in residential care, who often feel helpless and hopeless. They require help to achieve a "discomfort-hope balance," that is, "sufficient discomfort to exert pressure for action and sufficient hope to channel the pressure into action" [Moore-Kirkland 1981]. Too much discomfort and/or too little hope can immobilize anyone. Workers can enhance the youngster's hope by, for example, talking about the relationship between the present and the future, asking about his or her aspirations and wishes, and considering life goals.

Empower the Child.

Many seemingly small ways can be found to empower the child to act in his or her own behalf. The more one is involved in choosing a course of action, the more motivated and competent one becomes. In particular, children and youths can be encouraged to make decisions, to exert any possible ownership and control over their lives, and to feel that they can have an effect on their environment. For instance, workers can offer children a variety of possible activities and ask them to select the ones in which they want to engage. Similarly, in the example given earlier, the 14-year-old girl who is anxious about her forthcoming visit home can be encouraged to help chose the time, frequency, and conditions of her home visits.

Provide Opportunities for Success

Perhaps the most effective means of building a person's motivation is to provide opportunities for successful experiences in important areas of functioning. Direct care workers can help each child or youth to be *good at something*; for example, they can make assignments and offer opportunities for the child to achieve a goal and to sense the excitement that accompanies accomplishment.

Workers can also give positive feedback, which reinforces the youngster's self-worth. As underscored by psychologists, a person's ego is strengthened through his or her active participation in successful transactions with the environment, the resulting feelings of efficacy, and the cumulative development of a sense of competence [White 1963]. In short, competence feeds on competence, and direct care workers can facilitate this process by relying on their skills as adults who value and support young people in their strivings toward growth.

Restructuring the Environment

Finally, the ecologically oriented, competence-centered perspective high-lights the importance of modifying, enriching, or restructuring the environment. Competence flourishes through a nutritive environment that is suited to young people's needs and qualities, mobilizes their strengths, and supports their natural life processes [Maluccio 1981a].

This principle is particularly relevant to residential care, with its emphasis on the therapeutic use of the milieu in behalf of each child or youth. Direct care workers can use various approaches in restructuring the environment for this purpose. For example, they can modify dining room arrangements so that meal-times are more conducive to constructive social interaction. They can remove obstacles in the path of a child's drive toward industry and mastery, as with the boy failing in school, who might be transferred into a smaller class where he could receive individualized attention. They can mediate in the child's life space to strengthen coping abilities in such critical places as the school and the peer group. They can enrich a child's environment by providing aids (e.g., tutoring) or social supports (e.g., a foster home for weekend visits) [Whittaker and Garbarino 1983].

Promoting Workers' Competence

By following these and other principles flowing from a competence-centered perspective, direct care workers can do a great deal to foster the competencies of children and youths in interpersonal and group situations arising from the daily routine of residential life. This is not an easy or magical process, however; on the contrary, it requires that workers be able to play complex and multiple roles. They must provide cognitive and social stimulation, offer direct support, and serve as role models. These roles demand competent workers who have the requisite personal qualities as well as a variety of skills in individualizing, advocacy, communication, and direct influence.

As with children and youths, the development of competence in direct care workers also requires a supportive and nutritive environment that is conducive to their personal and professional growth, an environment enabling them "to carry out their roles and use and develop their potentialities" [Maluccio 1981b]. In short, the principles suggested by the competence perspective apply to the direct care staff as well as to children or youths. Along with professional training, workers need recognition, positive feedback, and support from supervisors and administrators if they are to be able to give young people what they need. Those who feel competent are best able to engender a sense of competence in others.

In a residential environment that is conducive to the development of competence in staff members as well as in residents, many opportunities emerge for child and youth care staff members to learn and grow by using existing knowledge as well as contributing to the development of further knowledge. Thus, in relation to the concepts and principles presented in this chapter, workers can examine which ideas or guidelines tend to work for them, and why; the kinds of situations or children or problems with which they are most effective; the additional principles that work best for them in practice; ways of refining or modifying the concepts and principles that have been delineated; and ideas or guidelines that do not work and should therefore be discarded.

Through such continual examination of their practice and reflection about the issues and problems that emerge, obtaining feedback from colleagues and young people about their performance, and sharing their findings and experiences with supervisors, peers, and others, direct care workers can not only refine their own skills, but also contribute to the testing and retesting of theory and the dynamic interplay between theory and practice. In so doing, they may well experience the exhilarating feelings of discovery and satisfaction, thus enhancing their self-concepts, sense of empowerment, and, ultimately, their competence.

REFERENCES

Angyal, A.   1941.   *Foundations for a Science of Personality.* New York: Commonwealth Fund.

Bronfenbrenner, U.   1979.   *The Ecology of Human Development.* Cambridge, MA: Harvard University Press.

Deci, E.   1975.   *Intrinsic Motivation.* New York, NY and London, England: Plenum Press.

Eisikovits, R.   1983.   No exit: Residential treatment and the "sick role" trap. *Child Care Quarterly* *12*: 36–44.

Eisikovits, Z., and Guttmann, E.   1985.   Doing Competent Child and Youth Care Work. Mimeographed.

Garbarino, J.   1982.   *Children and Families in the Social Environment.* New York: Aldine.

Germain, C.B., and Gitterman, A.   1980.   *The Life Model of Social Work Practice.* New York: Columbia University Press.

Gladwin, T.   1967.   Social competence and clinical practice. *Psychiatry 30*: 30–43.

Hartman, A., and Laird, J.   1983.   *Family-Centered Social Work Practice.* New York: The Free Press: pp 307–309.

Hobbs, N.   1982.   *The Troubled and Troubling Child.* San Francisco, CA: Jossey-Bass.

Maier, H.W.   1977.   Child welfare: Child care workers. In *Encyclopedia of Social Work* (17th issue). (Vol. 1). Washington, DC: National Association of Social Workers: pp 130–134.

Maier, H.W.   1979.   The core of care: Essential ingredients for the development of children at home and away from home. *Child Care Quarterly 8*: 161–173.

Maier, H.W. 1981. Essential components in care and treatment environments for children and youth. In Ainsworth, F., and Fulcher, L.C. (eds.), *Group Care for Children: Concept and Issues*. London, England, and New York: Tavistock: pp 19–70.

Maluccio, A.N. 1974. Action as a tool in casework practice. *Social Casework* 55: 30–35.

Maluccio, A.N. 1979. Promoting competence through life experiences. In Germain, C.B. (ed.), *Social Work Practice: People and Environments*. New York: Columbia University Press: pp 282–302.

Maluccio, A.N. (ed.). 1981a. *Promoting Competence—A New/Old Approach to Social Work Practice*. New York: The Free Press.

Maluccio, A.N. 1981b. Promoting client and worker competence in child welfare. In *The Social Welfare Forum—1980*. New York: Columbia University Press: pp 136–153.

Maluccio, A.N. 1983. Planned use of life experiences. In Rosenblatt, A., and Waldfogel, D. (eds.), *Handbook of Clinical Social Work*. San Francisco, CA: Jossey-Bass: pp 135–154.

Maslow, A.H. 1954. *Motivation and Personality* (2nd edition). New York: Harper & Row.

Matsushima, J. 1982. Therapeutic programming reevaluated: A recreational event as a therapeutic experience. *Residential Group Care & Treatment* 1: 51–61.

Mesibov, G.B., and LaGreca, A.M. 1980. Normalizing services for children with special needs. *Community Mental Health Review* 5 (1–4): 1, 4–14.

Moore-Kirkland, J. 1981. Mobilizing motivation: From theory to practice. In Maluccio, A.N. (ed.), *Promoting Competence: A New/Old Approach to Social Work Practice*. New York: The Free Press: pp 27–54.

Pierce, L.H., and Pierce, R.L. 1982. The use of warmth, empathy, and genuineness in child care work. *Child Care Quarterly* 11: 257–266.

Redl, F. 1959. Strategy and techniques of the life space interview. *American Journal of Orthopsychiatry* 29: 1–18.

Shulman, L. 1984. *The Skills of Helping Individuals and Groups* (2nd edition). Itasca, IL: F.E. Peacock Publishers.

Small, R.W., and Fulcher, L.C. 1985. Teaching competence in group care practice. In Fulcher, L.C., and Ainsworth, F. (eds.), *Group Care Practice with Children*. London, England, and New York: Tavistock: pp 135–154.

Smith, M.B. 1968. Competence and socialization. In Clausen, J.A. (ed.), *Socialization and Society*. Boston, MA: Little, Brown and Co.: pp 270–320.

Sundberg, N.D., Snowden, L.R., and Reynolds, W.M. 1978. Toward assessment of personal competence and incompetence in life situations. *Annual Review of Psychology* 29: 179–211.

Walsh, J.M. 1985. A model community-based residential treatment program. *Child Care Quarterly* 14: 48–55.

White, R.W. 1963. Ego and reality in psychoanalytic theory. In *Psychological Issues* (Vol. 3). New York: International Universities Press: p 3.

Whittaker, J.K., and Garbarino, J. 1983. *Social Support Networks: Informal Helping in the Human Services*. New York: Aldine.

4

Immediacy in Residential Child and Youth Care:

The Fusion of Experience, Self-Consciousness,

and Action

EDNA GUTTMANN

I wish the days were less eventful . . .
If only the incidents occurred one at a time . . .
Had I had some time to think what to do . . .
  —From the wonderings of a child-care worker

These and similar wonderings are perhaps universal in the experience of being a child or youth care worker. A day without overlapping "incidents"—would that be child or youth care work? When on the job one has to act, to reply to each situation while it is still happening. Also, one is immersed in the continuous flow of happenings without control over their timing or sequence.

"Immediacy," the concept we use to capture the realm of occurrences in residential group care as well as their rhythm and timing, includes the experiencing of a situation, becoming aware of its effect on oneself, and acting while it is occurring, as part of the flow of events. It is acting on an incident and knowing that as soon as it is over or most probably even before it is, another incident will follow, yet not knowing what that one will be like.

Let us begin our slow motion replay of immediacy with some vignettes that capture it as it occurs in residential child and youth care work.

I. *It is a quiet morning in the cottage.* The children have left for school, and you, the child-care worker, are walking around the premises. It is hard to imagine how noisy and messy the place becomes in the afternoon. As you walk through the rooms, scanning the space, you suddenly find a room that is not empty. There is a boy, in bed and covered up to his chin, reading a book. Calmness is over, as you sense that something is wrong with what you see. You stand there, staring at him, realizing that you will be judged re-sponsible and that the boy, who is on probation and should have been in school, is now likely to be thrown back into his troubled family. Your muscles are tensing . . . the boy notices you. Suddenly time starts running—you are faced with a situation that cannot be ignored. You must decide how to act. Now! The boy is staring at you, obviously understanding the potential con-sequences of his behavior. You must put into effect a decision you have not yet made. Your mind is flooded with possibilities of action that chase each other: Get angry at him and quickly send him to school? Tell him to get up and wait for your decision? Be kind and ask him understandingly if something is wrong? Or just make sure he knows that you have noticed and let him decide how to act?

You also have an opinion concerning some facts, such as how much you like this boy, and what he is missing at school now compared to what he gets through reading. What is more dramatic, however, is your sudden remembrance that going back to his abusive family may mean the beginning of the end. Time flows on as you consider the advantages, disadvantages, and possible consequences of each option for action . . . you are weighing them . . . . As you keep thinking, you keep losing time. You are almost out of time and still have not decided. Something inside pushes you: "Go on, do some-thing." But the question remains: "What?"

II. *As usual, you arrive at work in the afternoon.* You plan to talk with the children, to hear their stories, and to help them do their homework. Each day before entering, you know what awaits you, yet it is a new experience every time.

As you enter, children run toward you, stand all around you, touch you. They all speak at once; you hear voices, not words. You know that each of them wants you to spend the next hour only with him or her. They hold you, cling to you, and leave you no private space. You realize you should do something before you have no air to breathe. All your wishes now concentrate on gaining your space back. What can be done? Several options run through your mind: send the children firmly away, back to their rooms; make a tentative list of whom you will meet when; or just choose your favorites and work or play with them. You know who got your attention yesterday, who gets attention from other staff members, whom you prefer to spend time with. As they go on holding you, pushing each other, and speaking, it is becoming increasingly clear that you need to do something. The situation, the children, yourself—all expect you to act. But how?

III. *The residential setting is noisy outside.* You are a female youth worker, sitting calmly and quietly with an adolescent boy in his room; he is sharing some private stories. Suddenly, a group of his friends rushes in. They are speaking fast, all at once, among themselves and to him. You understand that they want something, yet you don't know what. All you know is that you have been interrupted and that you want them out. As you consider action possibilities (asking them to leave; waiting until they go), you realize that the longer you wait, the more remote is the chance that you will be able to get back to the conversation.

Whether you just wait or ask them to leave, they eventually go. The atmosphere is quiet again, but no longer calm. It has become tense. You ask the boy if he wants to continue the conversation, and his reply is, "I want you!" As you realize how strongly this boy feels toward you, you experience your body differently than before.

Your greatest need is for time to decide what to do. How do you get out of this without hurting him (or yourself)? Then you realize that he has risen to embrace you. You are left with just a fraction of your space. He is conquering it. As space shrinks, you lose the sense of time. You think simultaneously about how to explain to this young man that this action is the wrong thing to do and how to overcome the temptation to accept. Struggling with these pros and cons, you realize that you ran out of time. There is no more space for weighing. You must act while not yet having decided how and while wondering what will happen next.

Each of these vignettes captures some of the daily experience of being a child or youth care worker. Each has been distilled from its context for analytic purposes; however, in everyday residential life such happenings are contextualized by other events, people, and experiences. That is, immediacies take place within the context of events that occur simultaneously in the same space, of other children and staff members who are there, of the worker's experiences during that day, his or her perception of previous dealings with those involved, the preceding experiences of the other participants in the incident, and the pressures of the daily routine.

This chapter centers on the experience of immediacy in residential child and youth care work and on the nature of the worker's life—with and in immediacies—as well as on ways of handling both oneself and the situations. Only through the isolation of immediacies from each other, and by the handling of each one as a separate universe, can one successfully work through the stream of events that structures everyday life in residential child and youth care. The first part of this chapter deals with each experience in its immediacy as singled out by the worker, describing both the experience and its handling. The second part deals with the stream of immediacies, describing how this flow is experienced and handled, and shows how successful handling of the stream of events depends on the successful handling of the individual incidents. Finally, we tie the two parts together through a case example. (Note that the experiential order of immediacies moves in the other direction, from workers finding themselves in a stream of immediacies to isolating single immediacies from the stream. The order is inverted here for analytic purposes.)

Immediacy

An immediacy experience emerges in a work situation in which one finds oneself, from which one must single out an event on which to act. The sense of immediacy involves an element of simultaneity: the worker is part of a situation, must single out (frame) a specific event for action, and needs to be in tune with the continuous flow of incidents that make up the subsequent work environment. One must decontextualize the event in order to respond to it, yet the response must take into account the interconnection between the specific event and the stream of acts and events that surrounds it.

The complexity of an immediacy lies in the simultaneity of consciously experiencing a whole situation while taking action on parts of it. From an existential, phenomenological perspective, experiencing a situation, being conscious of it, and acting comprise what Heidegger [1962] called "being-in-the-world," or being involved with occurrences. This imbeddedness is composed of two entities: "being-in-itself" and "being-for-itself." The first, "being-in-itself," is the experience of incidents as they strike us on the sensory level, disconnected from and uninfluenced by any previous experiences [Natanson 1970; Sartre 1956]. The second, "being-for-itself," is the same experience mediated by consciousness, in which one is both introspective, or observant of oneself, and also considers a variety of action alternatives [Douglas 1977]. These two concepts are used here as heuristic tools to understand both the immediacy of a single child or youth care event and the stream of immediacies that, taken together, make up the universe of child and youth care work.

Being-in-Itself

As being-in-itself is characterized by the primacy of nonmediated experience and by the preclusion of any cognitive process [Keen 1970], it may be said that, in the being-in-itself experience, the self is both the core of one's existence and the context through which one makes sense out of the surroundings.

When the world around us changes abruptly as an outcome of an unexpected event, our experience of being-in-itself is altered. This reaction is usually mani-fested by bodily or spatiotemporal experiences that are blurred by the newness of the event. One may sense trembling, one's hands may get cold or shake, one may feel a heat wave within the body, get a headache, or suddenly feel tired. One can feel suffocated by the shrinking space; time may seem to pass too quickly . . . Due to the newness of the experience, one is affected without being able to identify precisely what is happening. For example, when you find the boy in his room instead of in school, you realize something is happening to you, yet you cannot tell what; you are overwhelmed. This momentary sense of being over-whelmed involves both spatial and temporal components.

Spatial Aspects of Being Overwhelmed

When the body is regarded as the zero point in organizing one's experiential world, space can be divided into outer and inner [Bollnow 1961]. The outer space is broad, unknown, and open for exploration; the inner is familiar, private, and delimited enough for us to own it; it is the area of the protected. While separated by clear boundaries, outer and inner spaces coexist in a functional relationship.

When one is overwhelmed, one's "lived space" suddenly becomes severely constricted. This sensation is not, however, associated with moving the occurrences from the insecure and ambiguous outer space to the known, owned, and protected areas of the inner space. Rather, the inner space is permeated by the characteristics of the outer space; that is, unfamiliarity, insecurity, and unlimited openness. Under these conditions, the boundaries between inner and outer space disappear, and one loses one's competence in moving the events from the unknown and boundless to the known and owned.

In immediacy situations, inner space shrinks and is emptied of any familiar content, thus becoming unpredictable, like outer space. One is not certain any longer about "what's happening." One's usual patterns of handling situations disappear. Familiar, normally used patterns of coping are no longer present or available, and there is nothing else in their place. One cannot move or act; one is overwhelmed.

Temporal Aspects of Being Overwhelmed

Time is usually considered to be flowing continuously from past to future at a certain speed. One's "lived time" is constituted from one's unique way of experiencing its flow [Minkowski 1967]. Furthermore, one's lived time is linked to objective (physical) time by simultaneity [Heidegger 1962]: one experiences oneself together with the continuous flow of events in the environment, and several unrelated events may take place at the same time. In an immediacy situation, the sense of being overwhelmed can be attributed to one's inability to differentiate between the situation and the experiencing of oneself, as well as to the difficulty in distinguishing between simultaneous events and the immediacy situations. For example, in the third vignette, when the boy expresses his feelings toward the youth worker, she is unable to identify that he and his actions are separate from her experience of tension, her feeling of shrinking space, and her vanishing sense of time. Nor can she distinguish clearly her interactions with the boy from the staff conversations she hears outside, from the screaming boys next door, or from her observation of another boy who is just entering the scene. Consequently, the sense of flow of time is disrupted; one no longer experiences it as fast or slow. The personal experience of the flow of time is lost; one is overwhelmed.

The spatiotemporal experience of being overwhelmed is instantly confronted by one's need for confidence, continuity, and competence. While emerging from this initial stage, one first regains the ability to differentiate among simultaneous experiences—both between what is happening to oneself and what occurs in the environment, and among various environmental occurrences themselves.

The interaction between the spatial and temporal experiences and the associated cognitive and emotional processes leads one toward such questions as, "What is happening to me?" "How do I experience what is happening to me?" "Why do these processes happen rather than others?" Questions like these pave the way to consciousness, or what has previously been termed being-for-itself.

Consciousness and Being-for-Itself

Consciousness is always *of* something. It is being oriented toward something, attending to it, and thus being open to the world [Sartre 1956; Luijpen and Koren 1969; Natanson 1970]. When one attends to, is oriented toward, and is open to one's self, we speak of self-consciousness. This process follows and transcends experience. An essential element in self-consciousness is distance, or the boundary between the person and what he or she is conscious of [Sartre 1956; Johnstone 1970]. One must be far enough from what one wishes to be conscious of so that one is able to objectify it, to get above and beyond it, and, thus, to get to know it [May 1958].

Being-for-itself is making the self the object of its own inspection [Natanson 1970]. This action is done through introspection or systematic inner observation [Douglas 1977], not only as a means of intensifying consciousness, but also as an aid to deciding upon action. Decision making is choosing among action alternatives [Macquarrie 1972], a choice through which one commits oneself to an unknown future and becomes engaged with that future [Marcel 1950]; that is, deciding is actualizing freedom: one thrusts oneself toward an unknown future by acting on the basis of one's preference in the present [Berdyaev 1955].

Actualizing freedom is a complicated task under regular spatiotemporal conditions, and it becomes much harder in the context of an immediacy. In regular situations, the difficulty stems from the commitment one makes to a single choice, which forces one to give up other options. In immediacy situations, where one's time and space are severely limited, the experience of choosing is one of being pushed to decide without having enough space or time to weigh the options. In other words, the difficulty emerges not only from the commitment that follows the decision, but also from the necessity to choose under difficult conditions. In immediacy situations one must decide without having the freedom to choose; one must act without having the freedom to do so.

The sequence from consciousness through distance, to introspection, to making choices and carrying out actions can be elucidated by the following example: In the first vignette, upon seeing the boy in his room instead of in school, the child-care worker senses that something is wrong. The worker starts being conscious when thinking, "Why is the boy not in school?" "Why do I feel that my muscles are tensing up and that I am losing time?" and, finally, "How am I to decide what to do?" Then the worker weighs options for action: Send the boy to school? Ask what is wrong with him? Tell him to wait till evening for a decision? The worker chooses one option according to his or her knowledge and feelings about the boy, the consequences of such behavior, the classes being missed at school, and other situational and boy-related characteristics. If the worker decides, for example, to send the boy to school, he or she risks that the child will be angry or even refuse, thereby forcing the worker to go through a second immediacy. Even though there was not enough time and space to weigh all potential options, however, the worker has chosen and acted: he or she has experienced the immediacy consciously.

So far, the components of an immediacy have been analyzed. It should be noted that action will take place only in immediacies that are experienced consciously by the worker. This cannot always be assumed, because one may experience an immediacy and not be conscious of it as such. Matrix 1 illustrates these possibilities.

Not being conscious of an experience means remaining overwhelmed, being unable to move beyond being-in-itself, and consequently not acting. The event is bypassed, as if one perceives its existence intuitively rather than consciously (item 2). Only an immediacy that is consciously experienced (item 1) has the potential to be acted upon.

Action may occur whether one is experiencing being-for-itself or not. In other words, action is not always the outcome of the combination of conscious experiencing, sorting out options, making a choice among the options, and deciding. When being-for-itself is not part of the way one experiences immediacy, one may consciously experience that something is happening, but not sort out the options or make conscious decisions upon which future action is based. Under these conditions, one is merely acting automatically, either on the stimulus-response level or in accord with preconceived response sets to certain kinds of environmental demands. The difference between action that emerges from being-for-itself and one that does not is the level of understanding of the actor. For example, child-care workers who find themselves surrounded by youngsters asking for attention may experience the limited space and ask themselves what is happening and what can be done. Due to time constraints and the feeling of no air

MATRIX 1

The Experience of an Immediacy With and Without Consciousness

	Experiencing	Not Experiencing
Being Conscious	1. Asking oneself, "What is happening?" and moving to being-for-itself	3. Irrelevant to immediacy
Not Being Conscious	2. Bypassing the event	4. Irrelevant to immediacy

to breathe, they may just push the children back with their hands or shout at the children to go away. They may also think that children should always be in their rooms doing homework in the afternoon and, independent of the situation, send each of them to his or her room every day.

It should be mentioned that not acting may also have varying qualities, depending on whether one is experiencing being-for-itself; that is, one can choose not to act, such as when one experiences an immediacy consciously, sorts out the options, and chooses to exercise the freedom not to act. One can, however, experience an event consciously and not act because the opportunity has already passed. One is stuck in one's own consciousness. For example, standing in front of the boy who should have been at school, the worker may think of sending him to school, asking the youngster what is wrong with him, or not responding and letting him decide what to do. Alternatively, the worker may decide to leave the room without taking any action. The worker may also stand there, watching the boy and being preoccupied with wondering, "What is happening?" and, "How do I experience it?" When the worker is flooded by such questions and is hence unable to answer them, he or she will be unable to act.

When the possibility of acting or not acting is placed on one dimension, and that of being-for-itself or not being-for-itself on the other, Matrix 2 is derived.

When an immediacy is handled as shown in item 1, the worker acts by conscious choice after knowing and understanding his or her options. He or she is immersed in, and is becoming through, the immediacy. When an immediacy is handled as shown in item 3, the worker consciously chooses not to act, and is becoming through that decision. "Becoming" is used here in the sense of the

MATRIX 2

Acting or Not Acting on an Immediacy While Being-for-Itself or Not Being-for-Itself

	Action	No Action
Being-for-Itself	1. Becoming: presence, responsibility, "being oneself"	3. Choice not to act—becoming
Not Being-for-Itself	2. Automatic action—on stimulus-response level or based on preconceived response sets	4. Stuck in own consciousness; the event bypassed the worker

emergence of oneself from decisions and actions (or conscious non-actions) in immediacy situations. One is then choosing one's own self rather than action possibilities outside of one's self [Berdyaev 1955]. One becomes what one does in immediacy situations. In this context, becoming means presence, responsibility, and being oneself.

Let us briefly elaborate on the components of becoming. *Presence* means being engaged and involved in a situation while capable of transcending oneself toward the other with whom one is engaged in that situation. Being present is being available to others spatially—being *here*—and temporally—being *now* [Natanson 1970]. Thus, in the third vignette, the worker's presence in an immediacy situation is being *there then*, understanding the boy's passions, letting him express them, being moved by them, and showing him that she is moved even though she decides not to accept his advances.

Responsibility is both awareness of what the action chosen means to oneself and readiness to accept and deal with the consequences of one's choices, whatever they may be [Wild 1963]. In the context of immediacy, a tension exists between time constraints and the options for responsible action that are under consideration. One cannot brainstorm endlessly concerning options in immediacy situations. Choices must be made within the time- and immediacy-related parameters that determine the stock of options available for action. In this context, being responsible means understanding that these parameters work both inclusively and exclusively: that is, temporal and situational parameters determine which action choices are plausible and which are not. It also means knowing why one has chosen a given option rather than another, and the expected results of the choice. For example, when the worker decides to explain to the boy why she cannot accept, she knows that this choice is because of her values and the nature of her relationship with the boy at the present time. She also know that he may feel hurt, although she is ready to accept that result and to stay with the situation in order to try and help him understand. She is aware of what both of them might gain if she were to accept his offer, and that he might not have been so shocked at her refusal had she told him first that she needed time to weigh his offer. Nevertheless, she decided to do what she did.

Being oneself is acting on the basis of one's own personal and occupational values and beliefs rather than situationally and according to what might be preferred by those who may observe the action. Being oneself is making decisions that are coherent with one's beliefs. This coherence transcends situations: the emerging self is unitary and beyond immediacy, although subject to change on the basis of experience. It is the reflection of one's holistic being in an ever-emerging stream of situations.

Being oneself consistently and holistically as a child-care worker constitutes the backbone around which isolated immediacies become part of what we earlier termed a stream of immediacies. In other words, the worker's self gives continuity and coherence to otherwise isolated immediacy experiences. The competence of child and youth care work may reside in simultaneously isolating an immediacy (to make it manageable) and viewing it as part of a stream of immediacies. What follows is an examination of the stream of immediacies and how the worker navigates it.

The Stream of Immediacies

Experiencing the stream of immediacies means experiencing a succession of singled-out events. The worker is expected to work each of these through, while possessing no control over their timing, their speed of occurrence, their content, or their participants. What is primary in the stream of immediacies is that the events keep occurring independent of one's influence. Like the flow of time or the stream of consciousness [James 1890], it is beyond one's control.

Although it has not been defined or analyzed as such, the concept of the stream of immediacies can be found in the child care literature, particularly in the context of describing strain and stress in everyday child-care work [Littner 1957] and coping with strain. In the former sense, it has been described in terms of "stressors," experienced as a sense of "having to handle too many events at once" [Barrett and McKelvey 1980; Reed 1977]. Thus, immediacies are described in behavioral rather than experiential terms. Coping strategies mentioned range from organizational to individual ones [Barrett and McKelvey 1980]. Our description focuses primarily on individual strategies, what Barrett and McKelvey term "self-management" techniques.

Even these approaches, which attempt to describe how self-awareness evolves in handling the stream of immediacies, do not deal with the experience of awareness integratively. They stop after the initial stages: identifying the stressor [Shannon and Saleeby 1980], assessing its effect, and suggesting ways of coping [Barrett and McKelvey 1980; Mattingly 1977]. For each stage, they describe responses that may occur, including avoidance of contact with clients [Maslach and Pines 1977], lack of concern with clients, deterioration of quality of work, absenteeism [Shannon and Saleeby 1980], and alienation [Daley 1979; Freudenberger 1977]. What follows here is an attempt to show what the experience of being-in-the-stream of immediacies is for the child-care worker. Again, as in the foregoing discussion of single, isolated immediacies, we first discuss the experiencing, then the consciousness, and finally, the handling of the stream of immediacies.

Being-in-Immediacies

Experiencing the stream of immediacies or being-in-immediacies means observing them, experiencing each immediacy in isolation, and knowing that as soon as it ends or even before that moment, another will emerge. When there is a break in the stream, the experience is one of anticipation—wondering what will happen next, and when. The experience of following the events and that of waiting for the next immediacy to occur emerge through bodily sensations, spatial and temporal perceptions, and emotions, in ways similar to the experience of each immediacy in isolation.

The bodily sensation of immediacies as well as that of waiting is one of tension, of standing on guard and being alert. One may experience one's body as a spring, ready to extend in the direction of the next event, or as being so filled with immediacy events that it is going to explode. This sense of almost-explosion is connected to the main spatial experience of immediacies: being flooded. This sensation occurs when the pressure of events to be handled overloads one's inner space; the resulting overflow may lead the person to lose track of what is happening. At that point, the events may become estranged or unfamiliar, they fade away, or, to use spatial terminology, they move to the outer space. An event that could have been dealt with is lost.

In temporal terms, the stream of immediacies is characterized by simultaneity and loss of time. One is trying to follow the events in order not to lose them, yet one experiences them as slippery, difficult to grasp. They are more so because their occurrence is simultaneous—either several things are happening at once or one is dealing simultaneously with an event and with the expectation of others.

The sense of overflow, loss, or inability to grasp everything at once may bring about the experience of becoming "emptied," or unable to be "there," "with it," or present. This feeling, in turn, may make one's working life in the residential setting seem meaningless and lead one into a world of absurd and false appearances, as one's basic ability to co-constitute the world and the self is called into question. Thus, the stream of immediacies sweeps away the constellation of our present existence, and there is a sense of loneliness, emptiness. One is deserted, and without any direction. It is the "experience of nothingness" [Novak 1970]. In this state, one feels that one has achieved nothing, that one's energy has been wasted. One is self-deceived [Nietzsche 1967]. Standing alone, deserted, in the middle of a false and meaningless world, one asks how to live through it, how to find meaning.

The very dreadfulness of being-in-nothingness makes it fascinating as well. Once having discovered that there is nothing there, the worker can invent any world he or she wants to, and live it. "Immediacy" and "failure to swim with the stream of immediacies" become metaphors, just as "handling them," "letting them pass," or "just collecting them in the album of one's past." The frightening quality of nothingness faces one inevitably with the choice of how to live it.

Living the stream of immediacies, as opposed to being swept by them, means being able to differentiate; that is, to delineate and separate discrete immediacies, and to develop self-understanding concerning their timing, their beginnings, and their endings. Consciousness of the stream of immediacies as a composite entity is composed of awareness of a succession of discrete events. It is moving toward answering the question, "How can I live it?" This search is "being-for-itself" in the stream of immediacies.

Consciousness and Being-for-Itself

Differentiating among immediacies and asking, "How can I live it?" enables the worker to observe himself or herself through the day and to search for the answers. Being-for-itself in the stream of immediacies can occur only when conscious action (presence, responsibility, and being oneself) characterizes each immediacy alone. In this way, one lives his or her professional life in the stream of immediacies reflectively [Schon 1983]. The reflective quality enables the worker to move from one immediacy to another.

In the third example, when other boys entered the room and interfered with the worker who was sharing a friendly talk with a boy, the worker was faced with an immediacy. She experienced the discontinuity, became conscious of it, and chose an action. That specific immediacy ended. The boys left, and it became quiet again. The worker made it clear to herself that she had handled the immediacy and, simultaneously, was prepared for the next one, the boy's expression of his need for intimacy with her. This declaration is a new immediacy in the stream, not mixed with the previous one. Such differentiation is what enables a worker to act on each new immediacy and keeps him or her from being swept on by the stream of immediacies, thus losing involvement with the occurrences in his or her working life.

By placing experience on one dimension and consciousness on the other, Matrix 3 summarizes the experience of the stream of immediacies.

Only the worker who experiences the stream consciously (item 1) has the potential to handle it. Otherwise, one is likely to be swept on by the stream of immediacies.

So far, we have attempted to describe and analyze the possibility of experiencing the stream of immediacies consciously, yet how does reflective experiencing lead to action?

Action can occur whether one is being-for-itself in the stream or not. When one is being-for-itself and acts, one is simultaneously becoming in each immediacy

MATRIX 3

The Experience of the Stream of Immediacies With and Without Consciousness

	Experiencing	Not Experiencing
Being Conscious	1. Asking oneself, "How do I live it?"; differentiating among the immediacies	3. Irrelevant to the stream of immediacies
Not Being Conscious	2. Being swept along by the stream of immediacies	4. Irrelevant to the stream of immediacies

and differentiating among them. In other words, one who is open to and oriented toward oneself is authentic, present in the immediacy, and chooses responsibly. In addition, these actions have the quality of being situationally appropriate. One can also act without being-for-itself in the stream of immediacies, however, and without differentiating among them, even though one is becoming in each immediacy alone. In that case, the worker is acting automatically with the stream rather than on it. His or her actions are divorced from their situational context. While they may make sense as separate instances, it is a way of acting that resembles a broken nickelodeon, whose songs are unrelated to what has been dialed on it.

Feeling flooded and, hence, being unable to differentiate among immediacies may also prevent one from acting. Unable to respond to the stream of immediacies, one attempts to keep up with the events, fails, and loses track of them. Yet one may also take no action while being-for-itself. This choice is only a theoretical possibility, because, if one goes consciously with the stream and differentiates among immediacies, one is becoming in each of them and cannot avoid acting. (Such "action" may include deciding not to respond, as has been noted previously in this chapter.)

The possibilities of acting or not and of being-for-itself or not in the stream of immediacies are brought together in Matrix 4.

When one handles immediacies, as shown in item 1, one is simultaneously handling each immediacy and the stream as a whole. The components of this way of acting include becoming, reflection, knowledge utilization, knowledge of the self and the world, and existential integrity. Let us briefly examine the importance of these concepts in the context of handling the stream of immediacies.

Becoming in each immediacy, comprising presence, responsibility, and being oneself, "pulls the self into a coherent unity" [Macquarrie 1972]. It aids in handling immediacies by helping to differentiate among them.

MATRIX 4

Acting or Not Acting on the Stream of Immediacies While Being-for-Itself or Not Being-for-Itself

	Action	No Action
Being-for-Itself	1. Becoming, reflection, knowledge utilization, knowledge of self and the world, existential integrity → selfhood	3. Irrelevant to the stream of immediacies
Not Being-for-Itself	2. A broken nickelodeon (automatic, situationally inappropriate action)	4. Flooded with immediacies, trying to follow them but losing them

Reflection, from a phenomenological point of view, is a retrospective disclosure of the meaning of experiences and actions used to obtain a descriptive and analytic understanding of them [Colaizzi 1978]. Being reflective at the end of a set of immediacies is being-for-itself; it is thinking, "What were the events?" "How did I experience each of them and the stream as a whole?" "What alternatives for action did I have in each immediacy?" "How did I choose the one that I did?" "What could have happened had I chosen other actions?" "How did I differentiate among immediacies?" In other words, it is analyzing retrospectively how one lived the stream.

So far, this phenomenological reflection leads the worker to the accumulation of practice knowledge, what was referred to in Chapter 1 as "tacit knowledge." To get beyond the particular stream of immediacies and to become better equipped for streams to come, one must bring the categories grounded in practice and derived from phenomenological reflection to higher levels of abstraction and integrate them with relevant theoretical knowledge: one should engage in *knowledge utilization*. This process, in turn, leads to developing hypotheses for alternative avenues of action, but it does not necessarily mean that the worker acts on them.

This continuous interaction between a reflective self and reflective action brings one, ideally, to an understanding of oneself and the world as they co-constitute each other. One is gaining knowledge of oneself and the world that cannot be achieved in any other way. One is being-in-the-world that he or she is co-constituting with "existential integrity" [Kirkegaard 1944]. That is, one knows and understands one's unique and holistic being, which is the road to attaining "selfhood."

Let us join the child-care worker handling events during her working day. The stream of immediacies in a film strip would appear as follows: she is sitting in a quiet room, sharing a friendly conversation with a boy; other children burst into the room; she tells them that they have interfered; they leave the room; the boy expresses a need for intimacy with her; the worker clarifies to him the boundaries of their relationship. In each immediacy (event), the worker made a choice according to her values, knowledge, and occupational beliefs. She reached out to the boy and allowed for sympathy to develop; she told the children that they were interrupting and assumed that they were mature enough to make the decision to leave; she declined the boy's offer, because it was incompatible with her values and potentially harmful for him.

In each of these seemingly trivial immediacies, the worker was faced with a dramatic choice. When reflecting on this stream of immediacies in the evening or in her free time, the worker is playing back the strip, her reactions to the immediacies, and the way she lived with them. The reflection includes alternative possibilities for action in each case and alternative strips or scenarios of what could have happened if another action had been chosen at any point. "What if I had told them to leave immediately, instead of just saying that they were interrupting?" "What if I had accepted his advances?" The worker is thinking retrospectively, reflecting on the way she swam in the stream of immediacies, the choices she made, and the implications of these choices for the situations and for herself.

Thus, conscious choice and reflection on it enrich the worker's practical knowledge about handling these types of immediacies. She is also capable of integrating immediacies into categories of practical knowledge and of using theoretical knowledge to develop, enrich, and analyze alternatives in her practical action categories. The understanding of how working situations and the participants, including herself, co-constitute each other leads her to develop competence in generalizing beyond, and thereby also to transcend immediacies, while it simultaneously allows for the uniqueness or idiosyncratic characteristics of each of them.

REFERENCES

Barrett, M.C., and McKelvey, J.   1980.   Stresses and strains on the child care worker—typologies for assessment. *Child Welfare* 59(5): 277–285.

Berdyaev, N.   1955.   *The Meaning of the Creative Act.* Translated by D. Lowrie. New York: Macmillan-Collier.

Bollnow, O.F. 1961. Lived space. *Philosophy Today* 5(1/4): 31–39.

Collaizzi, P.F. 1978. Learning and existence. In Valle, R.S., and King, M. (eds.), *Existential Phenomenological Alternatives for Psychology*. New York: Oxford University Press: pp 48–71.

Daley, M.R. 1979. Preventing worker burnout in child welfare. *Child Welfare* 58(7): 443–450.

Douglas, J.D. 1977. Existential sociology. In Douglas, J.D., and Johnson, J.M. (eds.), *Existential Sociology*. London, England: Cambridge University Press: pp 3–73.

Freudenberger, H.J. 1977. Burnout: Occupational hazard in child care work. *Child Care Quarterly* 6(2): 90–99.

Heidegger, M. 1962. *Being and Time*. Translated by J. Macquarrie and E.S. Robinson. New York: Harper and Row; London, England: Routledge and Kegan Paul.

James, W. 1890. *The Principles of Psychology* (Vol. 1). New York: Holt, Rinehart and Winston.

Johnstone, H.W. 1970. *The Problem of the Self*. University Park, PA: Pennsylvania State University Press.

Keen, E. 1970. *Three Faces of Being: Toward an Existential Clinical Psychology*. New York: Appleton-Century-Crofts.

Kirkegaard, S. 1944. *Training in Christianity*. Translated by W. Lowrie. Princeton, NJ: Princeton University Press.

Littner, N. 1957. *The Strains and Stresses on the Child Welfare Worker*. New York: Child Welfare League of America.

Luijpen, W.A., and Koren, H.J. 1969. *A First Introduction to Existential Phenomenology*. Pittsburgh, PA: Duquesne University Press.

Macquarrie, J. 1972. *Existentialism*. London, England: Hutchinson and Co. Ltd.

Marcel, G. 1950. *The Mystery of Being* (Vols. 1, 2). Translated by G.S. Fraser and R. Hague. Chicago, IL: Regnery.

Maslach, C., and Pines, A. 1977. The burnout syndrome in the day care setting. *Child Care Quarterly* 6(2): 100–113.

Mattingly, M.A. 1977. Sources of stress and burnout in professional child care work. *Child Care Quarterly* 6(2): 127–137.

May, R. 1958. Contributions to existential psychotherapy. In May, R., and Ellenberger, H.F. (eds.), *Existence: A New Dimension in Psychiatry and Psychology*. New York: Basic Books: pp 37–91.

Minkowski, E. 1967. Spontaneity. In Lawrence, N., and O'Connor, D. (eds.), *Readings in Existential Phenomenology*. Englewood Cliffs, NJ: Prentice-Hall.

Natanson, M. 1970. *The Journeying Self*. Reading, MA: Addison-Wesley.

Nietzsche, F. 1967. *The Will to Power*. Edited by W. Kaufman. New York: Random House.

Novak, M. 1970. *The Experience of Nothingness*. New York: Harper and Row.

Reed, M.J. 1977. Stress in live-in child care. *Child Care Quarterly* 6(2): 114–120.

Sartre, J.P. 1956. *Being and Nothingness*. Translated by H.E. Barnes. New York: Philosophical Library.

Schon, D.A.   1983.   *The Reflective Practitioner.* New York: Basic Books.

Shannon, C., and Saleeby, D.   1980.   Training child welfare workers to cope with burnout. *Child Welfare* 59(8): 463–468.

Wild, J.   1963.   *Existence and the World of Freedom.* Englewood Cliffs, NJ: Prentice-Hall.

Part 2

*Working Life with Children
and Youths*

5

Providing a Development-

Enhancing Environment:

The Child and Youth Care Worker as Observer

and Interpreter of Behavior

ANITA WEINER

It is 8:30 in the evening, and the group is settling down for its evening activity. Some of the children still have homework to finish in their rooms, but most are in the common room ready to continue work on a collage they are making for the exhibit next week.

Suddenly, the lights in the cottage go out. Pandemonium breaks loose. At least three of the children, ages eight to 12, are always terrified in the dark, and they need immediate attention. (These three share a room, and a hall light is left on for them all night.) The child-care worker, who has been with the group for six months, calls out to the group in as loud and confident a voice as possible, so that they will hear her, know where to locate her physically, and be reassured by her vocal presence: "I am going to get the big flashlight. Anyone who wants to can come with me." She starts to walk slowly toward the front closet, while calling out the names of all the children and asking them where they are. She takes particular note of the responses of the frightened ones.

At the closet, a few of the children have gathered, and she finds the flashlight easily. With the flashlight on, she collects the three she is particularly concerned about and announces that she is going to the fuse box in the back of the cottage. She invites them all to join her and asks whether any of them have ever been in a blackout before, and, if so, what they did when it happened. Everyone has a story, and they are all busy talking together when she reaches the fuse box and discovers that the control lever is down. She flips the lever up and the lights go on.

The children disperse back to their various activities, but the worker discerns that Rubin, age ten, has a guilty look on his face and seems unsure whether to stay near her or to move away. She strongly suspects that someone pulled the lever down on purpose, since all the electrical equipment in the cottage had recently been checked and approved, but her only clue is the look she caught on Rubin's face.

This suspicion is not the only concern on the worker's mind. She has noticed that, for three days now, Sheila has not been showing her usual enthusiasm for food at mealtimes; the worker had decided to have a talk with her once the group got started on the collage. Sheila is a quiet, unassertive child of 11, but she had usually been the first one seated at the table for a meal, and one of the most enthusiastic eaters. Naturally, the blackout was a far more dramatic event in the life of the group, but there is something about the way Sheila has been looking and acting lately that may warrant equal time in the worker's range of concern. Now she must decide whether, how, and when to relate to Rubin, to Sheila, and to the three fearful children who are waiting for her at the entrance to the common room.

Let us now leave our worker with her concerns, which are typical in the ebb and flow of a group care setting, and return to the three overlapping elements of the situation that can be used to enhance normal developmental processes. It is the direct care worker who creates the immediate context in which the children arrange their physical and emotional world, and it is within this context that children and workers struggle with their day-to-day challenges and interactions. Through these interactions, both children and workers can develop the competencies to cope with life's developmental tasks.

Since the ability to provide an appropriate context for development and interaction is essential in residential care, two questions arise that this chapter addresses: What are the components of an appropriate context for development? How can the ability of a worker to provide such a context be enhanced?

This chapter first deals at length with the components of an appropriate developmental context and the ecology of a caring environment. The child's broader life situation, particularly family relationships, are then discussed. Finally, the ways in which the ability of the worker to provide such a context can be enhanced are addressed in the last section of the chapter.

The Components of Caring Interaction

The beginnings of our scientific concern for caring interactions with children occurred in the 1940s when Ribble [1943] claimed that infants have a right to mothering, which "includes the whole gamut of small acts by which an emotionally healthy mother may consistently show her love for her child, thus intuitively stimulating emotional responses in him." By the 1980s, the concept of caring had replaced mothering, but many of the original components are still valid and appropriate.

In a flurry of studies on the nature of mother-child relationships during the 1950s and 1960s [e.g., Bowlby 1958; Mahler and LaPerriere 1965; Spitz 1965; Winnicott 1960], most researchers confirmed the importance of attachment, in the context of warm, stimulating, long-term relationships, for the normal development of children. As we are now learning, attachment is both a process of child-caregiver interaction and a result of the interaction. Some kinds of interactions are more likely to promote attachment and to enhance development, and some are less likely to do so.

In a step toward defining the quality of mother-infant interaction, Ainsworth [1974] developed a sensitivity-insensitivity scale that tests a mother's ability to observe her baby's signals, to interpret them correctly, and then to respond to them promptly and adequately. She found a relationship between a mother's ability to "see things from her baby's point of view" and the child's sense of security and growing exploratory capacities. Seeing things from the child's point of view requires that the mother focus her attention on the child, observe the child's thinking, feeling, and behaving, and then interpret these observations appropriately. To accomplish this task, the mother must be sufficiently separated from the child to see the child as a separate entity, yet sufficiently involved to interpret correctly what she has observed.

It is the mother's sensitivity to her child's signals that stimulates attachment in the child, and this attachment is essential for normal development. When it is not the mother but another caregiver who shows such sensitivity, the child develops an attachment to that person. According to Schaeffer [1971], attachments probably develop most readily to those caregivers who are able to interpret a child's behavior appropriately and to adapt their own behavior to the specific needs of that child, caregivers who see "care giving and care receiving as a symphony of human interactions" [Maier 1987]. Maier also claims that the "give-and-take process for tuning in and locating a joint rhythm occurs in attachment formation in all ages of life. This process of tuning in and finding common strands of attachments is one of the essential features of child care work" because it is a fundamental component of caring interactions.

Thus, when a child's needs are sensitively observed and interpreted, in addition to the feeling of well-being that results, the child learns to observe and interpret his or her own needs more clearly and to define them in ways that potentially lead to more gratifying empathic interaction with others. Gratification in interaction with others can lead to warmer and more stimulating relationships that, in turn, may create deeper attachments. The direct care worker who has skills in observing and interpreting the behavior of children may well be on the way toward providing those children with the foundation for a lifetime of caring, satisfying interactions.

Our task now is to define some of the cues or signals that the direct care worker is asked to observe and interpret in order to enhance caring interaction. These signals can be relayed at moments of high interactional intensity—that is, "in-action" signals—or at quieter times, an issue discussed in more detail later.

Reading Body Language

People of all ages use their bodies to express their emotions. The process of socialization teaches us to control much of what we say so that we learn to express that which is socially acceptable, or what we want others to hear. Body language is much harder to manipulate; it can therefore generally be relied upon as a more accurate cue to what the person is feeling. Children are often even less conscious of their body language than adults, and the signals they send can be rich and numerous.

Within the range of human emotions, there are continuums that move from the milder to the more extreme: fear-terror, anger-rage, pleasure-joy, concern-high anxiety, hesitation-paralyzing indecision, and sadness-grief are familiar examples. Children express these emotions differently, some expressing terror through frantic activity, for example, others through paralysis of activity. The direct care worker can observe clearly that some strong emotion is being felt, but other cues may be necessary to interpret what the child is experiencing.

Several conditions have an influence on the worker's ability to observe and interpret sensitively a child's emotional body language. First, strong emotions do not occur in a vacuum, and they invariably arouse an emotional response. If workers are having trouble coping with strong emotions in their private lives, it will be far more difficult for them to observe and acknowledge that a child is also having difficulty. The extra burden of handling the child's emotion may be unwelcome, and the body language may remain unread. (Conversely, the child who is under extreme stress will also be unable to respond at his or her usual level of astuteness.)

A related problem is the immediate context of the emotion. Children like Sheila, in our introductory vignette, whose personal crises are unrelated to the sudden, dramatic darkness, would be less likely to have their stress signals read, had the child-care worker been less sensitive and skillful, than the three children whose fears are related to the darkness.

Use of Space

We express ourselves in the ways we place our bodies in space. How and where children choose to sit at the table, whether alone or with others, and which others, tells us something about how they define themselves. A child who sits in the corner, or always sits next to the worker, is saying something. Sitting next to the worker may be a sign of seeking greater attachment, feeling a need for support, or acknowledging comradeship; sitting away from the worker may be a thrust toward independence or a leadership challenge. Although interpretations are variable and need to be situationally verified, they are, nonetheless, useful guides for day-to-day observations. Children may, indeed, tend to show by their use of space the extent and the nature of their connectedness with those around them.

Tempo, Patterns, and Rhythms

From the moment children wake up in the morning, and throughout their waking hours, a certain tempo of life can be discerned. Some children wake up with a bang, eager to begin the day, and approach each new encounter with zest. Among these children are some who are unable to sustain their energetic beginnings, and a pattern of leaps and lags accompanies their days; others tend to move breathlessly from leap to leap. For a child who approaches transitions with caution and needs time to prepare, however, a too-eager "good morning" can be experienced as a painful jolt.

From the earliest moments of life, each new being presents to the world signs of his or her life rhythm, and a caregiver's capacity to read these signs and to respond accordingly provides the framework for caring interaction. Thus an important component in caring interaction is the capacity to observe the tempo and rhythms of children individually, as well as in their interaction with one another. When a change in the pattern occurs, it may be a sign of growth and health or a signal of distress, and its occurrence needs to be noted as such.

Other Nonverbal Cues: Behavior Speaks

The boy who rushes past the worker on his way into the cottage, flings himself on the bed, and covers his head with his pillow is certainly sending off dramatic cues as to his immediate distress. Sheila, who generally comes enthusiastically to the table and helps herself generously but has now not been eating well for three days, is giving more muted signals. But the behavior of Rubin, who seems to have tampered with the fuse box lever, is exceptionally loud and dramatic, although it requires particularly subtle skills in interpretation. He is communicating indirectly through powerful symbols. Rubin's action to control the source of light may speak to his need for greater control in his life, whether objective control over the behavior of others or subjective control over his own fears. He has shown ingenuity and competence in his ability to trace the source of light for his cottage, but he has chosen to convey his message through behavior that arouses anxiety in those around him. Observing the guilt on his face is the first step in a caring interaction. Interpreting his action in terms of both the competency of its enactment and the signal it imparts is the next step. It should be noted that, had he channeled his need for mastery into acceptable activities in the electrical workshop instead, the interpretation might have been even more difficult to attain, perhaps leading to a more dramatic expression if the activity itself did not meet the need.

Verbal Cues and Signals

Verbal cues tend to be somewhat more tricky than direct body language. We are socialized into acceptable modes of communication, and we sometimes say the opposite of what we feel. Nonetheless, verbal cues can never be completely ignored. Particularly when a child says that he or she is frightened or angry or sad, he or she is transmitting information that should not be overlooked, since social norms generally dictate that such direct verbal expression of strong feelings be avoided. The child may be covering up an even less acceptable feeling or may be showing sufficient trust to express true feelings verbally. Even though the worker may have no solution at hand, just the fact of listening fully and feeling with the child at a time of stress can certainly be a source of comfort. One of the components of caring interaction is the capacity to listen actively and empathetically [Gordon 1970].

The Ecology of a Caring Environment

"Human beings change their physical and social environments and are changed by them through a process of continuous reciprocal adaptation. When it goes well, reciprocal adaptation supports growth and development of people, and elaborates life-supporting qualities of the environment" [Germain and Gitterman 1980].

Several ecological aspects of life in a residential setting are within the potential control of the direct care worker and tend to form either a responsive or a depersonalizing framework for the developmental tasks at hand. By observing the effect of these aspects of the environment, a worker can evaluate their contribution to the enhancement of competencies and to normal development processes as a basis for determining, and working toward, any needed change.

The Physical Environment

Visiting a home adds considerably to our knowledge of a family, and the individuality of each family member can usually be felt within the context of his or her room. A residential cottage may provide standardized equipment for all the children in care, but unless the rules are extremely rigid (which may reflect and contribute to an unresponsive ecology), there tends to be a different "feel" about each room and about each individual's space within the room. How children arrange their belongings tells us something about their values and their priorities. Which picture a child decides to display always contains an announcement with emotional content, and having no picture can be a statement as well. The direct care worker's responsiveness to expressions of individuality encourages a sense of belonging and enhances a child's ability to make creative use of the space in which he or she lives.

Time and the Rhythm of Caring

Children in group care often face largely nonresponsive, depersonalizing environments. These aspects have been emphasized most particularly in the works of Bowlby [1958]; Provence and Lipton [1963]; and Spitz [1965], with respect to preschool institutions, but they pertain to group care at all ages [Goffman 1961]. One of the more blatant of these aspects is the rigid use of time and its routines.

Routine, in and of itself, is certainly not harmful. For most children in care, it can be comforting and a source of security and support. It provides the necessary external limits that convey caring and concern. Problems arise, however, when routine becomes disassociated from the rhythm of caring, and when its dictates take precedence over responsiveness to need. Constant vigilance on the part of direct care workers is required, therefore, to discern when a routine is operating so as to create or foster depersonalization.

Sometimes a new person, coming into a routinized situation, can observe consequences that have become invisible to those who have been involved in the situation over time as a result of their familiarity with it.

> A new director at a preschool residential institution discovered that, when she arrived each morning at 7:30, most of the 60 small children in the home showed signs of tension and frustration, which gradually dissipated during the day.
>
> One morning, she came at 6:30 and found the children awakening normally, without any signs of tension. The direct care workers, however, expecting their replacements an hour later, were busy keeping the shades down and the children quiet and in bed. They explained that the activities related to waking and dressing were not in their jurisdiction as night workers. At a meeting called that day, the child-care workers agreed to a schedule change by which they would arrive at 6:30, so that the children could awaken to an atmosphere that was more in accordance with their needs.

By keeping the shades down and expending considerable energy in keeping the children in bed, the night workers had certainly been observing the behavior of the children, but the focus of their interpretation of that behavior did not relate to the legitimate need of children to feel the opportunity for freedom of movement and contact with the world on awakening. Any solution that was responsive to the needs of both the children and the workers would have been equally satisfactory, since the goal was to reach a rhythm of caring that would enhance normative development. All daily routines should be subjected to such tests of appropriateness from time to time in order to reassess their responsiveness to the rhythm of caring.

There are other aspects of time and the rhythm of caring that warrant consideration, such as the need for maximum flexibility in the children's contacts with family and friends. Are weekend leave arrangements geared to the routines of the institution or to the powerful pulls and shoves these weekends inevitably arouse in both the children and their families? Are parent visiting schedules sufficiently flexible to encourage even the most reluctant, ambivalent parent? More broadly, when is the need to be alone more important for growth and development than the need to learn to work and play together with the group? In many ways the rhythm of caring should steer a course between allowing the child to do what he or she wants to do, and gently guiding the child to conform to social expectations.

Quiet Times and Active Times

One of the endemic problems of direct care work with children is the urgency or immediacy of needs that require on-the-spot decision making. Those who have had direct experience with the group care of children can usually bring to instant recall a favorite tale of horror, a time when they were confronted with a dramatic crisis and had to make an immediate, authoritative decision. These are the "trials by fire" that all children subject adults to, knowingly or not; they seem particularly overwhelming in the group care situation, where the worker's ability to observe and interpret behavior is subjected to a test of action under the scrutiny of many anxious, watchful eyes. Will this be the time that the worker will show his or her "true colors"? Will the worker show that he or she is incompetent or really can't stand children? Perhaps, and then who will "win" the contest of strength and authority?

There is probably no single formula available that applies to all such moments of confrontation, and there is no single "right" reaction. The worker in our illustration found herself in such a situation, and she had many alternatives available. Her responses in action at the time of the blackout probably gave a feeling of reassurance to the children. Despite the pandemonium around her, she found a way to relate both to the specialized needs of the particularly fearful children and to the needs of the others. She managed to observe the expression on Rubin's face, and the interpretation of that will guide her reactions with him during the evening. It is reassuring to consider, however, that within the context of a caring environment such as the one she seems to have created, even a serious blunder or misinterpretation can usually be straightened out and worked through.

The more carefully the worker observes each of the children in care during the quiet moments, when life is proceeding relatively smoothly, the better equipped the worker will be when an on-the-spot interpretation has to be made. The more caring and responsive the day-to-day environment provided by the worker, the more latitude will generally be given by children who may be the victims of misinterpretation at a moment of crisis. This reaction depends also, of course, on the child's history of disappointments, which may make some children particularly vulnerable and harder to appease.

The Child's Broader Life Situation

Research on children in placement has been emphasizing strongly the importance of parents and the home environment [Fanshel and Shyne 1978; Maluccio and Sinanoglu 1981; Weiner and Weiner 1990]. "The ecological emphasis on the dynamic transactions between people and their environments highlights the crucial importance of the biological family in the growth and functioning of children in placement" [Maluccio 1981]. Thus, despite the physical distance and the opportunities for attachments to direct care workers, parents remain important to children in care. Even with minimal contact or a history of abuse, the influence of the parents is usually permanent and should not be impugned or denied. Genetic endowments such as the child's physical appearance, sex, health history, innate intellectual capacities, and basic personality traits all reflect his or her biological parents and ancestors and are also a continuous part of the child's reality.

Without the knowledge necessary to take cognizance of this aspect of the child's reality, the direct care worker may underestimate the significance of the parents in the child's inner life, or the worker may feel that he or she is in the position of rival for the child's primary attachment. Thus, Jenkins [1981] conceptualizes the placement situation in terms of the more familiar custody battle for children of divorce: "The biological parent is in this sense in the same situation as the noncustodial parent in divorce, who has a real struggle to remain a significant figure in the child's life." As in divorce, acknowledgment of the child's need to remain in contact with and attached to the noncustodial parent can help free the child for deepening attachment to the direct care worker.

By acknowledging the child's hidden loyalties, the worker can take them into account when observing changes in a child's verbal and nonverbal behavior. When a child who is usually an enthusiastic eater, like Sheila, loses interest in food for a few days, one of the interpretations that must be considered is a possible change in the pattern of interaction between the child and the parents. Perhaps Sheila has had no contact lately and feels despair, or perhaps the anticipation of a coming visit has aroused anxiety. Or perhaps it is not her parents who have been the source of her problem, but rather her relationship with a sibling, a grandparent, an aunt or uncle, or even a former teacher or a friend not in the residential care setting.

Although the direct care worker may, in many settings, have little direct influence on what happens in the homes of the children in care, knowledge of those happenings is an important element in the sensitive interpretation of observed behavior.

The Role of the Direct Care Worker

Although reviewing behaviors and their interactional contexts can be a helpful tool, it is not enough. The process must be incorporated by the worker if it is to be used flexibly and effectively. Since those workers with growth-enhancing abilities generally appear to have a natural familiarity with the needs of the children in their care, however, why subject such workers to an enhancement process that may cause awkward self-consciousness?

In their books on child development, Winnicott [1964] and Kaplan [1978] stress the concept of normalcy in parenting. Winnicott points to the immense contribution made by the "ordinary good mother" who benefits her child and society "simply through being devoted." Kaplan insists that the "less than perfect" mother is generally adequately equipped to guide her young child successfully from "oneness to separateness," from infancy to individuality. "A mother need not match up with her infant's illusion of perfection in order for the infant to thrive and be whole. A mother survives best when she allows herself the imperfections of the ordinary mother."

Can the same be said for the direct care worker? As with intuitive parenthood, healthy instincts and natural self-reliance in a caregiver make the daily interactions with dependent children more pleasurable for both worker and child. Why try to enhance the skills available intuitively to many such workers, and probably inaccessible to most inadequate workers even after such an attempt at enhancement? Will a direct care worker who becomes a more conscious observer and interpreter of behavior lose the intuitive ability that made his or her relationship with the children satisfying? In Buber's terms [1970], will it lead to the establishment of an "I-it" rather than an "I-thou" relationship? These are questions faced by all who are involved in communicating empathic skills and the acquisition of an informed or trained presence of mind.

Reynolds [1965] identifies five stages of learning that students of social work pass through in their efforts to master basic helping skills. The first involves acute consciousness of the self, a stage marked by distress that requires the mobilization of energy that is expressed differently by different individuals. Among direct care workers, this stage might express itself in flight from the task at hand or in aggressive self-defense. The instructor provides security by "helping the learner to plant his feet in the solid ground of personal adequacy he already has."

During the second stage, the learner begins to have some idea of what is expected and, in a sink-or-swim effort, may hit upon a response that is favorably received. Criticism at this stage can do harm; the goal of the instructor is to create an atmosphere that is both protective and stimulating.

In the third stage, the learner experiences a sense of understanding the situation, but still does not possess the power to control his or her activity, and the automatic responses of the past are still utilized. The instructor's role is one of patience and reassurance.

It is in the fourth stage that the learner achieves a sense of relative mastery in which he or she can both understand and control behavior. The fifth is the stage of learning to teach what one has mastered. The parallels to the development of youngsters in group care should be noted.

Gordon [1970], in his Parent Effectiveness Training Course for improving the observation and interpretation skills of parents in their daily interactions with their children, identifies four stages in the process of learning interactional skills. He begins with the "unconsciously unskilled" stage, when parents (and direct care workers) interact with their children without awareness of the fact that there are skills available that could help them. Many direct care workers are operating at this stage.

The second stage, resembling the first two stages of Reynolds, is the "consciously unskilled" stage. Parents become aware of the availability of interactional skills but are not yet using them. Feelings of inadequacy and guilt often accompany this phase. During the third stage, the parent becomes "consciously skilled" and tends to feel awkward as the newly acquired skills are haltingly applied. If the parent persists in using these new skills, the stage of being "unconsciously skilled" is reached, with comfortable integration of the new skills into all of life's interactions.

It is clear that the acquisition of empathic skills is a process that generally evokes resistance and creates a sense of awkwardness. The stage of self-consciousness one experiences before integration of the new skills can be experienced as a movement into "I-it" from the more familiar "I-thou" relationships of the past. As with any meaningful change, there is a feeling of vulnerability when defenses are lowered so that change can occur, although this transition is, it is to be hoped, only a temporary one. This is true for the experienced worker with considerable intuitive ability as well as for the anxious, well-defended beginner. Nevertheless, the benefits for the direct care worker and, of course, particularly for the children in care, are immense: for the worker, a deeper, more satisfying caregiving experience; for the children, opportunities to learn about themselves through the eyes of a sensitized adult, to grow and develop in a development-enhancing environment, and, above all, to form a warm relationship with a skilled observer and interpreter of behavior.

Summary

Caring interactions that enhance growth and deepen attachments are based on the sensitive observation and interpretation of a child's behavior. Children give cues and signals that can be observed through emotional body language; through the use of space; through the expression of life tempo, pattern, and rhythm; through the use of verbal cues; and through direct behavior.

In addition to caring interactions, the ecology of a caring environment includes the interaction between children and their physical life space and vigilant awareness of the effect of time and its tendency toward depersonalizing routinization. The significance to children of their families should never be underestimated despite geographical distance and meager contact.

It is hoped that the more knowledge gained by direct care workers through sensitive observation and interpretation during moments of peaceful existence, the better equipped they will be to respond with care when decisions must be made on the spot. The enhancement of their skills of observation and interpretation can create a more satisfying caregiving experience for them and an improved developmental environment for the children in residential care.

REFERENCES

Ainsworth, M.D.S. 1974. The development of infant-mother attachment. In Caldwell, B.M., and Ricciuti, H.N. (eds.), *Review of Child Development Research 3*. Chicago, IL: University of Chicago Press.

Bowlby, J. 1958. The nature of the child's tie to the mother. *International Journal of Psychoanalysis* 39: 350–373.

Buber, M. 1970. *I and Thou*. New York: Charles Scribner's Sons.

Fanshel, D., and Shyne, A.W. 1978. *Children in Foster Care: A Longitudinal Investigation*. New York: Columbia University Press.

Germain, C.B., and Gitterman, A. 1980. *The Life Model of Social Work Practice*. New York: Columbia University Press.

Goffman, E. 1961. *Asylums: Essays on the Social Situation of Mental Patients and Other Institutions*. New York: Doubleday.

Gordon, T. 1970. *P.E.T. Parent Effectiveness Training*. New York: Peter H. Wyden, Inc.

Jenkins, S. 1981. The tie that bonds. In Maluccio, A., and Sinanoglu, P.S. (eds.), *The Challenge of Partnership: Working with Parents of Children in Foster Care*. New York: Child Welfare League of America.

Kaplan, J. 1978. *Openness and Separateness: From Infant to Individual*. New York: Simon & Shuster.

Mahler, M.S., and LaPerriere, K. 1965. Mother-child interaction during separation-individuation. *Psychoanalytic Quarterly* 34: 483–498.

Maier, H.W. 1987. *Developmental Group Care of Children and Youth: Concepts and Practice*. New York: Haworth: pp 40, 42; also in Ainsworth, F., and Fulcher, L.C. (eds.) 1981. *Group Care for Children: Concept and Issues*. London and New York: Tavistock: pp 23, 25.

Maluccio, A. 1981. An ecological perspective on practice with parents of children in foster care. In Maluccio, A., and Sinanoglu, P.S. (eds.), *The Challenge of Partnership: Working with Parents of Children in Foster Care*. New York: Child Welfare League of America.

Maluccio, A., and Sinanoglu, P.S. (eds.). 1981. *The Challenge of Partnership: Working with Parents of Children in Foster Care*. New York: Child Welfare League of America.

Provence, S., and Lipton, R.   1963.   *Infants in Institutions.* New York: International Universities Press.

Reynolds, B.   1965.   *Learning and Teaching in the Practice of Social Work.* New York: Russell & Russell.

Ribble, M.   1943.   *The Rights of Infants.* New York: Columbia University Press.

Schaeffer, R.   1971.   *Mothering.* Cambridge, MA: Harvard University Press.

Spitz, R.A.   1965.   *The First Year of Life: A Psychoanalytic Study of Normal-Deviant Development of Object Relations.* New York: International Universities Press.

Weiner, A., and Weiner, E.   1990.   *Expanding the Options in Child Placement.* Lanham, MD: University Press of America.

Winnicott, D.W.   1960.   The theory of parent-infant relationships. *International Journal of Psychoanalysis 41*: 585–595.

Winnicott, D.W.   1964.   *The Child, the Family, and the Outside World.* Hammondsworth, Middlesex, England: Penguin.

6

Promoting Social Competence: Implications of Work with Mentally Retarded Children and Adults in Residential Settings

SHUNIT REITER
DIANE NELSON BRYEN

Rosie, a mentally retarded adolescent living in an institution, was taken by her direct care worker to a department store to buy underwear in the course of a social education program. A satisfactory choice was made and paid for. Having successfully supervised this novel transaction, the direct care worker became interested in some clothing and left Rosie for a short while to her own devices. The worker's attention was sharply recalled to her client when she sensed some public commotion. To her consternation, she discovered Rosie embarking on a striptease in her desire to try on her new garments [from Gunzberg and Gunzberg 1973].

When Yaron was 15 months old, he was separated from his mother and placed in a residential nursery. Observations of his early days in the nursery revealed that by the fourth day, his behavior had deteriorated markedly. He had lengthy spells of sad crying that merged with the din of the other children and went unattended by the nurses. His play was listless, he sucked more, ate and drank hardly at all, and walked with a slow, shambling gait. On the fifth day, Yaron's misery attracted added attention from the nurses, but they could not comfort him or interest him in toys. He ate nothing all day. No nurse had direct responsibility for him, so their concern was dispersed and ineffectual. Occasionally, he shouted angrily at no one in particular, and in a brief contact he smacked one nurse's face. By the ninth day, Yaron cried from the moment he awoke, hanging over his cot and shaking with sobs. Only one of the nurses was not new to him, and he was often slumped motionless on her lap. Thereafter, Yaron alternated between long periods of apathy to food, people, and activities, and brief, intense bouts of aggression [based, in part, on Robertson and Robertson 1971].

Tamar, a resident of an Israeli institution for moderately and mildly handicapped children and adolescents, was invited to a wedding. To prepare for this special occasion, she went to the hairdresser in town. Coincidentally, one of the cottage supervisors from the institution was also there, although she could not easily be recognized under the hair dryer. She could, however, observe Tamar as the girl stood at the door, being "very polite" and waiting for someone to approach her and invite her inside. At most such establishments in Israel, it is expected that clients will walk inside and inquire how soon and from whom they can get service. Thus, as Tamar kept standing at the door, the hairdresser started to giggle and pointed a finger at her, saying, "She must be retarded."

Tom is a mentally retarded ten-year-old who has been in an institution for moderately and severely retarded persons for three years. According to his child-care worker, he is typical of the group for which she is responsible. She described Tom as being "very good": he completes all his tasks when told; upon completion of tasks he just sits and waits or rocks himself; he does things with people or objects only when told to do so; he eats any food placed in front of him, and when finished, he waits; he allows other children to take food and objects from him; he always stops and waits for help when a new or somewhat difficult task is presented to him. She summarized Tom's behavior by reiterating what a good and obedient little boy he is.

Each of these vignettes highlights various serious difficulties in the development of social competence in residents of institutions that cannot be completely accounted for on the basis of their being mentally retarded or developmentally young. Rosie's behavior was clearly socially inappropriate. Is her inappropriate behavior a direct result of her mental retardation? Gunzberg and Gunzberg [1973] think not. They go on to say that, "quite oblivious of the need for privacy to which she had never been accustomed in ward life, Rosie simply transferred her way of living in the institution to the community." Many non-retarded young people in institutions have similar difficulties.

Young Yaron's problems were quite different from those of Rosie. He was depressed, listless, and frequently angry, most probably because of his separation from his mother, his lack of ego maturity due to his very young age at the time of separation, and his inability to establish a substitute mothering figure from whom security and comfort could be obtained. Like Rosie, Yaron was also at the mercy of a compliancy-demanding environment and of the institution's failure to provide an adequate substitute caregiving object [Spitz and Wolf 1946]. Also like Rosie, his social (and, in this case, emotional) problems were not just internally based. The absence of a primary care worker who was directly responsible for him, who could respond to his signals of distress, and who could comfort him, compounded an already potentially traumatic situation, his early separation from his mother.

Tamar is overcompliant, as evidenced by her being unduly polite and waiting for someone to approach her and invite her in, despite the cultural norm in Israel of entering and requesting service. This behavior reduces her effectiveness in transacting social affairs in the community. In addition, it attracts negative attention and ridicule from others. Overcompliance may even have inadvertently been taught by residential staff members who see compliant behavior as positive (or at least expedient).

Finally, we have Tom, whose social problems are perhaps the most far-reaching and debilitating. He is extremely passive and reactive to the demands of others, and he retreats from tasks that are new or slightly difficult. Rarely, if ever, does he initiate interactions with either his social or his physical environment. Instead, he behaves as though he is a victim of his environment. The phenomenon of learned helplessness [Seligman 1975] is further compounded by the fact that his care worker views his helplessness, or his compliance, as she calls it, quite positively and inadvertently fosters it.

Some of the problems faced by these four young people and many others living in institutions cannot be eradicated by direct care workers, no matter how good our intentions or how skillful we may be. For example, Rosie, Tom, and

Tamar are mentally retarded and will experience some difficulty in learning that is simply beyond our control. Similarly, we can do little to change the reality that Yaron was separated from his mother at too young an age—before his ego had developed adequately and before he had developed an adequate object concept so that he could re-create his mother symbolically in her absence. Care workers can do much, however, to promote social competence and emotional well being, and it is to these ends that this chapter is written.

Before proceeding to practical strategies that direct care workers can use to promote social competence and emotional well-being in young people in a variety of out-of-home residential group care settings, existing knowledge pertaining to social competence, social-emotional development, and factors affecting social competence is presented briefly for several reasons. (See also Chapters 2 and 3.) First, principles of learning and development can help to guide the selection and use of particular strategies. In addition, a sound knowledge base can provide support for many of the helpful practices already being used intuitively by many residential child and youth care workers, enabling them to communicate more effectively the what and the why of their actions with clients—an important skill in asserting one's role as a valued and valuable member of the residential staff.

Social Competence: What Is It?

Social competence can be viewed as the ability to cope with the natural and social demands of one's environment. It includes skills, capacities, motivations, knowledge, and personality attributes, all of which are applied to interact with the immediate environment more or less effectively. According to Leland [1977], to interact with the immediate environment effectively, a person must "take from the environment the cues and behavioral guides critical to successful comprehension of the demands of that environment, and having comprehended these demands, he must through his own processes [and intentions], adjust his behavior and modify his approaches to develop individual strategies to deal with these demands." Since this concept is quite broad and abstract, it may be helpful to define social competence in more familiar terms, such as interpersonal relations, social behavior, adaptive behavior, social interactions, social skills, adequate self-image, self-acceptance, initiative, and cooperativeness, all of which describe particular components of the concept of social competence.

In terms of what is learned and taught, social competence includes three interrelated content categories: (1) performance skills (the what; for example, vocalizing "Hello"); (2) societal norms (the when and where of skill utilization: for example, saying "Hello" to known people when you first greet them and not to people who are strangers or to a staff member every time contact is made with him or her during an activity); and *(3) value judgments* (the why of skill utilization: for example, social greetings such as saying "Hello" that reflect the value of being polite while maintaining some physical distance, rather than ignoring familiar persons or touching them).

These three social competence factors—skills, norms, values—cut across two general concepts of social competence, one of which is "daily living skills" and comprises those social competencies that enable the individual to act independently within a social setting. Within this general category are more specific competencies, such as dressing, toileting, washing, moving from place to place within and between settings, and so forth. One basis for this category of competencies is the value of being as minimally dependent on others as possible. The second category is the social-interpersonal. Here, the goal is not independence from others, as with daily living skills, but rather to promote and sustain interpersonal and, thus, interdependent relations with others. Thus, becoming more socially competent means being able simultaneously to develop skills that enable independence and promote interdependence with others.

Examples are given in Table 1 to illustrate these two general categories of social competence, as well as the three factors that influence the successful learning of all social competencies. The examples provided in Table 1 are drawn from problems experienced by Rosie and Tamar. As can be seen from this table, social competence "lies in the relational system and as such must be evaluated (and taught) from an interpersonal perspective" [Prutting 1982].

Social Competence and Institutionalization

Much has been written about the potential harmful effects of large institutions on the social competency of their clients. Since an extensive literature already exists, possible negative effects of institutions are mentioned only briefly here. Many mentally retarded people living in large public facilities, for example, have been found to withdraw from social interaction [Peters et al. 1974] and to express their frustrations and anger ineffectively [Boe 1977; Felsenthal and Scheerenberger 1978]. They have also been found to be dependent and suspicious [Zigler 1978] and to feel helpless to influence their environments [DeVellis 1977; Veit et al. 1976]. Additionally, Zigler [1978] and others have found that the residents have strong needs for social approval even though they are wary of adults. Similar effects have been reported among the non-retarded.

Because many more social problems have been found among young people living in large institutions than among those with similar problems living in the community, current research [e.g., Burkhart and Seim 1979; Tjosvold and Tjosvold 1983] has focused on the effects that large institutions and care practices within

TABLE 1

Categories and Factors of Social Competence

Categories	Skills (What)	Norms (Where and When)	Values (Why)
Independent-living competencies	Dressing/undressing	Appropriate times and places to dress/undress	Body should be covered in public situations
	Use of private and public telephones	Correct hours for making business and personal phone calls	Makes social/business communication more efficient when time and distance prevent face-to-face interaction
	Time-telling	Appropriate times and places to check time and the need to regulate behavior accordingly	Punctuality makes for smooth social transactions and shows regard for other people
Social-interpersonal competencies	Initiating a conversation	Socially acceptable situations to initiate a conversation and with whom	Interpersonal interactions, intimacy versus privacy
	Introducing oneself to others	Acceptable social circumstances that call for identifying oneself	Social interactions are based on a mutual appraisal of others' identities
	Saying "I'm sorry."	Response to other's cues of pain, hurt, or discomfort	Respect and concern for the feelings of others

them might have on the social competence of their residents. It should be noted, however, that not all large institutions produce such negative consequences, nor are small, community residences completely free of these hazards. In fact, a group of British researchers [King and Raynes 1968; Raynes and King 1968; Tizard 1960, 1964, 1970] found that the size of the institution was not, as had been expected, the most important factor affecting the quality of life of its residents. The nature of the organizational structure (i.e., client orientation versus an orientation to the maintenance of the status quo) appeared to be the critical variable determining the quality of the client's life in the institution.

Thus, certain patterns of institutions and caregiving practices within them hinder the development of social competency. They include rigid routines and strict regulations; limited and inadequate interaction and communication between staff members and residents; lack of privacy and lack of private space and possessions; lack of stimulation; and rapid turnover of direct care workers—to describe just a few. These and other restrictive conditions result in clients' poor self-images, boredom and self-stimulation, and lack of secure attachments to others. Educational programs are often lacking, and when they are provided, they most frequently focus on daily living skills only. In addition, programmatic efforts are often restricted to the learning of isolated skill performance (e.g., tying one's shoes), rather than the kinds of skills, norms, and values summarized in Table 1. Indeed, the list of potentially debilitating effects of institutionalization is long and has been extensively documented [cf. Zigler 1978; Tjosvold and Tjosvold 1983; Edgerton et al. 1975].

Rather than focusing on the negative effects of institutions, however, we should view the promoting of social competence in residential settings from a positive analysis of the environment. Three general orientations to institutional life and clients provide an appropriate framework: (1) life in institutions should be as normalized as is appropriate to the capacities and needs of the clients; (2) insofar as possible, the circumstances that lead to institutionalization should be viewed as developmental disabilities (with developmental solutions) rather than as deviance; and (3) the management style of the institution should be client-oriented rather than institution-oriented. Each of these perspectives is discussed briefly below.

Normalization

The normalization principle holds that all institutions should strive to create an environment that is as culturally normal as possible. This concept originated in the Scandinavian countries in the early 1970s and, at first, was focused mainly on residential services for the mentally handicapped [Nirje 1969]. Its application has now been broadened to include services for all devalued persons, such as the handicapped, the disadvantaged, and the aged.

Wolfensberger [1972] defined normalization as the "utilization of means which are as culturally normative as possible, in order to establish and/or maintain personal behaviors and characteristics which are as culturally normative as possible." Thus, this orientation refers to what is generally done and valued by most people in a given society. For an institutional environment to be normalized, clients must have some personal possessions, have a certain degree of privacy, have access to community activities (e.g., movies, restaurants, houses of worship); work or attend school in a place other than the cottage; not be constrained to overly strict routines and schedules regarding bedtime, toileting, and eating; and have some degree of choice concerning the type and quantity of food, leisure activities, and so forth. Although age is a major factor influencing decisions about what is normative for a particular client, chronological age alone is not sufficient to determine either the goals or the means of staff-client practices; the client's developmental status must also be taken into account. Thus, we come to the second orientation guiding institutional life and client-care practice.

Developmental Orientation

To create a normal yet appropriate environment, residential settings must provide their clients with activities and experiences that are tailored to their developmental needs, which do not necessarily coincide with chronological age. This perspective may also require providing those make-up experiences that clients missed in earlier stages of their development but that are basic to the mastery of social competence.

Referring back to our opening vignettes, Rosie should have had the opportunity to experience privacy; personal clothing; time and space for solitude; and the contrasting aspects of private, primary group, and public activities, all accompanied by sensitive and well-adapted feedback regarding the situational appropriateness of private versus public behavior. Yaron needed the opportunity to form a secure attachment to one caregiver, even if that could not be his own mother; this means the presence of a stable, consistent, and responsive care worker. For Tamar and Tom, opportunities to initiate, sustain, and terminate activities, to have choices, to negate the actions of others and not always to comply with their dictates should have been provided. These experiences are crucial to the development of initiative, judgment, and other adaptive behaviors.

A developmental orientation assumes that, irrespective of their handicaps, clients follow the general course of development experienced by non-handicapped people [cf. Kahn 1975, 1977; Inhelder 1968]. This development is sometimes delayed or arrested not just because of those handicaps, but as a result of inadequate care practices and restrictive institutional environments. With the implementation of developmentally based strategies, however, further growth and development can occur. In contrast to a development orientation, a restrictive environment is one that assumes (albeit sometimes unconsciously) that people with handicaps are different from the rest of society—an assumption that they are qualitatively deviant and thus need deviant environments. Consequently, the goal of these environments is corrective rather than developmental.

A developmental perspective does not mean that corrective and/or remedial strategies are never used. Indeed, there are some clients who, after years of institutionalization, have developed coping strategies that are deviant and require extreme treatment approaches. As a general guideline, however, it is best to start with strategies that are based on developmental principles. Only after a substantial period of time has passed without evidence of even limited growth should the care worker apply remedial approaches that are based on the notion that the client is deviant.

Many theories exist that describe and attempt to explain cognitive development [e.g., Piaget 1952, 1963]; social-emotional development [e.g, Erikson 1950]; attachment formation [Bowlby 1953]; and social learning [e.g., Bandura 1965]. On the basis of these theories, several principles and many strategies can be derived and effectively used by care workers.

Client Orientation

The third orientation that should guide the care worker in the selection and use of caregiving strategies is a primary focus on the needs of the client rather than on the efficiency and status quo of the institution. Like all social organizations, institutions experience a continuing tension between activities and interactional styles that are geared to the smooth and efficient operation of the setting, on one hand, and the needs and interests of the members, on the other. Unfortunately, it is particularly easy to neglect the social-emotional and developmental needs of clients in group care settings so that the institution can run smoothly and efficiently. When this situation occurs, transactions between care workers and clients are limited in both quantity and quality and are frequently characterized by expedience. For example, when daily routines are conducted, instead of showing the clients what needs to be done and why, and instead of talking to them during the actual routine, care workers may perform the activity for the client or they may rely on abrupt commands without modeling how to do it and without the important supportive communication.

Client orientation is affected by a multitude of management factors, not the least of which is the decentralization of decision making. King and Raynes [1968] reported that the care of mentally retarded clients in residential settings was more resident-oriented when those in charge of the daily living units housing the clients (i.e., care workers) participated in several aspects of decision making. Similarly, Raynes et al. [1977] found that the provision of resident-stimulating care was positively related to the extent to which the care workers perceived themselves to be involved in the making of decisions related to their work and the clients in their care. Thus, it seems clear that a client orientation is one that is responsive to the participation of both care workers and clients in decisions and actions that affect their daily lives.

Practices and Strategies of Effective Care Work

Child and youth care workers "provide the main source and substance of care experience and are the pivotal people in the residents' daily lives" [Maier, this volume]; their role is therefore critical in providing effective strategies to promote social competence. Strategies based on the three orientations just described that provide a framework for effective and caring caregiving are suggested below.

Normalization in Practice

Embodied in the normalization principle are many physical, spatial, and temporal events that affect every aspect of a person's life. Effective implementation of this principle transforms the institutional environment from being impersonal, sterile, and rigid to being personal, personalized, and flexible.

Strategies that affect the physical and spatial environment include the following:

1. Clients should have personal and private space for sleeping, for receiving friends and guests, and for keeping their personal possessions. Even where large wards do exist, temporary partitions can be erected to maximize private space, and brightly painted boxes can be used to store personal belongings. Without private space for the clients and their possessions, clients cannot learn to differentiate between public and private behaviors (you will recall Rosie), nor can they learn the difference between "mine" and "yours."

2. Clients should be permitted and encouraged to have, display, and use personal belongings (e.g., clothes, toys, photos) that they choose rather than those belongings that are communal or are chosen by others. Without these possessions, clients can neither learn the difference between "mine" and "yours" nor express their individuality. Futhermore, possession of one or more personal and favorite objects serves the emotional function of providing security to the client in times

of stress or discomfort (you may recall the cartoon character Linus and his ever-present blanket).

3. Clients should be able to decorate their personal area with personal photos, drawings, or other favorite objects. In so doing, not only is one able to display one's personality and interests, but also establishes one's actual home, with all that is idiosyncratic to his or her home environment.

4. Communal areas, such as dining rooms and bathrooms, should be comfortable, personal, and welcoming. This goal might mean placing flowers on the tables, providing pleasant and comfortable furniture, hanging photos and artwork on the wall, and hanging bright curtains at the windows. Without a safe and pleasant physical environment, the cottage can never be a desirable home for clients or a pleasant place for care workers to spend their working hours. Furthermore, if the most basic physical needs for comfort and security are not met, the client will not be free to proceed toward learning more sophisticated skills.

5. All living spaces should be free of unpleasant odors (e.g., the smell of urine or disinfectant) and, to whatever extent is possible, free of intrusive noises (e.g., excessive screaming). The reasons for this goal are much the same as those for the preceding strategy.

6. Clients' activities should not be confined to one physical area. Eating, work or school, and recreation should take place in different locations within the institution and, as much as possible, in the surrounding community. The more they are exposed to different contexts and the people and activities associated with them and the more experiences they have that are embedded in a range of contexts, the more likely it is that clients will learn situationally appropriate behaviors. Overpoliteness, as shown in the behavior that made Tamar "look retarded," will be less likely to occur as clients learn to adapt skills to the norms and situational demands of different environments in and out of the institution. Having different activities in different locations has the additional advantage of fostering the learning of transportation skills, even if the transportation occurs by foot within the institution itself.

Normalizing the temporal environment is furthered by the following strategies:

1. Basic daily activities, like bathing, toileting, and sleeping, should not be done rigidly, en masse. Instead, the timing of these activities should as much as possible reflect the individual needs of the clients. All people have different toileting schedules, require different amounts of sleep, and have, within limits, different patterns of bathing. To require that all clients go to sleep and arise at the same

time, and toilet and bathe at the same time, not only ignores their individuality, but also demands that clients be responsive to the operation of the institution rather than the institution being responsive to their needs.

2. Weekend schedules and activities should differ from and be more flexible than the weekday schedules of work and/or school. The reasons for this difference are twofold. First, time is learned and understood by event markers—of which schedules and activities are but two. Thus, different weekend schedules temporally mark off the weekend from the weekdays. Second, all people need a break from the more rigid and hectic flow of weekday work schedules. It should not be assumed that institutionalized young people and their care workers are exceptions.

3. Clients should have adequate time (and space) during meals to enjoy not only the nutritional aspects of eating, but the social aspects as well. Mealtimes are important opportunities to learn new eating and social skills and can serve as the starting point for all kinds of human development. In fact, several publications have been devoted to describing the many potentials for learning and socialization during mealtimes [e.g., Perske et al. 1977]. These authors, some of whom are care workers, summarize the ideal mealtime as an opportunity for

> Feeling comradeship and belonging
> Relaxing and being less defensive
> Communicating in many ways, with voice, eyes, body, taste, smell,
and touch
> Laughing and feeling joyful
> Being accepted exactly as you are, and being glad you are you
> Making choices
> Having all the time you need
> Heightening all the senses
> Feeling full, satisfied, and relaxed
> Taking in nutrition for growth and good health

4. Care workers should eat with the clients (at the same time and at the same table) so that personal interaction and the modeling of appropriate behaviors can occur. (See also the reasons described in item 3 above.)

5. A balance between free and leisure time and the more rigid schedules of work or school should be sought (i.e., punctuality at work and school is contrasted with the freedom in time and space of leisure). Not only is this balance necessary, as described in item 2 above, but clients need to learn skills in managing their free time. Clients who are always programmed tend not to learn or tend to unlearn basic exploratory and play behaviors that characterize normal free time. This behavior is clearly illustrated in the vignette about Tom.

These normalizing strategies are not meant to be exhaustive. In fact, it would be impossible to itemize all aspects of a more normalized environment. Care workers can generate many, many more strategies by reflecting on the physical, temporal, and spatial aspects of their own personal lives and, wherever possible, relating these to the lives of those in residential care.

Client Orientation in Practice

For the institutional environment to be responsive to the social-emotional learning needs of its residents, its management style must tilt toward that rather than toward expediency and administrative convenience. These strategies can help to move the institution toward greater focus on the needs of its residents:

1. All daily activities should have as their goal not just the expedient completion of the activity, for example, handwashing, but rather the client's learning how, when, and why to do something. This may seem self-evident, but it is often overlooked because it takes more time to model, communicate while doing, experiment with, and try each activity again than to preempt the client's own faulty attempts. Each daily living activity should be viewed as a context for teaching/learning self-help and social skills and, therefore, be afforded the necessary time and patience.

2. Clients should be given choices, whenever possible, in selecting their clothing, games, food, leisure and work activities, friends, workmates, and so on. Unless they experience choices, clients are unlikely to develop initiative, judgment, and understanding of and responsibility for the consequences of their actions, nor will they learn the many reasons for communication. Futhermore, without choices, an individual unfortunately learns the subtle but profound message that the environment is all-powerful, and the person is simply reactive to the needs and wishes of others. Both Tom and Tamar are examples of overly compliant behavior that can be explained, in part, by the lack of choices offered to them.

3. Clients should be given the opportunity, within reasonable bounds, to refuse food, clothing choices, activities, and so forth, presented by staff members. Just as choices offer rich opportunities for learning, the ability to refuse the choices made by others teaches clients that they are people with unique interests, desires, and needs, and that they have some power to express them.

4. Clients should be able to express, in nonviolent ways, negative feelings, frustrations, anger, and so forth, without fear of reprisal. Without this freedom, clients inadvertently learn to believe that they are helpless to influence their environment. This belief not only hinders the development of social competence, but it is likely to spread to all aspects of their learning.

5. Clients should be encouraged to initiate interactions with staff members and not just to react to the staff's initiatives. While often bothersome, especially when staff members have chores to do, client-initiated interactions are the key to forming secure attachments and to learning many important interpersonal skills. Indeed, the cases of Yaron, Tom, and Tamar show the adverse effects of an environment that has not been responsive to their initiation.

6. To the greatest extent feasible, clients should participate in decisions that affect their daily lives in the institution. Some reasons for this have been discussed earlier, vis-à-vis the care worker; others are described in items 2 through 5 above.

7. Interactions with clients should reflect each client's uniqueness, needs, and abilities. This aim means calling them by their names and recognizing and acknowledging their interests, temperaments, and fears. For some clients, dependency or "holding-on" behavior may be needed despite the general institutional goal of teaching independence. For others, a gentle nudge toward doing something more independently may be called for.

Again, it is impossible to list all of the many strategies that reflect a client orientation. Operating within the conscious framework of providing clients with an emotionally responsive environment helps care workers to generate additional strategies in the course of the work.

Developmental Orientation in Practice

A developmental orientation implies that new skills and abilities grow out of and build on earlier, more basic, and sometimes qualitatively different abilities and skills. It further implies that the development of these abilities has an orderly hierarchy that normally cannot be bypassed. It assumes that most of the problems of young people in group care are developmentally based; that is, they reflect uneven rates of growth and development. In most individuals, some developmental domains lag behind others (for example, cognitive development in the mentally retarded) and do not match chronological age; both the lags and the disparities often appear as problems. For effective and caring child and youth care work, staff members must be able to take cues from the clients' behaviors to assess approximately where the client is developmentally (what he or she knows and doesn't know, can and cannot do, and so on). In addition to intuition, familiarity with developmental theory (i.e., the stages and processes) and developmentally based assessment tools will help in determining the client's level of development and appropriate interventions.

The following general strategies illustrate the application of basic developmental principles:

1. View the client's behaviors, even those that appear to be bizarre or unconventional, as purposeful rather than random or without meaning. For example, even self-stimulating behavior has a purpose. It may serve as a source of stimulation when environmental stimulation is either lacking or out of the client's reach. It may indicate to you the client's need to explore and understand his or her physical environment. Developmental principles clearly indicate that all behavior, that of humans and other animals, has purpose. Even Tom's excessive thumb-sucking may be viewed as an example of purposeful behavior, perhaps an attempt to return to earlier, more secure events or to reduce tension and discomfort.

2. Provide the client with a caregiver who can be a stable, responsive, and secure social base for emotional attachment. This principle is expressed in many caregiver behaviors, including the following:

Knowing and responding to the client's distress signals

Accurately interpreting the intent of the client's communications

Responding to the client's communication initiatives

Approaching the client to express positive feeling by smiling, touching, holding

Reacting positively when the client seeks you out

Providing the client with pleasant, even entertaining attention and interaction

Talking to the client during routine caregiving activities

Showing a willingness to listen, negotiate, and, wherever possible, comply with the client's wants, needs, moods, and interests

The responsiveness of the care worker leads to emotional security on the part of the client, with positive cognitive as well as social-emotional developmental consequences. If the client is securely attached, he or she will have the emotional freedom to venture away from the worker to explore the physical and social environment.

Maccoby [1980] describes why a secure attachment yields definite cognitive advantages. To a person who is young developmentally (i.e., a young child or a severely retarded person), the physical environment is not only unfamiliar but also quite complex, because the developmentally young person has not yet attained an understanding of objects and their functions and consequently cannot predict how the environment will respond to his or her actions. As long as the client can control the worker (a lesson that is learned gradually over time) by knowing how to signal distress and being able to count on a protective response, he or she is free to explore the complex environment.

If, however, the client cannot count on the responsiveness of the worker, he or she will feel helpless in the face of novel (thus potentially discomforting) situations. As a result, the client will be reluctant to explore objects, people, and events in the environment, unless they are wholly familiar. It should be apparent that, without the freedom to explore the novel, learning is greatly impaired. In our examples, although Tom's case best illustrates this developmental need, Rosie, Yaron, and Tamar also show by their rigid behavior that this developmental need has never been fully met in the institution.

3. The client has to explore and manipulate the social and physical environment in order to master it. A secure emotional environment, as described in item 2 above, is a necessary condition for learning, but certainly not a sufficient one. Developmentalists and educators, such as Piaget [1952, 1963] and Dewey [1933], describe learning as "learning by doing or acting." Therefore, clients must be afforded the opportunity and even encouraged to explore and manipulate objects in their environments, even if their explorations are initially idiosyncratic and nonfunctional.

4. Related to the foregoing principle is the developmental principle that clients need interesting, meaningful, even novel activities if interest is to be maintained and learning is to occur. At least two strategies apply. First, the client's environment must be rich in interesting objects and activities, and these objects must be within the reach of the client (as opposed to being locked in a closet due to fear of loss or breakage). Second, even activities of daily living, such as dressing, washing, and eating, must be somewhat enjoyable and entertaining. Transforming daily routines into stimulating and interesting transactions can be accomplished by creative and caring care workers.

5. Learning demands must be within or only slightly beyond the client's developmental levels. If learning demands are too difficult for the client, not only will failure result, but the client will also feel constant frustration, as well as receiving feedback from the environment that he or she is incompetent. This feeling of incompetence is likely to spread to other areas, even those where the client may have initially experienced success. Sensitive care workers must balance the introduction of new and more demanding levels of performance with feedback from the client's behavior, attitudes, and motivations in order to judge whether learning demands are attainable. Simply stated, neither low nor overly high and unrealistic expectations foster growth and development.

6. Most clients are adaptive to environmental demands and norms prevailing in the institution. Adaptation to environmental demands is a basic principle for survival, not just in humans but in animals as well. Since the care worker is the most proximate expressor and mediator of institutional and societal norms, his

or her behavior is crucial. Modeling of positive social behavior by the worker is consequently a powerful source of client learning. Modeling of respect, warmth, and the value of caring interactions with clients and other staff members is an important source for clients to learn the same.

7. The learning of most basic skills and knowledge occurs in a social context, through transactions with other people. This is especially true in learning social skills, norms, and values; that is, learning to become socially competent. Direct care workers must therefore be continually engaged in the teaching/learning process with clients even (or especially) when teaching occurs in traditionally non-teaching settings. Translated into practice, this means that care workers must be relatively free from routine housekeeping chores (except as these are part of the daily living curriculum), so they can engage in positive social transformations. In addition, they must view themselves as change agents and not simply as housekeepers. Finally, care workers must view their clients as growing persons who are and can be responsive to realistic learning expectations, not as persons or objects incapable of change.

8. Learning to become more socially competent requires a variety of mean-ingful cues and contexts (e.g., natural cues embedded in a variety of contexts, input from the care worker), not isolated teaching activities where context is unchanging or disregarded. As noted earlier in this chapter, social competence embodies learning performance skills, norms, and attitudes, and it is in the normal course of daily events in a variety of social and physical contexts that people are taught all three aspects concurrently. The process can and should occur in residential group care as well.

Too frequently in actual practice, however, only skill development is taught, and generally through artificial and isolated teaching activities, rather than in the course of natural, ongoing life events. As a result, not enough attention is given to the motivational aspects (generally embedded in the natural context) or to the norms and values that underlie the skill being taught. This practice contradicts the commonly accepted developmental principle that social competence depends as much on one's willingness (i.e., motivation and values) and on the right judgment as to when and where to exercise a certain skill, as on the mastery of the skill itself. Thus, most developmental teaching/learning activities should take place in natural contexts, where all three aspects of social competence can be learned.

It is also important to note that, in addition to the general strategies that can be incorporated into the daily routines of the clients, there are self-contained programs that focus on developing social competence. These programs generally require some degree of special training, and they typically supplement the ongoing, interpersonal work that care workers provide. Interested readers may refer to the following sources for further details regarding the goals and methods of these programs: Adams [1979], Coyne [1980], Elwyn Educational Materials Center [1978], Gunzberg [1978], Jackson [1981], Kelly [1979], Lancion and Giulio [1982], Mays [1977], Moxley [1981], and Rhoades [1980].

Concluding Remarks

We have identified three general orientations and a series of strategies reflecting these orientations that, if implemented appropriately, will facilitate the growth of social competency in young people living in institutions. Of course, many other issues affecting the work of care workers exist. The following discussion concerns several of these issues that, if not attended to by direct care workers, administrators, and society in general, will hinder the implementation of the suggested strategies and will result in a poorer quality of life for care workers and their clients.

Since the strategies presented in this chapter are based on current knowledge, theory, and research, upgrading the professional standards, qualifications, and training required of care workers is one way to enable care workers to translate existing knowledge into effective practice. With professionalization, however, can come an undue focus on objective knowledge about the how, what, and why of direct care practice. There are risks as well as benefits in this approach. Objective knowledge can replace sound intuition. Therefore, a balanced and sensitive combination of knowledge and intuition must be the goal of professionalization efforts.

The role and status of the direct care worker are issues. Historically, the role was inordinately restricted to housekeeping activities, leaving little time for active work with clients. In this chapter we have taken the position that care workers are pivotal in promoting the development of social competence in the clients with whom they work. We would also like to suggest that the role of the care worker be broadened further to include that of active advocacy for needed institutional change.

Much like the clients residing in the institution, direct care workers are likely to feel the direct effects of administrative policy and management. As a result, they can be the best antennae of the need for change. Unfortunately, while the role of care workers is critical, they are seldom the persons who have the greatest input and control in determining management style, the nature of the physical environment, and the treatment orientation of the institution, which have a profound effect on their lives and those of the clients. Therefore, if implementation of the three orientations and the suggested strategies is to occur, not only are sound knowledge and intuition needed by the direct care worker,

TABLE 2

Necessary Conditions, Obstacles, and Means for Effective Care

Necessary Conditions	Obstacles to Implementing Necessary Conditions	Means/Resources for Overcoming Obstacles
1. Respect for clients	1a. Negative attitudes toward clients	1a. Role playing; sensitization and simulation activities; meeting with families; knowledge about the clients' difficulties
	1b. Poor working conditions	1b. Flexible work routines; dialogues with supervisors and administrators; greater societal value for the care worker
2. Interaction with clients	2a. Negative attitudes toward clients	2a. Role playing; sensitization and simulation activities; meetings with families; knowledge about mental retardation
	2b. Insufficient time to interact	2b. Flexible work routines; sharing maintenance chores with other staff; lower client/staff ratios
	2c. Restricted view of the care worker's role	2c. Redefining the role of the care worker; professionalization of the care worker
	2d. Lack of positive interaction skills	2d. In-service training; brainstorming sessions with other care workers; observation, modeling, and self-analysis of worker/client interactions
3. Translation of care worker's intuition into effective strategies	3a. Lack of awareness or value of care worker's intuitive knowledge	3a. Sharing ideas, views, and approaches with other care workers and staff; engaging in

(Table 2—continued)

TABLE 2 (Continued)

Necessary Conditions, Obstacles, and Means for Effective Care

Necessary Conditions	Obstacles to Implementing Necessary Conditions	Means/Resources for Overcoming Obstacles
		dialogues with supervisors and administrators
	3b. "Helplessness" in translating intuitive knowledge into practice and in articulating ideas to others	3b. Professionalizing the care worker; providing flexible work schedules; sharing maintenance chores with other staff; redefining the role of the care worker; brainstorming with others
4. Basic knowledge of growth and development	4a. Lack of opportunities to acquire knowledge	4a. In-service training; professionalization through course work, professional meetings, workshops
	4b. Negative view of client (e.g., not capable of growth and development)	4b. Role playing; sensitization and simulation activities; meetings with families; knowledge about mental retardation
5. Translation of knowledge into practice	5a. Insufficient time to interact	5a. Flexible work schedules; sharing maintenance chores with other staff; lower client/staff ratios
	5b. Restricted view of care worker's role	5b. Redefining the role of the care worker; professionalization of the care worker
	5c. Negative view of client (e.g., not capable of growth and development)	5c. Role playing; sensitization and simulation activities; meetings with families; knowledge about mental retardation

	5d. Conceptual problems in translating knowledge into practical strategies	5d. Discussions and brainstorming about what the knowledge means and how it relates to daily interactions.
6. Advocacy for needed environmental changes	6a. Lack of awareness of what changes are needed	6a. Role playing and sensitization activities; meetings with clients and their families; brainstorming about what changes are needed and feasible means for obtaining these changes; sensitive observations
	6b. Fear of and/or inability to articulate reasons for changes	6b. Organizing support groups, including other staff and professionals to share ideas, concerns, fears, and to develop advocacy skills
	6c. Lack of responsiveness from administrators	6c. Organizing parent groups and other external groups (e.g., legal, legislative) to provide additional pressure for change.

but also the active cooperation of policy makers and institutional administrators. Direct care workers may need to facilitate this process actively.

Translation of knowledge into effective practice can take place only if there is access to existing knowledge, respect for the direct care worker, administrative support, and positive attitudes toward the clientele. Unfortunately, there are many obstacles to the achievement of these conditions. A concluding schema presented in Table 2 offers a realistic process for identifying *(1)* the necessary conditions for effective care, *(2)* potential obstacles to providing this care, and *(3)* means and resources for overcoming many of these obstacles so that the strategies suggested in this chapter can be implemented.

REFERENCES

Adams, P. 1979. *Sonoma Developmental Curriculum: Instructional Program* (Vol. 2). Sonoma, CA: Casa Brande Center.

Bandura, A. 1965. Behavioral modification through modelling procedures. In Krasner, L., and Ullman, L.P. (eds.), *Research in Behavior Modification.* New York: Holt, Rinehart and Winston.

Boe, R.B. 1977. Economical procedures for the reduction of aggression in a residential setting. *Mental Retardation 15:* 25–28.

Bowlby, J. 1953. Some pathological processes set in train by early mother-child separation. *Journal of Mental Science 59:* 265–272.

Burkhart, B., and Seim, R. 1979. The effects of institutionalization on retardates' social independence. *Journal of Mental Deficiency Research 23:* 213–218.

Coyne, P. 1980. *Social Skills Training: A Three-Pronged Approach for Developmentally Disabled Adolescents and Young Adults.* Portland, OR: Oregon University Health Services Center.

DeVellis, R.F. 1977. Learned helplessness in institutions. *Mental Retardation 15:* 10–13.

Dewey, J. 1933. *How Do We Think.* Chicago, IL: Henry Regnery Co.

Edgerton, R.B., Eyman, R.K., and Silverstein, A.B. 1975. Mental retardation system. In Hobbs, N. (ed.), *Issues in the Classification of Children* (Vol. 2). San Francisco, CA: Jossey-Bass, Inc.

Elwyn Educational Materials Center. 1975. *Personal Adjustment Training* (Vols. 1, 2, and 3). Elwyn, PA: Elwyn Institute.

Erikson, E. 1950. *Childhood and Society.* New York: Norton.

Felsenthal, D., and Scheerenberger, R.C. 1978. Stability and attitudes of primary caregivers in the community. *Mental Retardation 16:* 16–18.

Gunzberg, H.C. 1976. Assessment and evaluation in social education. *Research Exchange and Practice in Mental Retardation 2:* 95–112.

Gunzberg, H.C., and Gunzberg, A.L. 1973. *Mental Handicap and Physical Environment.* London, England: Bailliere Tindall.

Inhelder, B. 1968. *The Diagnosis of Reasoning in the Mentally Retarded.* New York: The John Day Co.

Jackson, H.J.   1981.   Social skills assessment and training for mentally retarded persons: A review of research. *Australian Journal of Developmental Disabilities* 7: 113–123.

Kahn, J.V.   1975.   Relationship of Piaget's sensorimotor period to language acquisition of profoundly retarded children. *American Journal of Mental Deficiency* 79: 640–643.

Kahn, J.V.   1977.   Piaget's theory of cognitive development and its relationship to severely and profoundly retarded children. In Mittler, P. (ed.), *Research to Practice in Mental Retardation* (Vol. 2). Baltimore, MD: University Park Press.

Kelly, J.A.   1979.   Group skills training to increase the conversational repertoire of retarded adolescents. *Child Behavior Therapy* 1: 323–336.

King, R.D., and Raynes, N.V.   1968.   Patterns of institutional care for the severely subnormal. *American Journal of Mental Deficiency* 72: 700–709.

Lancion, I., and Giulio, E.   1982.   Normal children as tutors to teach social responses to withdrawn mentally retarded schoolmates: Training, maintenance and generalization. *Journal of Applied Behavior Analysis* 15: 17–40.

Leland, H.   1977.   Adaptation, coping behavior, and retarded performance. In Mittler, P. (ed.), *Research to Practice in Mental Retardation* (Vol. 2). Baltimore, MD: University Park Press: p 151.

Maccoby, E.E.   1980.   *Social Development: Psychological Growth and the Parent-Child Relation.* New York: Harcourt, Brace Jovanovich.

Mays, M.   1977.   *State of Ohio Curriculum Guide for Moderately Mentally Retarded Learners.* Columbus, OH: Ohio State Department of Mental Health and Mental Retardation.

Moxley, D.   1981.   *Socialization Games for Mentally Retarded Adolescents and Adults.* Springfield, IL. Charles C Thomas.

Nirje, B.   1969.   The normalization principle and its human applications. In Kugel, R., and Wolfensberger W. (eds.), *Changing Patterns in Residential Services for the Mentally Retarded.* Washington, DC: U.S. Department of Health, Education and Welfare.

Perske, R., Clifton, A., McLean, B.M., and Stein, J.I.   1977.   *Mealtimes for Severely and Profoundly Handicapped Persons.* Baltimore, MD: University Park Press.

Peters, E.N., Pumphrey, M.W., and Flax, B.   1974.   Comparison of retarded and nonretarded children on the dimensions of behavior in recreation groups. *American Journal of Mental Deficiency* 79: 87–94.

Piaget, J.   1952.   *The Origins of Intelligence in Children.* New York: International Universities Press.

Piaget, J.   1963.   *Psychology and Intelligence.* Patterson, NJ: Littlefield.

Prutting, C.A.   1982.   Pragmatics as social competence. *Journal of Speech and Hearing Disorders* 47: 123–134.

Raynes, N.V., and King, R.D.   1968.   The measurement of child management in residential institutions for the retarded. In Richards, B.W. (ed.), *Proceedings of the First Congress of the International Association for the Scientific Study of Mental Deficiency.* Reigate, Surrey, England: Michael Jackson.

Raynes, N.V., Pratt, M.W., and Roses, S.   1977.   Aides' involvement in decision-making and the quality of care in institutional settings. *American Journal of Mental Deficiency* 81: 570–577.

Rhoades, D.   1980.   Group counseling: An effective intervention with the mentally retarded. *Training Quarterly on Developmental Disabilities 1:* 7–17.

Robertson, J., and Robertson, J.   1971.   Young children in brief separation: A fresh look. *Psychoanalytic Study of the Child 26:* 264–315.

Seligman, M.E.P.   1975.   *Helplessness.* San Francisco, CA: W.H. Freeman & Co.

Spitz, R.A., and Wolf, K.M.   1946.   *Anaclitic depression: An inquiry into the genesis of psychiatric conditions in early childhood.* In Freud, A., Hartman, H., and Kris, E., The Psychoanalytic Study of the Child (Vol. 2). New York: International Universities Press: pp 313–342.

Tizard, J.   1960.   Residential care of mentally handicapped children. *British Medical Journal 1:* 1041–1046.

Tizard, J.   1964.   *Community Services for the Mentally Handicapped.* New York: Oxford University Press.

Tizard, J.   1970.   The role of social institutions in the causation, prevention, and alleviation of mental retardation. In Haywood, H.C. (ed.), *Social-Cultural Aspects of Mental Retardation.* New York: Appleton-Century-Crofts.

Tjosvold, D., and Tjosvold, M.M.   1983.   Social psychological analysis of residences for mentally retarded persons. *American Journal of Mental Deficiency 88:* 28–40.

Veit, S.W., Allen, G.J., and Chinsky, J.M.   1976.   Interpersonal interactions between institutionalized retarded children and their attendants. *American Journal of Mental Deficiency 80:* 535–542.

Wolfensberger, W.   1972.   *The Principle of Normalization in Human Services.* Toronto, Ontario, Canada: National Institute on Mental Retardation.

Zigler, E.   1978.   National crisis in mental retardation research. *American Journal of Mental Deficiency 83:* 1–8.

7

From Warehouse to Greenhouse:

Play, Work, and

the Routines of Daily Living in Groups

as the Core of Milieu Treatment

F. HERBERT BARNES

"If you guys don't load the truck, nobody's goin' nowhere," shouted the youth care worker. "I'll just sit here in the shade all summer. It's no skin off my nose!" Rebellious earlier in the day, the boys hardly changed their positions in the hot June sun. No one moved toward the canoes, the camping gear, or the provisions that were to accompany the group on its nine-day trip into the Maine wilderness. "Don't you guys have any appreciation for all the work we put into arranging this trip?" barked the worker. "We try to do something nice for you, and look what happens!"

I n different ways, the foregoing experience is repeated in child and youth care settings daily, whether in the presence of daily routines like cottage cleanup, recreational activities, or major events like the canoe trip. The incident can even be viewed as a metaphor for life in many group care settings—the workers do the work and the clients "take it or leave it." This chapter proposes a way of looking at the daily life experience in group care that will enable programs serving children and youths in residential treatment to capitalize on the phenomenon of group life as a positive, developmentally appropriate, growth-producing experience.

Play, work, and cottage routines are viewed as the content of an overall curriculum for learning through experience. So that the meaning of experiential learning is not simply taken for granted and its applicability to the work of residential treatment left unspecified, it should be noted that the concept of experiential learning includes both learning by doing and relationship learning. Although this is the primary goal, it becomes impossible to avoid seeing the new possibilities and new responsibilities for child-care workers that emerge through this curriculum approach to care, learning, and treatment: a new way of looking at the child-care worker as both "milieu manager" and "here-and-now educator." The child-care worker can then plan and orchestrate the ingredients of a learning milieu in the daily living of residential treatment, as in the approach used by the child-care workers staffing the canoe trip described more fully later.

To fail to operationalize group care fully on a developmental or educative model, to equate care with custody and control, and to see the child-care worker primarily as a behavioral manager and social controller reflect the lack of a clear and conceptualized application to group care of those principles of experiential learning that have been successfully applied in other sectors, primarily in summer camps and schools founded in the progressive education era [Arieli et al. 1990].

Experiential Learning as a Basis
for Group Care

Winsor [1963], in describing the discovery-learning (learn-by-doing) approach that formed the basis of the work of Lucy Sprague Mitchell in teaching young children, stated:

> Helping children to discover the wonder of the world about them— to grasp ideas, to perceive relationships, to take the long leap into new ideas and more complex relationships—is the learning-curriculum approach which is the school's great (and too often unused) power in fostering the mentally healthy, socially productive development of all children.

She noted further that those ideas were relevant not only to teaching young children but that

> the principles which underlie this work are as applicable to children today as they were in the experimental school of the 1930's. Adaptation of technique is, of course, necessary . . . . The important point is that the method of learning how to observe and what questions to ask and relating these discoveries to other bodies of information remains. It can be applied to any environment and to any time.

How much more important—and more difficult—this task is with older youths who have been denied such opportunities in their earlier years!

In his now classic *Democracy and Education*, Dewey [1916] explains the social media as educative.

> Social environment forms the mental and emotional disposition of behavior in individuals by engaging them in activities that arouse and strengthen certain impulses, that have certain purposes and entail certain consequences. The child growing up in a family of musicians will inevitably have whatever capacities he [sic] has in music stimulated, and, relatively, stimulated more than other impulses which might have been awakened in another environment. Save as he takes an interest in music and gains a certain competency in it, he is "out of it"; he is unable to share in the life of the group to which he belongs. Some kinds of participation in the life of those with whom the individual is connected are inevitable; with respect to them, the social environment exercises an educative or formative influence unconsciously and apart from any set purpose.

He further states that

> just as the senses require sensible objects to stimulate them, so our powers of observation, recollection, and imagination do not work spontaneously, but are set in motion by the demands set up by current social occupations [Dewey 1916: 19–20].

He calls this, "The unconscious influence of the environment."

In a chapter entitled "Play and Work in the Curriculum," he discusses the place of active occupations in education—learning by doing:

> The desirability of starting from and with the experience and capacities of learners has led to the introduction of forms of activity in work and play, similar to those in which children and youth engage outside of school. Experience has shown that when children have a chance at physical activities

which bring their natural impulses into play, going to school is a joy, management is less of a burden, and learning is easier.

Sometimes, perhaps, plays, games, and constructive occupations are resorted to only for these reasons, with emphasis upon relief from the tedium and strain of "regular" school work. There is no reason, however, for using them merely as agreeable diversions. Study of mental life has made evident the fundamental worth of native tendencies to explore, to manipulate tools and materials, to construct, to give expression to joyous emotion, etc. When exercises which are prompted by these instincts are part of the regular program, the whole pupil is engaged, the artificial gap between life in school and out is reduced, motives are afforded for attention to a large variety of materials and processes distinctly educative in effect, and cooperative associations which give information a social setting are provided. In short, the grounds for assigning to play and active work a definite place in the curriculum are intellectual and social, not matters of temporary expediency and momentary agreeableness. Without something of the kind, it is not possible to secure the normal estate of effective learning; namely, that knowledge-getting be an outgrowth of activities having their own end, instead of a school task. More specifically, play and work corresponded, point for point, with the traits of the initial stage of knowing, which consists in learning how to do things and in acquaintance with things and processes gained in the doing [Dewey 1916: 228–229].

These are the two levels of concern and attention in child-care work referred to earlier.

Bruner [1970], speaking at a Bank Street College Conference about the benefits of learning as an approach to occupy children and teachers (equivalent in this sense to child and youth care workers), says:

> The child must be encouraged to get the full benefit from what he [sic] learns. This is not to say that he should be required to put [it] to immediate use in his daily life, though so much the better if he has the happy opportunity to do so. Rather, it is a way of honoring the connectedness of knowledge. Two facts and a relation joining them are and should be an invitation to generalize, to extrapolate, to make a tentative intuitive leap, indeed, even to build a tentative theory. The leap from mere learning to using what one has learned in thinking is an essential step in the use of mind. Indeed, plausible guessing, the use of the heuristic hunch, the best employment of necessarily insufficient evidence—these are activities in which the child needs practice and guidance. They are among the great antidotes to passivity.

Bruner's idea of the "happy opportunity" to put into immediate use the full benefits of what the child learns readily connects to milieu treatment, which offers a unique opportunity to do exactly that.

Dewey [1916: 32–33] further employs the concept of the unconscious influence of the environment to address the questions of control.

> When others are not doing what we should like them to do or are threatening disobedience, we are most conscious of the need of controlling them and of the influences by which they are controlled. In such cases, our control becomes most direct, and at this point, we are most likely to make the mistakes just spoken of . . . . In all such cases of immediate action upon others, we need to discriminate between physical results and moral results . . . . A child may have to be snatched with roughness away from a fire so that he shall not be burned. But no improvement of disposition, no educative effect, need follow. A harsh and commanding tone may be effectual in keeping a child away from the fire, and the same desirable physical effect will follow as if he had been snatched away. But there may be no more obedience of a moral sort in one case than in another . . . . When we confuse a physical with an educative result, we always lose the chance of enlisting the persons' participating disposition in getting the result desired, and thereby of developing within him an intrinsic and persisting direction in the right way.

> In general, the occasion for the more conscious acts of control should be limited to acts which are so instinctive or impulsive that the one performing them has no means of foreseeing their outcoming. If a person cannot foresee the consequence of his act, and is not capable of understanding what he is told about its outcome by those with more experience, it is impossible for him to guide his act intelligentlly. In such a state every act is alike to him. Whatever moves him, moves him and that is all there is to it. In some cases, it is well to permit him to experiment, and to discover the consequences for himself in order that he may act intelligently next time under similar circumstances. But some courses of action are too discommoding and obnoxious to others to allow of this course being pursued. Direct disapproval is now frequently resorted to—shaming, ridicule, disfavor, rebuke, and punishment are used. Or contrary tendencies in the child are appealed [to] to divert him from his troublesome line of behavior. His sensitiveness to approbation, his hope of winning favor by an agreeable act, are made use of to induce action in another direction.

> These methods of control are so obvious (because so intentionally employed) that it would hardly be worthwhile to mention them if it were not that notice may now be taken, by way of contrast, of the other more

important and permanent mode of control. This other method resides in the way in which persons use things; the instrumentalities with which they acomplish their own ends. The very existence of the social medium in which an individual lives, moves, and has his being is the standing effective agency of directing his activity.

This holistic approach, which incorporates subject matter, facts, and experience into the exploration of young people and combines that with an active, participatory role for the teacher, forms a common, shared process that can provide a health and learning-oriented basis for the work of residential treatment. To apply this thinking to understanding a construct for residential treatment, I would propose that the whole be conceptualized as a combination of ingredients that are the common, shared interaction of children and their workers: care, learning, and treatment. Taken together, as an integrated approach to program, they provide the ingredients for a holistic notion of practice.

Care

Regarding care, workers must be nurturing persons. They must be interested in the young people of the age with which they are working; they must be able to empathize with them and understand and appreciate their situation. Since limits are a part of care, children need adults to act in ways that adults can be expected to act, which includes setting limits. When done as an intrinsic part of the adult-child relationship and in an overall educative orientation, setting limits is non-authoritarian and, in its own way, quite nurturing. It is a misuse of the group, however, to have all of the nurture of children in residential care provided by the staff. Staff members, as good group workers, should facilitate the nurturing qualities of other children for their peers. A group, to be worth anyone's being involved in the experience, must provide unique benefits to the residents, and the quality of peer nurture is certainly one of those.

Learning

Learning can be seen as what the group does: for the group, its curriculum; for the workers, their pedagogy. And, as noted, twofold learning is always in process: the merit of the activity in its own right—its worth as learning or experience or fun—and the developmental and pedagogical meaning of the activity, which is what elevates it into treatment.

Treatment

Treatment is the awareness that workers bring—the conscious use of program ingredients as opportunities of daily living for growth and development against the background of pathology that children bring to their residential experience. Treatment is the process of changing Dewey's "unconscious influence of the environment" to a conscious influence derived from purposeful plans and conscious intervention that comes through a thorough understanding of the treatment needs of the group and its members. The child-care worker is in a unique relationship to children and content—one that creates an excellent and continuing possibility for being the facilitator of this kind of discovery learning. To create the proper basis for that learning, however, it is important to look at the construct of the group.

Composition of the Residential Group and Its Purposes

Basic to a healthy, developmental approach to residential group care is a clear definition of the group not as "kids and keepers" or as a totally child-centered group of children, but as people, both children and staff members, whose purposes are care, learning, and treatment. The child-care worker of Figure 1 illustrates the "kids and keepers" model, with the child-care worker as outside and supervising the children's group yet not a fundamental part of the adult group, that sophisticated ring of professionals who, from their different disciplinary vantage points, surround the residential group.

The composition of the group as charted in Figure 2 suggests much more the inclusion of the direct care worker—in Figure 2 termed an *educateur*, as explained below—as an interacting part of the children's group even though the child-care worker maintains a peer identity with co-professionals from other disciplines in the circle surrounding the group.

The recommended concept of the group, therefore, is one that includes not just the children, but the combination of children and staff members as they work together. The workers are group members by virtue of their role and are responsible, as part of the joint action of children and staff members together, for the three elements of the group's tasks—care, learning, and treatment.

The Role of the Child and Youth Care Worker in Group Care

What kind of worker does it take to carry out activities that are educational, work that is developmentally appropriate, and routines that are the result of

Figure 1. Treatment and care—illness orientation. Fragmented model in which the child-care worker or youth worker manages the daily living situation and provides social control while sending the children to individualized special services, which are perceived to be the treatment.

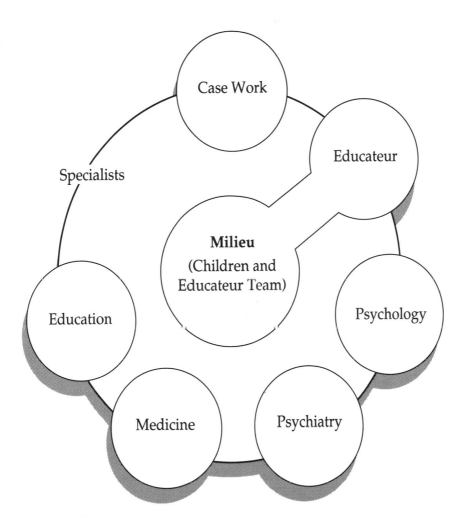

Figure 2. Milieu treatment—integrated and holistic orientation. Integrated model in which the joint action of children and educateurs provide care, social control, and treatment opportunities. Specialists are still used, but as technical resources outside the milieu.

group planning rather than merely arbitrary exercises in unproductive, boring, repetitive tasks?

In many countries, the worker who carries these responsibilities performs them as a professionally designed task for which there is an identified professional training and clear professional status equivalent to the professional status of other human service disciplines. The *educateur* in France and the *barnevernpedagog* in Norway would view these responsibilities as part of their regular professional work.

That we largely lack such a definition in the United States need not make it impossible for us to recognize our ability to provide residential work of this same quality here. Indeed, in residential centers across the country, there are American child-care workers who, because of their response to individual young people in residential treatment and the demands of the group in which they live, are in fact transdisciplinary workers, who develop programs with their groups, provide counseling in the life space, deal with behavioral and management issues through effective use of peer group and counseling interventions, provide care, nurture, and structure as required by growing children, and do the whole with an educational rather than a social control focus.

When the child-care worker of Figure 1 is used, the design of the program will inevitably appear as shown in Figure 3. Care, counseling, and activities are all separate services provided by separate staff persons, and it is usually the child-care worker's responsibility to send the child to the other two-thirds of the milieu treatment program.

If the child-care worker functions as shown in Figure 2, however, the milieu program can achieve a much more integrated and flowing design, illustrated in Figure 4.

In this model, with the child-care worker operating as a transdisciplinary professional who occupies a dynamic, participating role in the milieu with the group and also maintains a professional and collegial relationship with allied professionals outside the milieu of the children, the notion of milieu treatment becomes much clearer. The worker is involved in basic care and nurture and use of the residential unit and group as a basic caregiving situation. The worker's responsibilities include work with the group on management and program, designing it with the group and also carrying it out with them. Using activities both as a basis of experiential learning and as an arena for engaging the strengths and weaknesses of the performance styles of all group members, the worker is able to develop a structured group approach to helping young people identify their problems and solve them more effectively. The worker also has a role in counseling young persons to enable them to use the milieu treatment resources more effectively and in helping them to mediate between the emotional baggage they

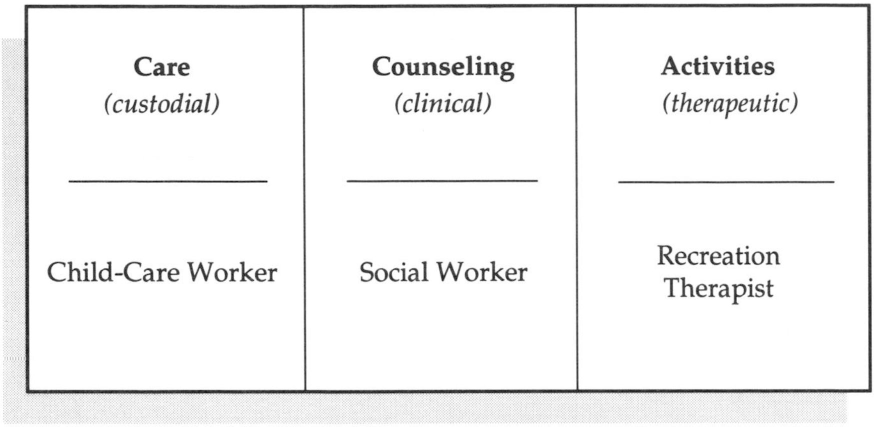

Care (custodial)	Counseling (clinical)	Activities (therapeutic)
Child-Care Worker	Social Worker	Recreation Therapist

Figure 3. A linear, fragmented, specialist model.

bring with them and the demands of the real-life experience in which they are engaged.

Two concepts enunciated by Redl [1957] contribute substantially to making the child-care worker a milieu treatment specialist: the life space interview, where the child care worker finds the equipment to provide both "emotional first aid on the spot" and "clinical exploitation of life events"; and the concept of mediation services needed by children to help them negotiate the mine field of practical daily living and its demands while burdened with the emotional baggage of traumatic episodes and incidents earlier in their development. In Figure 3, we find that the limited role of the child-care worker is based primarily on an earlier theoretical construct, the notion that the person who is engaged in the daily living activities with children and is placed in a position of setting limits cannot be the person who helps them to explore their innermost feelings and insecurities, because that purpose requires an atmosphere of neutrality in order to happen. Such an atmosphere of neutrality can be achieved in a therapist's office, distant from and out of the context of the daily living situation, but the unique opportunity of the milieu worker is to achieve that with the child within that context, as French educateurs and Norwegian barnevernpedagogs regularly do.

This is in keeping with their philosophy that the worker who is engaged with the young people in their activities is best situated and equipped to received their confidences because these confidences are more usually and normally shared in the context of activity. Equally, this philosophy contends that the worker who shares the confidences is the one best equipped to help the children use that material productively in negotiating the expectations of the daily living situation,

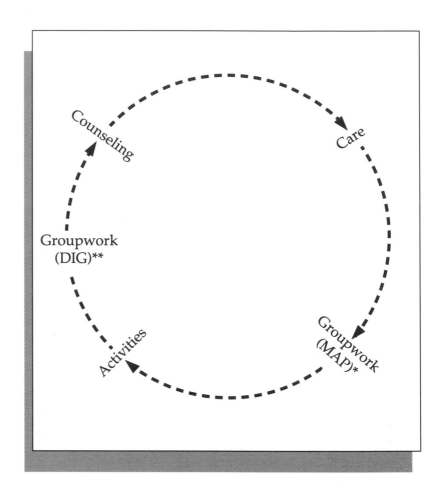

Figure 4. A circular, holistic, transdisciplinary model.

*MAP is an acronym for the Management and Program Group session, which is concerned with these functions.
**DIG is an acronym for the Development of Individual and Group session, a specialized, structured treatment meeting.
Note: Both group sessions are discussed in detail later in this chapter.

Redl's "mediating influence." This worker and style of functioning are illustrated in Figure 4.

Activities and Program Planning: Routines, Work, and Leisure Time

In many American agencies, the planning and management of activities is done by activity or recreation specialists outside the immediate residential living unit of the group. It is worth questioning, however, whether a search for expertise in activities or recreation is worth the fragmentation of the group and its child-care staff along yet another disciplinary turf boundary. In Europe, where the child-care worker is a professional, such fragmentation is much less likely to occur. One educateur, a participant in an international learning exchange for child-care workers, observed upon being in an American agency for some months that the way Americans defined the work of the child-care worker was curious. "Here," he said, "I do exactly half of the job that I do in France. The other half is done by two people, a social worker and an activity specialist" [Nicolais 1986].

Leisure Time Activities: Fun with a Purpose, and as an End in Itself

Though many highly specialized activities may best be provided cross-campus (mountaineering, soccer team, volunteer service to the community, photography club), many activities can be returned to the cottage. If activities are considered to be part of the group's overall curriculum, then planning for them and carrying them out by the group together with the cottage staff can be part of the cottage's regular daily life. The group interaction would be strengthened, and the staff-child relationship would become considerably more therapeutic.

The worker's role is further discussed later, but at this point it is important to connect the planning and management of activities with the group process. At a regular meeting during the week, the group, with its staff, can plan its own weekend activities, of which individual participation in specialized cross-campus activity groups may be a part. Suppose the group wishes to go, as a group, with its own group activities budget, to the movies. This brings about the discussion of the pros and cons of going to see a particular movie to the staff members, who know the children best and can best use the flow of discussion in helping the children.

What if the movie the group wants to see is "bad"? Why does the worker say it is bad? Does the worker believe the group should not be exposed to it? Perhaps the worker will say that the group should see the movie only if they all agree to pay close attention and discuss it when they return. Perhaps the group can split up, one part to see one movie and another to see a second choice. The point is that, even in something as simple as the group going to the movies, the planning and the doing can now become a participatory activity in which children feel involved together with staff members, rather than simply recipients of some other person's or the Activity Department's plan. It is likely that behavior problems in this movie-going arrangement will be far fewer and if they occur, they can readily be discussed by the group as a violation of a reasonable code of behavior for "our group." The problem could well be the focus of a special group meeting; it might also reveal information that the group needs to deal with on a deeper level in a different kind of meeting. The main point is that, when these activities are not the province of the group and its own staff, then the opportunities for developmental work with both individuals and group are diminished.

A more complex activity, such as a day's trip to the beach, could well profit from more advance planning through the work of subcommittees. Ideally, the following tasks come to mind: transportation (How will we get there? Will the workers drive? Is the bus available? Can we all get into two agency vans? Where is the gas money coming from?); food (What will we eat? When? Where? Is this part of the regular food budget or do we have to get the money from a special activities budget?); destination (What beach? How long does it take to get there? What route do we take? Is there some worthwhile interesting sightseeing on the way?).

All of these decisions might more easily be made by the staff and, unfortunately, during observation of group care programs in action, it is often apparent that they are. The point is not, however, just to have these tasks done, but to have them done in such a way that they are in and of themselves educational. Performance of the tasks should certainly be focused on the result to be achieved. Productless tasks are meaningless. Doing them, however, should also produce group spirit and individual enthusiasm, and the process should lead to an educational result—the two levels of concern of which the staff should always be aware. A combination of content and process such as this always carries within it the opportunity for building a closer relationship with peers and with staff members, and all of the possibilities for enhanced self-esteem that come with their successful completion.

Special Events

Birthdays, holidays, and other celebrations will probably be purely the group's business, such as what customs the group develops for celebrating the birthdays of its members. Others will be functions celebrated by the residential center as a whole, such as a sports banquet where the group sits together and cheers its successful members but is part of a much larger, schoolwide activity. Still other activities may also be campuswide but require special participation and planning by each cottage group, such as a one-day country fair at which each cottage takes the responsibility for a different booth or activity. Halloween, with all of its spectre of masks, disguise, and vandalism, needs special positive planning so that long periods of anonymity behind masks do not eliminate the operating social mores and encourage chaotic behavior. Addressing these problems through planning program components rather than social control strategies is the primary key to having a greenhouse rather than a warehouse, with child-care workers serving primarily as teachers and facilitators rather than custodians and agents of social control.

The Routines of Daily Life

Cottage routines or chores are an essential part of the child-care worker's regular daily practice diet. They are a constant for the children as well. Morning routines before breakfast or before going to school and chores each afternoon upon returning from school and before activities begin often seem to be viewed by all as negative. The following definition of "routine" in the *American Heritage Dictionary of the English Language*, when taken literally, becomes a definition of the problem as well: "A prescribed and detailed course of action to be followed regularly; a standard procedure . . . a set of customary and often mechanically performed procedures or activities." To do something in a routine way is to imply that it is lacking in interest, to do it in accordance with established procedure, in a habitual or regular way. In addition, tasks performed in routine ways are "lacking in interest or originality." It seems small wonder that these tasks are continual problems for children and staff members.

Might turning to the definition for "chores" provide greater inspiration? Not at all. The *American Heritage Dictionary* defines a chore as "A routine or minor task; any daily or routine domestic task." It further qualifies a chore as "an unpleasant or burdensome task." When child-care workers perceive routines and chores in this manner, they will inevitably have to use coercion and exercises of power to get children to do these "prescribed and detailed courses of action."

Would it not be much better to view these tasks as part of the group's total program and approach them differently? By involving the group in defining the scope of the domestic tasks and the best means for dealing with them through group process, the group could do its own prescribing and detailing of how the domestic work is to be done within the general guidelines set down by the child-care workers. The staff would then be placed in a facilitating rather than an enforcing position. The tasks would not be performed mechanically or in a rote way but rather according to the group's own plan, which would be subject to review in a later meeting if flaws were detected in it.

It is essential that workers be clear on the fundamental nature of any activity, and in the case of domestic chores it would seem that what workers ought to be talking about and planning and working on with children is the managing of the essentials of daily life as a total activity, demanding joint action and full involvement of children and staff members because "it's our place and, therefore, it's our project."

If the vehicle of a group meeting is used to identify responsibilities that the group must address, then the fine points of daily program and schedule can become part of the group's responsibility, and it can become the group's task to consider how to include all of the things that are required—group time, optional time, time for group activities, time for basic maintenance—and to manage the scheduling and allocating of the various responsibilities inherent in a group living situation. This process becomes a learning/planning, problem-solving aspect of an overall educative approach.

An often-heard criticism of this approach is that the staff members will be abrogating their authority, and essentially asking the children's permission to perform essential tasks. That argument is a straw man. To develop such an approach with the children does not mean that the workers lose their authority. Instead, it means that, rather than controlling the children, the workers are controlling the process and the content, leaving the children free to make choices, to learn by operating with some autonomy in a situation that is made secure for experimentation by the definition and structure which the workers provide.

This point can be illustrated with an example of directing children and then of the alternative, controlling the process.

> As breakfast was ending on a Saturday morning, Gary told the children he wanted them all to stay at the breakfast table after they were finished so he could give out the chore assignments. Immediately he began getting complaints: "Oh, that again. I wonder how long it's going to take this Saturday." "I always get the lousiest job," coupled with, "Here we go, watch him give Rob the best job, he's his favorite," and on down the list of complaints— usually numerous and usually reliable.
>
> Jim, however, a more experienced worker who understands that the goal isn't just to get the laundry done and the place picked up, started differently. As breakfast was ending, he said, "OK, gang, as soon as everyone is finished with breakfast and the cleanup is done, I'd like us all to meet in the living room so we can plan what we're doing today." "What's happening today, Jim?" asked one of the boys. "Well, that's what we have to discuss,

so let's hurry it up," said Jim. He then began busying himself with various aspects of cleanup, talking with the boys as they worked together. When they were all gathered in the living room, Jim opened the discussion by outlining the several things that were on line for the day. "This is the day we said we wanted to go to the mall to shop for Halloween. We also invited Mr. Smith, from school, to come to lunch, and of course we have regular Saturday cottage chores to get fitted in, too. What we'd probably better do is figure out whether we'll get this all in and still be able to go to the movies as several guys have suggested. Who wants to start us off with a strategy for how we do this?"[1]

Jim has set up a process in which, though leader, he is also a participant with the boys, helping all to share their ideas or gripes while making sure that they cover all the essentials in their planning, and that they make a group decision about the sequence and content of the day's events. Gary, however, will spend the morning being an enforcer, and the group will probably go off shopping or to the movies with unresolved conflicts that then spill over into the next activity.

Work in the Curriculum of Group Care

Work that exceeds the demands of everyday routines, although part of the essential stuff and material upon which adolescents thrive and define themselves, is often a controversial issue in residential programs because of the possibilities for exploitation. One state, trying to regulate this, put into formal regulations for institutions that work shall be permitted as long as the institution derives no tangible benefit from it! There must be some better way to prevent exploitation than to legislate the requirement that child work in the institution have no benefit, for work without a beneficial product has no positive meaning and, in another sense, is itself a form of exploitation.

Work is important to growing people, but for work to be developmentally important, it must have productive significance that they can comprehend. Work that is of importance to the group but not to the institution is probably of a highly temporary nature (dusting, picking up one's room, waxing the floor), but these are elements in the routine of daily living that we have discussed above. "Real" work is of a more lasting nature and fits both the young doer and the facility in which the work is done.

Valid and important work experiences can also be provided for young people in care by providing them with paid work experiences outside the institution. Holding down a part-time job, such as mowing a neighbor's lawn or bagging groceries in a store, is valid work experience that does not get into the dangerous arena of exploitation. Constructing a farm fence at the residential school, or building a new walk to the cottage, or making drapes for the living room are also valid work experiences, but these tasks do enter that arena where there is right and reason to be cautious.

In spite of all the difficulties, however, work remains one of the significant ways in which young people can develop competence that they themselves can measure, from which they can derive confidence, and which provides a core for the development of positive identity. It is not something that can be allowed to be lost in a maze of bureaucratic regulatory definition. Certainly, to include work as part of the agency's program, it must be thought through clearly, and the reasons for its being regarded as education made absolutely explicit. The example below, where production-oriented workshop experience was part of each student's daily experience, may elaborate this point.

As in other activities, work also has an intrinsic and a developmental purpose. Certainly the intrinsic purpose of a sidewalk is that people eventually can walk on it. The developmental purposes for the youngsters installing it, however, are clear: First, that they learn how to do that particular job and, more broadly, learn how to do a job and get it done. The doing of that job creates pride on the part of the doers as they see others actually making use of and deriving enjoyment from the product.

One residential center[2] developed its day program for each student with half the day being spent in an academic group and half in a production-oriented vocational training workshop. Earlier, these shops had been largely devoid of production value, being seen only as activities for hands-on learning—basically hobby shops. In the small engine shop, successive waves of students had been taking apart and reassembling the same power lawn mower. The instructor felt that the boys were capable of much more than this empty task and that more important work would be more challenging and provide better instruction, but this step had never been taken because of the bugaboo of work as exploitation.

This repetitive work that was safe from the criticism of exploitation (because it was so lacking in value) was a key incentive for the staff to rethink the role and nature of work in the program. The shop was converted to an auto and engine repair shop, and students began taking in real vehicles to be fixed and returned to the road. This shop gradually took on the maintenance of all the agency's vehicles, and, at one point, rebuilt a diesel farm tractor, saving the agency considerable money that could then be used to buy more advanced shop equipment. The day the tractor drove out of the workshop pulling a wagon carrying the instructor and the mechanics who had worked on the project was a great moment of pride for every student.

Was this exploitation? Applying the test of whether the institution derived benefit from the work, it certainly was. Knowing the students who worked on the project and knowing the feeling of pride they experienced as their product rolled out the door, the primary benefit clearly was the value of work as an identity-building, competence-promoting activity. Rather than concentrating on the end result, whether the work has benefit to the institution, perhaps the way to ensure the proper place for work in the residential curriculum of growing adolescents is to concentrate instead on the process approach. Here, the key questions are whether the work would be developmentally appropriate for youths in general, programmatically valid for these particular youths, and an activity about which they are enthusiastic. Then it is important that the agency think through all aspects of the work experience: purpose, time, who is involved, who supervises it, what are the individual's credentials and role, whether there will be a cash return from the work, and what safeguards are necessary to assure that the profits accrue to the students. It is equally important that the protocols be written and available to students, staff members, parents, purchasers of service, and licensing and regulating authorities.

Dewey [1916: 241–242] offered a clear definition of the relationship of play and work in the curriculum:

> It is important not to confuse the psychological distinction between play and work with the economic distinction. Psychologically, the defining characteristic of play is not amusement or aimlessness. It is the fact that the aim is thought of as more activity in the same line, without defining continuity of action in reference to results producted. Activities as they grow more complicated gain added meaning by greater attention to specific results achieved. Thus, they pass gradually into work. Both are equally free and intrinsically motivated, apart from false economic conditions which tend to make play into idle excitement for the well-to-do and work into uncongenial labor for the poor. Work is psychologically simply an activity which consciously includes regard for consequences as a part of itself; it becomes constrained labor when the consequences are outside of the activity as an end to which activity is merely a means. Work which remains permeated with the play attitude is art—in quality if not in conventional designation.

One other aspect of work in residential centers that is usually identified as exploitation and, to the author's mind, is exactly that, is work as punishment. It is exploitative in that it exacts services as retribution from people because of behavior unwanted by other people. (This definition is significantly different from work as restitution for acts of vandalism, theft, or carelessness.) Work as punishment (retribution), rather than teaching positive attitudes about work, teaches the youths about unilateral use of power; it generates resentment more than learning. There are other, more direct, more educational, and more appropriate ways of dealing with unapproved behavior than meting out work as a punishment, which destroys work as the valid confidence-building enterprise it can and should be. It also damages the relationship between the direct care worker and the young people; although this recognition may not be expressed, it is well known and resented that this game is one the worker is playing to win and that he or she has the power to do so, but often only at the cost of sacrificing larger and more fundamental goals.

When the work is entered into as restitution, however, and as a result of problem-solving dialogue between the staff member as the authority and the student as the malefactor needing to make restitution, it can be well safeguarded and so valuable as to make the staff member secretly delighted that the untoward event took place. An example illustrates this point.

> It was a Saturday morning, and a group of children were washing the bus and cleaning it out, getting it ready for a trip that afternoon. Karl, a big, athletic 16-year-old who had been sweeping the inside of the bus and around the area with a large floor broom, was now lost in a baseball reverie, swinging his broom as a bat at make-believe incoming fastballs from a hypothetical pitcher out there somewhere on the mound. Unfortunately, in Karl's mind the pitcher must have been exactly where the bus was, because, just as Karl swung at the incoming pitch, the head of the broom separated and went flying straight through the windshield of the bus. Karl was shocked and scared.
>
> The youth worker in charge of the activity proposed a meeting with the program director about what was to be done. Punishment was irrelevant, unthinkable, and unnecessary. Karl was already punished more than enough by his combined fear and embarrassment, and the boy and the staff all realized this. As the program director explained, "Even though it was an accident and we can all feel very sorry about it, there is the matter of a windshield that now needs to be replaced and no one, in working up the budget for this year, had thought to budget for replacing a $400 bus windshield, So, what do you suggest?" he asked Karl. Karl was flabbergasted. "I don't have $400," he said, "and I don't have any way to get it. I don't know what to do."
>
> At this point, the program director proposed to Karl a way to earn the money. The barn needed painting and if Karl felt that he could do quality work, up to the standards of the maintenance department, then he could have the job. Karl was given time to consider that with his youth worker, to go to look over the barn, and to talk to the head of maintenance. Meanwhile, the business office would figure out an hourly rate that Karl could be paid.

Karl, his worker, and the program director then met again. All agreed that that would be the plan, and Karl set to work.

Karl did good work, developing considerable pride in his accomplishment, which of course was obvious to himself and all others who observed him at work. He was as scrupulous about his time as he was about his work. At the end of the number of hours required to pay off the windshield, Karl came back to the program director to note that the debt was done but the barn was not. "I enjoy the work," he said, "and if you want me to finish the job, I'll keep right on working." This offer sounded great. The director said he would consider that with the maintenance department and the business manager.

The next day, they met again. "We all think that it would be great for you to continue and get the barn done," said the director. "OK," said Karl, "but I have some bad news for you. My hourly rate is higher." "Why is that?" asked the director. "Well, when I started the job I was a beginner, but now I'm an experienced painter and I don't work for the beginning hourly rate anymore." A compellingly practical argument, and a marvelous confirmation of developmental gains. Karl was rehired at the new rate.

Beyond Routines: Cottage Management and Maintenance

One step above routines and chores, cottage management and maintenance are the responsibility the group takes for its own residence. Frequently, the overtones between the staff and the children in this domain are negative, concerned largely with social control of the group to prevent acting out leading to vandalism, perhaps with damage that will attract the criticism of the maintenance department and/or administrative review of the child-care worker's competence to manage the group. The fear of negative group fallout and the possibility of physical damage that will attract criticism from other departments is an unfortunate element that can permeate the work of the child-care staff with the group and the cottage. Through combining an educational philosophy and clear concepts of group process, however, the focus of the work can change from preoccupation with social control. Children and youth care workers can set a new tone in the way that a group lives together and manages itself. To do so, three ingredients are essential.

Content is the first ingredient. It is essential that the workers recognize what they want to accomplish with the group and their combined stewardship of the residence unit given to their use. It is essential that the staff help the children to develop a sense of ownership. The second ingredient is *process*. Conversations about how best to use and care for the unit are the proper arena of concern of the group. Third is *budget*. It is important that there be genuine resources to work with and some actual permission to do so. If all maintenance is done by the maintenance department and the children are never permitted to take positive responsibility for the unit in which they live, it is quite likely that resorting to social control will be necessary to prevent them from doing damage. If, however, they are the agents of the unit's improvement, physical damage and accompanying maintenance bills can be reduced, as is shown in the following example.

In one residential setting, the interplay of all three of these ingredients created a completely different attitude about cottage management and maintenance. Each residential group was given control of a portion of the actual maintenance budget allocated to their cottage for repairing broken items, such as screens, doors, locks, handles, paint, trim, and furniture. The group was expected to use these funds in maintaining their unit as part of the overall cottage program. There was no illusion that these were extra funds and that the maintenance department still had the funds necessary to perform the maintenance even if a group slipped up. Thus, it became the responsibility of the group—staff and children—to maintain the quality of its own environment and to use the funds to cover necessary repairs, with the clear understanding that money not expended for repairs would be available to the cottage group for some other purpose to be determined by the group.

To add incentive and enthusiasm to the whole, an additional amount of actual maintenance budget was reallocated and set up as a damage fund to be used in case of some damage taking place outside the cottages. Decisions regarding incidents and expenditures from the damage fund were made by the campuswide Student-Staff Coordinating Committee, composed of children from each residential unit, staff members from residential units, and staff members from nonresidential program areas. All money in the damage fund not expended by the end of the fiscal year for covering breakage incidents was transferred to the activities budget, which was presided over by the Student Activities Committee, another campuswide, student-staff group. As the child-care staff was empowered to use all three ingredients—content, process, and budget—and to be involved with the children as participants, it was possible to redefine the content of maintaining the living unit from a series of social control issues to a curriculum for participation, learning, the development of ownership, and the fostering of pride.

Toward More Developmentally Productive Work: A Campuswide Example

The Farm Market Project was developed one summer at the same residential center cited in the preceding example. This facility for emotionally disturbed children and youths provided services to nine county child welfare agencies, several juvenile courts, and the City of Philadelphia. The project is offered here as an example, on the assumption that analogous programs developed elsewhere to fit local, current circumstances might be different in content. In these settings, programs might also be cottage-based rather than campuswide; the specifics are limited only by the ingenuity of those involved. Yet it is hoped that this example will provide a useful model for those seeking to undertake such efforts in locally appropriate form.

The staff in this facility had been concerned with increasing the competence of the program and staffing so that the agency could work more effectively with the difficulties of the disturbed children then being referred. It was felt at the time that to build the concept of a whole school working together, a core activity was needed to engage the energy of the whole place and to provide opportunities for individual children, regardless of competence, age, or experience, to be active participants and contributors. The staff was concerned that the activity finally decided on would assure that certain fundamental objectives would be met:

> That there be the requirement, built into the project, of children working together for the success of the whole
>
> That the children would be the leaders, the staff members the facilitators
>
> That there would be leadership positions for many and a clear, important niche for everyone
>
> That the project actively foster positive social interactions, cooperation, some specific skills, and the development of some peer group organizational structures
>
> That there would be some chance for the children, either as individuals, as a whole, or both, to make money, because their non-institutionalized peers did so during the summer
>
> That the project would be fun, because that's also what children do in the summer, have fun

This was a difficult set of objectives to meet. The program that the staff ultimately selected used many of the resources of the facility itself and capitalized on its relationship to the neighborhood.

The Farm Market Project was set up to operate like a business. It involved every student in the agency who wanted to be involved, regardless of age or sex, and made use of their talents and energies through participation on one or more committees. The enterprise was organizationally clear. It had an executive administration composed of a general chairperson, the chairperson of each of the operating subcommittees, and three staff members. The following six committees were regarded as essential.

The *Growing Committee* was responsible for plowing the land and planting and cultivating the crops; the *Harvesting and Transporting Committee* was responsible for exactly that—harvesting the crops and transporting them to the point of marketing. To carry out this mission, several of the students had to learn to drive the tractor, which certainly made that committee an exciting one on which to serve. The *Marketing Committee* was in charge of building and operating the stand and developing marketing strategies including advertising, distributing handbills around town, placing signs in stores, and determining prices through research in local markets and with grocery wholesalers.

The *Timekeeping Committee* was responsible for scheduling and certifying time worked by individuals—a critical function because the ultimate distribution of proceeds was based on time spent by each person as a worker in the project. The *Bookkeeping Committee* was responsible for keeping track of all expenditures and incomes, as well as payment of loans. To get the business under way, the school had purchased seed and fertilizer, an expenditure that would have to be reimbursed from the proceeds of the project. Gasoline for the tractor also had to be purchased by the project, but the use of the tractor was donated by the school. The *Administrative Committee* was responsible for coordination, making sure the committees worked together on the same time schedule; and it managed the distribution of proceeds based on the contributions of individual participants.

Each committee had technical assistance from selected staff members. The farmer, for example, was the technical assistance person to the Growing Committee and also to the Transportation Committee, since the group used his tractor. The business manager was the primary technical assistant to the Marketing Committee. The bookkeepers provided technical assistance to the Bookkeeping Committee and the treasurer, a senior child-care worker to the Administrative Committee, and so forth.

Each committee had its share of successes as well as its share of problems. The Growing Committee soon found that certain of their jobs were boring (hoeing, for example), while others' jobs were more exciting (e.g., handling the money). So the Administrative Committee soon had a problem to settle and handled it by allowing and facilitating a certain number of committee exchanges. Although keeping everybody going was a constant issue before the Administrative Committee, specific episodes of malingering needed particular attention.

A surprising problem was generated by enthusiasm—the desire to expand. Though some expansion was permitted (members of the Growing Committee going with the agency's food buyer to the wholesale vegetable market to pick up commodities that were short in the field), enthusiasm for adding new lines of merchandise and new additions to the market was resisted on staff advice. A major and unforeseen issue that took considerable energy and created a considerable problem for the project was what to do in midsummer with the embezzling treasurer. It was resolved after an investigation of the amount of missing funds, the interviewing of witnesses who had some observations to make, and confronting the treasurer with the evidence, which was followed by her resignation from that position and a planned program of restitution.

This project was only a part of the summer program, since many of the older students had summer jobs outside the agency, younger students were involved in summer school and summer activity groups, and cottages had many of their own residential unit activities. It was, however, a core element that summer to provide a unifying vehicle for the whole school, and it did its job. Students learned to work together and to resolve their difficulties. They also learned a whole new basis for relationship with the staff.

By astutely sharing technical assistance assignments through different sectors of the staff, it was possible to put children in relationship to staff members with whom they normally were not involved and also to put those children and staff members who were accustomed to working together into new relationships, in which they found new values and new interests in each other. These experiences contributed greatly to creating the kind of longer-range staff-child relationships we were interested in facilitating in the agency, and in modeling a concept for the authority of child-care workers with children and their groups as derived authority (derived from the workers being in charge of the process and technically interested in the content) rather than merely assigned authority (from the hierarchical structure of the agency alone).

Group Process in Group Care: The Key to the Greenhouse

It seems evident that all the approaches that have been described above depend essentially on the ability of the child and youth care worker to work effectively with and through groups. That process, too, must be planned with care and implemented with sensitivity. In one program-development situation in which the author was involved, two kinds of group sessions, each with its own style of groupwork and participation, were enunciated in order to maximize the potential for positive interaction and to provide additional clarification for workers about role and practice. This construct is suggested here as a way of providing direction for groupwork in the milieu in the hope that it can add significantly to the methodology of child-care work while providing necessary assurance for individual members of groups against the potential tyranny of youth groups.

The first group, titled from its function, Management and Program, is the MAP group. In this style of work group, the children and staff members together are concerned with all the issues of the management of the cottage and the development of its program. The group operates best when functioning in a truly democratic and parliamentary fashion. The chair should not always be a staff member. There are many opportunities in the conduct of such a group to carry out both its immediate business and its teaching role. If the chair is shared among the youth members of the group, they then have opportunities to learn how to interact, to lead, to participate, to follow, to derive consensus, to be exponents for and defenders of ideas, to understand and be able to participate in effective problem-solving and planning processes, and then to carry out and enjoy the results of those plans and decisions. The MAP group is task-oriented and functional.

Although it is easier to see how groupwork can be an effective tool in managing living and planning programs, it is also possible to harness the power of the peer group to deal directly with individual issues of its members and the dynamics of the group and its interactions. This type of group interaction has, however, a very different purpose: to deal with the Development of Individual and Group (DIG). Where the MAP group is task-oriented and functional, the DIG group is process- and performance-oriented and dynamic. Its task is to dig into the developmental issues of both the group and the individual members and to provide support, clarification, and even confrontation where that is necessary. Usually regarded in traditional, clinically based programs as completely confidential, the problems of individual youths are regarded in this construct as being of concern to their colleagues and highly susceptible to helpful intervention if the structure for positive support is built into the program. It is the purpose and design of the DIG group to accomplish this.

In programs that have developed a structure for peer group intervention and behavior, it is recommended that this group and its purposes be clearly separated from the program group and its purposes, and that the separation be maintained. The entire reason for having a group for each purpose is to ensure that the agenda does not become mixed, and that a general discussion about activities does not somehow evolve into a confrontation session on behavior. With a clear concept of differential, functional groups, it is more possible for staff members, as well as for children, to regulate the nature of discussions so that the potential for tyranny from the group is eliminated. In other words, a discussion that begins as a MAP group where the concern is planning some aspect of program cannot, because dissension arises during discussion, evolve into one focused on a particular group member and his or her own individual issues.

It is equally important that the DIG group not be permitted to drift into a MAP group. The group should decide that the DIG group is over and determine its next activity, which may be a MAP meeting, a snack, etc.

That each of these groups in its specificity of definition seems to be artificially constructed rather than simply evolved naturally could suggest their being contrived. To the extent that they are created structures, that is true. The whole of residential treatment, however, is a structured environment rather than a natural one. This structure is designed to maximize the value of the treatment center's peer groups and to provide a clear element of a unifying methodology for the staff.

In an agency where this kind of explicit group definition does not seem feasible, the workers need not be deterred from using the same principles. If workers accept this perception of group structure, then they will recognize, whether groups are explicitly established for these different purposes or not, that these functions are present: the worker must know which situation he or she and the group are in and deal with the group accordingly.

Putting the Pieces Together: A Program
Example as a Metaphor
for Group Care

With this background of group life as a developmental and growth-promoting activity, with the direct care worker as a broad-based facilitating resource, and with explicit models for groupwork in learning (MAP group) and treatment (DIG group), it is possible now to examine more deeply the kind of program reflected in the vignette that opened this chapter.

It is possible to amass large program pieces and carry them out successfully in the same way that the small experience of going to the movies is designed, implemented, and followed up. The Farm Market Project already described is one example. An example of a different sort follows, describing a summer project undertaken by a small residential treatment center. Through similar processes, complete group care programs can be derived to meet the needs of those involved in other group care settings.

The setting was a small residential treatment center in the White Mountains of New Hampshire.[3] In general meetings of children and staff members, planning had been looking ahead to the summer. Certain necessary projects had been identified: everyone wanted two new ski trails and those had to be cleared, the entrance road required rebuilding in three places because of washouts, several cabins needed repairs, and a start had to be made on building up the firewood supply for the winter. Local recreational ideas were proposed and particular summer events in the community were noted, but then the group centered its attention on planning a real adventure. What finally evolved was the "West Branch Canoe Trip."

This trip is discussed here as a major program undertaking to elaborate the concept of activity, with all of its concomitant aspects of planning, experience, learning, and interrelationships, as the core of milieu treatment. It should also be viewed as a metaphor for the whole of residential treatment planning and can serve as an illustration of the application of the principles that have been presented in this chapter.

The West Branch of the Penobscot River begins in Seboomook Lake in the wilderness of Maine and was to be the beginning of the proposed trip, which would then proceed through some exciting sections of white water and over some quite long and boring sections of flat-river paddling to the upper waters of Chesuncook Lake and down the entire length of the lake to the trip's destination at Ripogenus Dam. The trip would be undertaken by nine boys and three staff members, using four canoes and one large van to make the journey from Jackson, New Hampshire, to the wilderness of Maine and the shores of Seboomook Lake. Ultimately, the planning determined that the entire trip would require nine days, one day each for traveling out and back and seven days on the river. The staff knew well the old formula that high structure equals low pressure, so the children were introduced immediately to the rule of the six Ps, and it was quickly adopted as a motto: "proper prior planning prevents poor performance."

The planning period, which lasted about six weeks, included people working in small groups (three committees) on separate aspects of the whole trip. The Food Committee worked out detailed plans for menus and the supplies that would be necessary to meet the demands. It involved visits to the mountain supply store in town to consider dehydrated foods and to grocery stores to inquire into the best packages for other foodstuffs. The committee assembled the whole into a food plan that was manageable both in terms of budget and transporting in the canoes.

The Route Committee was responsible not only for understanding the canoe route but determining the best way to get to the point of embarkation and how to retrieve the van at the end of the trip for the return home. This group studied canoe guides, topographical maps, and New Hampshire and Maine road maps. They studied the country to be traversed by the canoes and drew up a canoe route map that highlighted special features such as flow of water, carries, fast water, anticipated distances per day of travel, and special features that they wanted to include on the trip over and back. With staff guidance, the group realized that they would be in the neighborhood of Mt. Katahdin, and the view of the mountain over Togue Pond from the Baxter Park road was one that should not be missed, so it was included in the route map for the return home.

The Equipment Committee had responsibility for everything from canoes to axes. Two canoes and one tent had to be rented; comparative pricing was required to make those decisions. All common gear had to be assembled and all personal gear had to be inspected as to its condition and appropriateness. Determinations had to be made about how much individual baggage any one person could take and still have room for his share of the common load. Whether individuals could take radios became a serious question for discussion, which the committee approached first from the point of whether there was room. The issue had, however, another dimension: were radios appropriate even if there was room for them? For that decision, the committee had to bring the question to the entire group, and there it was decided that radios were not part of a wilderness experience and should not be brought.

As committees delved into their work and developed the expertise necessary to complete their tasks, they also became the resource to whom one would turn for any kind of technical information regarding that particular area, and this became even clearer as the trip got under way. For example, though persons working on the food were not the only ones who did the dishes en route, they were the persons who were "in the know" and could (if they chose) answer the question, "What's for dinner?"

New definitions of adult authority began to evolve during the preparation and were further elaborated during the trip itself. Staff roles became defined around important and useful areas of expertise, for example, canoe management, river flow, fish, edible weeds, weather, woodland wildlife, geography, topography, and creative solutions to the boredom of long stretches of flat-water paddling. This interesting new basis for authority was an unanticipated development, but one so salient that more work was done on it upon return to regular program.[4]

Although the planning for the management of each day's itinerary and dealing with any special problems or opportunities was a task of the group as a whole, each morning saw two committees at work, one responsible for breakfast and one responsible for cleanup. Then the whole group met to look at river charts and topographical maps and plot the day's intended journey. This planning was based on the original chart plus any revisions en route prompted by the discovery of some special opportunity that was worth spending time on or making a detour.

The ideas from the pre-planning of each committee were called forth in this meeting, as were the contributions of individual staff members based on their particular areas of expertise. The boys too had begun to develop expertise in certain areas, depending on their interest or on the relationship with a staff member who might be particularly involved. Ideas stemming from those interests also had to be reviewed as part of the planning. This meeting might therefore initiate a whole new activity, such as exploring a tiny, remote village that was discovered by investigating a small checkpoint on the map, or happening on a series of ledges and chutes with fast-water action, which called for a quick change into bathing suits to enjoy several hours of recreation that had not been foreseen in the master plan.

White water is always exhilarating even when it is not navigable, and plans must be made for maneuvering canoes carefully down over ledges and shelves, but flat water can be boring; the longer it continues, the more boring it can become. Although exhilarating experiences seem automatically to bring out the best in everyone, occasions that will call that forth in the down times of flat-water boredom need to be created. During one episode of flat water, paddling turned out to be much easier after pulling ashore at a worthwhile spot to look for animal tracks; a fine beach suddenly appearing around the bend called for a stop to go skinny-dipping; and an abandoned cabin that might have been bypassed on a thrilling stretch of white water suddenly seemed to need exploration and a trip back in history to learn something about its origins and who might have used this remote outpost. Good exercises in imagination such as these were always given additional inspiration by reading at night around the campfire of Henry David Thoreau's travels over these same waters from Moosehead Lake, over Northwest Carry, and down the Penobscot into the system of lakes that leads to the Allagash.

Staff members found that it is important to keep aware of the need for change of pace, and that many of the most unobtrusive staff interventions were probably the most effective. One staff member always seemed able to reach into the depth of his pack and pull out a candy bar for everyone at the critical moment when a jolt of energy was needed; candy breaks became one of the interventions in the down times of flat-water boredom.

Staff members must also be alert to new learning opportunities that can help to manage the flow of activity, in ways that keep young people interested, and stave off the intrusion of negative "critical incidents"—behavioral expressions that stem from lack of involvement. For example, when the group was presented with the long, flat stretch of Chesuncook Lake, a tremendous distance with the destination completely out of sight and the sun beating down over what appeared to be an endless journey, the impossible was made possible by rafting the canoes together and creating a makeshift sailing rig, thus converting a situation destined to tax patience to the breaking point into a moment of a new and unusual high adventure and learning opportunity.

The point is that the staff is on duty (the children are "on vacation" because we are working!) and has to find ways to get through tough spots, whether because of hazards, heat, cold, or boredom. If such a trip is to be successful, however, it is also crucial that the staff enjoy the adventure with the children— and that the children perceive their own work contribution as essential. More broadly, it is important that any activity achieve its intrinsic goal, such as a successful art project or a competent team or a reasonably clean cottage; that it enhance the development of the young people involved; and that it be shared as a joint undertaking of children and staff members.[5]

The canoe trip was not a trip of high stress, great danger, solo in the wilderness, or survival. It was not a dangerous mission or one fraught with enormous need for technical competence. For its success, like success at daily group living in the residential center, it required good planning—the kind that could be enthusiastically shared by staff members and boys. It required the staff's conscientious management of the flow of events and the managing of the curriculum so that every one would have fun and an opportunity to participate appropriately. It required good attention to group process, so that the children were managing their own trip and making the decisions that affected their own activity.

Moving from the metaphor, the microcosm of the canoe trip, to the macrocosm of the residential center, it is apparent that the same elements are required.

Conclusion

More often than we like to admit, however, what we see when visiting a children's residential center is a group idly sprawled in front of a television set, with the residential staff members by themselves in the cottage office. At worst, they are getting out of the way of the children; at best, they are supplanting active child-care work—joint interaction of staff and children—with the writing of reports or some other tangible, adjunctive activity such as counting laundry or typing menus. Although they are available to the children, staff members in these situations are not a continuing part of their lives.

On further exploration in such a cottage, we are quite likely to find rooms with unpersonalized walls, uniform bedspreads, and few of those indications of real-life experience that one finds with the children and youths in the homes of one's friends and colleagues. Exploring a cottage kitchen may provide an equally barren experience of cabinets largely empty except for instant coffee and paper cups ("staff stuff") and portion-controlled leftovers in the refrigerator. Common rooms frequently exhibit a dearth of supplies. How many cottage living rooms have you seen that have bookshelves with actual books for children, rather than copies of Alice of Old Vincennes, 18 consecutive years of National Geographic, and two sets of the Encyclopedia Americana, editions 1968 and 1974, contributed by board members as tax deductions?

These staff members may be able to handle the white-water times: the shopping trips, the getting ready for school, the Saturday night trip to the movies.

But they are totally unequipped to manage the flat-water periods of cottage living. This arrangement may be satisfactory if group living is just the warehousing of children between major activities and clinical appointments, but the purpose of group care is to make being in care a developmentally rewarding experience. Group life must not be a warehouse but a greenhouse for encouraging growth, and the emphasis should be on education rather than on custody.

The treatment center and each living group must be perceived as places for positive social interaction and experiential learning. Then new approaches to developing child-care work can be undertaken so as to use all the elements of the daily living situation as the medium for treatment, as they occur, for the promotion of confidence and the building of competence on the part of each and every young person in the group with whom the worker is involved. Such a normalizing approach creates demand for more sophisticated child-care workers than are required when the focus for residential treatment is curing pathology and workers are regarded as providing custodial care between clinical appointments and therapeutic recreation. As competence-building comes more clearly into perspective, the true importance of activities, of work and play, becomes even more evident. They are the key elements in the structure of milieu treatment.

NOTES

*Several actual program or practice examples are used in the text to illustrate the points being made regarding a conceptual basis for program, a unifying methodology for workers and groups, a conceptual definition of role and practice of child and youth care workers, and program models that were designed to meet specified goals. These examples come from the experience of the author as executive director in three different agencies.

[1]Carson Valley School in Flourtown, Pennsylvania, a residential facility for 65 children and youths: The program and structure for managing routines, the Farm Market Project, and the example of the bus windshield come from this agency.

[2]Connecticut Junior Republic, Litchfield, Connecticut, a residential treatment center for 80 court-adjudicated boys: A complete new program design was developed—Positive Group Interaction (PGI)—which included the two task group models described in the text (MAP and DIG).

[3]Youthorizons, in its Spruce Mountain Program in Jackson, New Hampshire, carried out the canoe trip described here and is offered as a metaphor for the goals and complexity of residential treatment.

[4]Evolving a new definition of the basis and structure of authority and generating a new model for staff interaction and teamwork were not part of the original intent of the trip but, as these began to emerge, they were recognized and accepted. As a result, it was possible for the three staff members to continue to experiment with these newly recognized bases for authority and the more interactive quality of teamwork that these new lines of authority produced. The "model" was brought back from the canoe trip and worked on further by the whole staff,

which ultimately developed a different distribution of authority based on expertise and presence rather than on power and position. It is perhaps worthwhile to note that adventures such as this, which may be proposed as programmatic elements, may in addition serve as catalysts for development, just as the canoe trip itself is being used here as a metaphor for the totality of residential treatment.

[5]This idea brings to attention an additional important principle: *the staff is always working on two levels at the same time.* The first level of work and attention is in regard to the activity itself. The activity has meaning and intrinsic value of its own and should be entered into by the group with wholeheartedness or commitment of energy or whatever is appropriate to the nature of the task in terms of their group's purpose for being involved. Accepting the principle that the child-care workers are jointly involved with their children in the activity, be it a chore, a game, or a canoe trip, the successful completion of the activity itself and the involvement of all in it are specific and significant goals. The second level of attention for the staff is the meaning of the activity to the learning and the treatment of the children in care, the educative or clinical aspect of the staff's concern. This is equivalent in importance to the participatory level, because, if either is neglected, the program cannot succeed.

REFERENCES

Arieli, M., Beker, J., and Kashti, Y. 1990. Residential group care as a socializing environment: Toward a broader perspective. In Anglin, J.P., Denholm, C. Ferguson, R.V., and Pence, A. (eds.), *Issues in Professional Child and Youth Care.* New York: Haworth Press. (Also in *Child and Youth Services, 13*(1):45–58.)

Bruner, J. 1970. Conference presentation at Bank Street College.

Dewey, J. 1916. *Democracy and Education.* New York: Macmillan.

Nicolais, V. 1986. Personal communication, during his year as a participant in the International Learning Exchange in Professional Youthwork (ILEX).

Redl, F. 1957. *The Life Space Interview.* Washington, DC: Child Research Branch, National Institute of Mental Health.

Winsor, C.B. 1963. Foreword. In Mitchell, L. S., *Young Geographers.* New York: Basic Books.

8

Normalization for Youth Development

in Residential Care:

The Role of the Direct Care Worker

in Enhancing Vocational Development

and Job-Finding Skills

YECHESKEL TALER

Jacob, 13, developed behavior problems at school. As a result, it was decided that, due to "an unfit home environment, low income, and marital problems," it would be better for him to be removed from his home and sent to a residential group care setting providing intensive psychological treatment, academic studies, and vocational training.

The boy had some initial difficulty in adjusting to the institution but overcame it quickly. He studied automobile mechanics and acquired the skills with ease. He was a bit shy and lacking in self-confidence, but the other youngsters accepted him. All in all, he adjusted well and adapted himself both to his studies and to the institutional environment as a whole.

At the age of 17, Jacob completed his studies, receiving a good recommendation from his teachers, who believed that he would work well if provided with a suitably "personal" employment environment. He returned to his family, who received him well and were pleased that he had had training and possessed an important vocation. Jacob contacted the youth employment service to which he had been referred by a counselor at the institution. The counselor at the employment service, impressed by his credentials, referred him to an interview for a job as an auto mechanic.

Jacob arrived at the interview feeling very anxious. Upon being questioned about his past experience, he told of his stay at the institution, about his behavioral problems and his problems at home, and mentioned his credentials and recommendations. Because of the stigma of institutions and the behavior problems that Jacob had described, the head mechanic chose to hire another youth instead.

Jacob was referred for a number of additional interviews but was not hired; the pattern described above was repeated again and again. He began to lose confidence in his ability as an auto mechanic and to feel that maybe his recommendations were incorrect. He gradually stopped going to interviews and began to sit at home watching television or wandering around with a group of friends from his neighborhood. His relationship with his family also began to decline as a result of his failure to get a job.

Experienced child and youth care workers will recognize Jacob as another in a long line of young people who, having succeeded admirably (and through much hard work on the part of all concerned) in residential care, return to their home environments only to experience frustration and defeat. The "normalization perspective" [Wolfensberger 1980] has been proposed to deal with the problems that such transitions present, but it has been applied more frequently in community settings than in group care. This chapter deals with approaches to normalization through which residential direct care workers can protect their "investment" in their clients, specifically in the vocational development domain, within the residential context. To ignore the transition back to the community is to increase the risk that past progress may unravel.

Normalization

The normalization principle stresses the importance of "utilizing means as culturally normative as possible in order to establish, enable or support behaviors, appearances and interpretations which are as culturally normative as possible" [Wolfensberger 1980]. An important part of this principle in practice is the movement to bring as many as possible of those who have been institutionalized as deviant, many if not most of whom are young people, back to the community. This process is made more difficult to the extent that institutional or group care settings tend to isolate their residents from the outside world and habituate them to dependence on their more limited or limiting immediate environment. In this context, it is crucial that residential group care settings prepare their residents with the skills and knowledge they will need to cope successfully with life in the outside world.

To facilitate social integration, thus normalization, it is important to associate devalued people with positive and valued images. This image in western culture is that of a working person, so an indivisible component of a normalizing environment here is the opportunity to work [Nirje 1980]. If a devalued person is associated with positive characteristics (e.g., has a job), the positive associations will begin to compensate for, or balance off, the negative ones. For older youths returning to the community from an institutional existence, this aspect is crucial in reinforcing the personal normalization process and in determining the success of reentry into normal, independent living. For young persons without previous vocational experience, it may be particularly important in establishing whether they will be able to make a successful long-term adjustment.

Clinicians and researchers agree that two major variables related to the successful reintegration of institutionalized populations in the community are the availability of a social support network, and finding and being able to sustain a productive job [Ainsworth and Fulcher 1981; Whittaker 1979]. Neither of these requirements, which are (as we shall see) closely interrelated, can prudently be left to the post-institutional adjustment period. They should be pursued during the institutional phase and should be in place before discharge so that clients can avoid much unsuccessful flailing that may close opportunities for them and make it difficult for them to recoup. Furthermore, experience suggests that most will not get this kind of assistance in the community, and the need for reinstitutionalization may well result. Therefore, it is important that those who work directly with young people in residential environments be well versed in this area and able to make vocational development and planning, in the broad sense, an active part of the living-learning experience. The focus of this chapter, then, is on the role of the direct care worker in helping young people to acquire the skills and knowledge to sustain productive work, with emphasis on the importance of an effective social support system.

The Importance of Work

Why is work important? "Work is a human activity that produces something of acknowledged value. All three of the elements in that definition—activity, production, and value—are important for mental health. Mental health can be enhanced by activity, although all activities are not health-enhancing. Mental health is also enhanced by the reality and experience of producing something, and by the recognition on the part of others that the activity and its outcome have value" [The President's Commission on Mental Health 1978].

Neff [1985] and Akabas and Kurzman [1982] see five major tasks in work:

Work provides income for living.
Work enables one to utilize energy in a productive way.
Work enables creativity and productivity.
Work enforces social interaction.
Work has a strong influence on social status.

In the development of a career, a critical skill for a young person is that of job-finding. Success or failure at this point is known to have a significant influence on future career aspirations and development: for example, the realization of a useful and satisfying career progression, relegation to a series of low-wage, dead-end jobs, or long-term unemployment. What follows, therefore, is a general discussion on job-finding skills, to be applied later to the residential care situation.

The Job-Finding Task and Job-Finding Skills

In these days of specialization and emphasis on scientific research, we frequently find a narrow topic examined in great depth in isolation from others with which it is inextricably linked. Within the field of residential care and rehabilitation, three such topics have received considerable attention separately in recent years: how jobs are found, which methods are most helpful in job finding, and how social support systems affect job finding. When examined together, however, they are discovered to have a great deal of bearing on a crucial topic in reintegration, the return (or, in the case of most young people, the introduction) of the individual to the work force.

How Jobs Are Found

A wealth of survey research data has ascertained that the majority of individuals who seek jobs, whether or not they are handicapped and regardless of type of disability, deviance, age, and gender, find them through their own initiative rather than through organizations set up to achieve this goal [Bradshaw 1973; Farnel and Pitzalis 1978; Corcoran et al. 1980; Granovetter 1974; Jaffe et al. 1964; Jorgensen et al. 1968; Parkes 1954; Rees and Schulty 1970; Rosenfield 1975; Ruck 1963; Veglahn 1975]. Moreover, jobs are most frequently obtained through informal social support networks, that is, through friends or relatives. (In this chapter, the emphasis is on skills and methods used in finding a job in the most effective way, not on the significant but different problem of creating new and productive work opportunities for young people.) The research of Akabas et al. [1979] suggests that the pattern may be different in the case of the long-term disabled, however, since they appear to be more dependent on rehabilitation and placement agencies; this situation may reflect the dissolution of their informal social support networks over time. The implications for young people entering the job market are unclear, but it should be noted that those leaving residential care programs frequently do not have social support systems in place back home and may, therefore, be more dependent on formal, agency help. In addition, most will be entering the job market seriously for the first time.

Jones and Azrin [1973] use social reinforcement theory to explain the apparent superiority of informal methods under most conditions. They portray the employment process as an informal job-information network in which persons with early knowledge of job openings (employers and employed persons) pass this information on, selectively and privately, to their unemployed acquaintances. Thus, informal referral networks emerge. It is known that such networks are far more significant and effective in job finding than any formalized, bureaucratic means. For example, in one study of job finding, it was learned that two-thirds of the jobs were located through such informal networking [U.S. Department of Labor 1975]. Since getting a job begins with the discovery of available positions, social reinforcement factors become particularly important at this initial stage of the process. Other job seekers may be excluded from the informal information network either because they do not know people who are employed or because they lack resources to reward potential informants either tangibly or, more typically, in other ways.

Which Methods Help Most?

It has become clear, in recent years, that for individuals to find competitive employment, they need both marketable job skills and the ability to sell their employability. Studies in the field of vocational rehabilitation indicate that the major obstacle is gaining, rather than maintaining, employment. Research findings also show that the most successful programs are those that not only stress the need for job-finding skills, but actually train the client in these skills by using a variety of individual and group techniques aimed mostly at job-finding behavior, particularly in interview situations.

Many vocational counselors have, therefore, established programs designed to improve job-seeking skills, which have often focused on skills pertinent to the initial hiring interview, since employers appear to place primary weight on this first encounter. In one of the earliest studies of such programs, Rosenberg [1956] examined the effectiveness of group counseling sessions on filling out job applications. He learned that this method led to changes in the attitudes of job seekers and to increased success in finding jobs. Anderson [1968] and Purro et al. [1966] report successful placement results among handicapped clients in formal classes designed to teach them (1) to identify assets and describe them advantageously, (2) to anticipate questions about deficiencies and develop appropriate answers, and (3) to learn how to discuss their disabilities in a job interview. Other training and counseling programs developed along these lines showed similar results [McCleve 1972; Meoney 1966].

Pinto [1979] evaluated another job interview training program used in a rehabilitation setting in which clients underwent two one-hour training sessions aimed at improving both verbal and non-verbal target behaviors (making self-statements, seeking more information about the job and place of work, body position, positive eye contact, and the like). The program led to marked improvement in most of the target areas, with the training procedure itself, rather than simple practice in interviewing, considered to be the prime factor in the change. Stione and Geppert [1979] reported that clients who received training through role playing fared significantly better than those who did not.

A variety of studies have reported success with the use of "job clubs" in improving job-seeking skills and results [Azrin et al. 1975; Azrin and Philip 1979; Azrin et al. 1980; Taylor et al. 1976]. A range of formats is represented, all centered on group meetings, and the approach appeared to be effective with a wide range of participants in terms of age, sex, ethnicity, education, and mandatory versus voluntary participation.

These programs provide a wide range of approaches, many of which can be adapted to the residential setting, to help young people develop job-seeking competence. As these are applied by direct care workers and others, and if they are reinforced by social support networks built into the program and by the ecological arrangements in the institution, they can be translated by the young clientele into life competencies, such as writing effective resumes; skills in selling oneself in an interview situation (e.g., answering difficult questions, appropriate use of eye contact and other body language, being able to present one's assets, and showing enthusiasm about the job); use of informal support networks (friends, relatives, neighbors, and so on); and the like. These competencies should be seen as key normalizing factors both within the institution and, as residents move out, in facilitating their reincorporation into their home communities.

The Role and Uses of Social Support Systems

Support systems play a crucial role in "continuing social aggregates that provide individuals with the opportunities for feedback about themselves and for validation of their expectations about others, which may offset deficiencies in these communications within the larger community context" [Caplan 1974].

The key characteristic of these social relationships that facilitates healthy development is that persons are treated as unique individuals. Other people are interested in them in personalized ways and are sensitive to their individual needs, which they consider worthy of respect and satisfaction.

Social support may be continuous or intermittent, provided by one significant other or by many and varied relationships. It is usually aimed at helping the individual cope with general continuous life events and/or with acute needs or crises. Yet, whatever their specific nature, supports, says Caplan [1974] consist of three elements: significant others help individuals mobilize their psychological resources and master their emotional burdens; they share their tasks; and they provide them with needed resources in the form of money, material, tools, skills, psychological support, and/or cognitive guidance as these may be needed to improve their handling of their circumstances.

The supportive others function in two ways as buffers against defective feedback. First, they may help one actively by collecting and storing information and interpreting otherwise incomprehensible sets of cues, thus helping the individual to find a safe path. Second, they may act as a refuge or sanctuary to which the individual may return for rest and recuperation between his or her forays into the stressful environment, as an "island of stability and comfort in the turbulent sea of daily life."

According to Caplan [1974], the best-known natural support system is the marital and family group; when functioning adequately, the family provides the essential elements of sensitivity, respect for the needs of its members, and effective communication. Another common natural support system can be found in others who have coped or are at present coping with similar problems, the mutual help groups that range from housewives meeting over a cup of coffee to discuss daily living problems to formal organizations such as Alcoholics Anonymous.

Most people who seek aid tend to do so within the framework of informal social support networks rather than through professional agencies and helpers; help provided in this mutual fashion not only tends to be freer of stigma but often is more satisfying, because it allows the individual to be both a giver and a receiver, thus fostering a sense of personal integrity and independence. In this context, the acquisition of vocational skills is not only critical in and by itself, but also can be instrumental in providing an opportunity to experiment and understand social support networking and its influence on youths' overall development.

The importance of the social support system, the informal network of contacts from which one receives support, is not specific to vocational adjustment. A growing body of theoretical formulations and empirical research indicates the crucial role that one's social support system plays in the restoration and maintenance of physical and mental health and its importance in social functioning of all kinds [Caplan1974].

Social support as used here refers to "a set of interconnected relationships among a group of people that provides enduring patterns of nurturance . . . and contingent reinforcement for efforts to cope with life on a day to day basis" [Whittaker et al. 1983]. Although empirical evidence on the relationship between social support and job finding is scant, sufficient indications point to its importance. In the context of mental health, Caplan [1974] suggested that, beyond a specific domain of life such as jobs, social support is crucial for the overall mental well-being of individuals and their ideas of themselves.

If social support systems are given centrality in residential group care settings, they can have far-reaching implications. On the peer level, direct care staff members can help youths learn to make the living group into a social support system. The staff can also provide a support network for the youngsters in seeking productive employment and in other ways. Efforts to broaden family involvement in a youth's vocational concerns, as these evolve during the period in residence, provide one means of broadening the network and facilitating transition, something that can usefully be expanded to other significant figures in the community as well.

To illustrate further the relevance of the foregoing discussion to residential care, let us return to our earlier example and ground our discussion to the situation of the young client, Jacob, mentioned there.

The Direct Care Worker and
Vocational Development

A few months later, Jacob went to visit the institution he had attended. His youth care worker was happy to see him and asked how he was doing at home and at his job. Jacob hesitated, feeling embarrassed, before he told the worker that he had not found a job; he added that he was happy but did not understand why he had not been hired even though the staff at the institution had given him good recommendations.

The counselor mentioned that he had recently read of a group being formed at a youth agency near the boy's home to provide training in job-finding skills. Jacob was hesitant because of his lost confidence, not believing that anything would really help him. When the counselor encouraged him to give it a try, however, Jacob promised to contact the agency to find out about the training.

He arrived home, called the agency, and was given an appointment a day later. During the interview, Jacob told of his experience at job interviews and how he had presented himself and his skills and abilities as an auto mechanic, and he demonstrated this pattern in a brief role play between himself and the counselor. The counselor strongly suggested that Jacob join a group of youngsters who had experienced similar problems in presenting themselves and had had difficulty in finding jobs. Jacob agreed to give the program a chance. The group met for a period of two weeks, during which there were six four-hour meetings. This intensive experience provided suggestions on developing and using a social support network by contacting neighbors, friends, and family to find out about job openings. The participants learned how to write a resume, fill out a job application, and speak on the telephone with a potential employer where the aim was to obtain an interview rather than the job itself. The role-playing method was used in rehearsing telephone contacts. They then learned how to behave and present themselves during the interview so as to emphasize their skills and abilities and their interest in the job appropriately, and how to answer difficult or embarrassing questions.

Most of the role playing was done in pairs, where the youngsters aided one another by providing feedback on the process. At this stage, much use was made of videotape. At the last session, each youngster was required to appear as he or she would for a real interview, using the skills learned, including dressing properly, making use of body language, and completing the interview in a positive manner.

Jacob became well integrated in his group. He found a few friends who helped each other during role playing and provided information on job openings. Thus, the group itself turned into a source of support for each member. Armed with all this "wisdom," Jacob spread the word concerning his interests in finding a job. His uncle, who knew about his efforts, contacted one of his friends, who was the foreman in a large auto repair shop and was looking for applicants for two job openings. Jacob arrived at the interview ready and excited. This time he did not mention his past at the institution or his behavioral problems, information that was irrelevant to the job. He did emphasize his knowledge of automobile mechanics, his experience with different kinds of motors, and the kinds of equipment he was familiar with and had used in the past.

Toward the end of the interview, the manager asked Jacob if he had any questions, and Jacob replied that he would like to see the work platform. The manager was glad to show him around. Jacob pointed out equipment he knew about and even asked when he could start working. The manager replied that he had other applicants to interview but would notify him within a week. Jacob explained that he would not be home much the following week because he would be busy looking for a job and asked if he might contact the manager on his own initiative within a few days. The manager agreed. Within two days, Jacob was informed that he was hired.

What can be generalized and learned from this example and its successful resolution?

> The most effective way to get information about available jobs is through informal social support networks.
>
> Job-seeking skills can and should be learned, as are other social skills.
>
> The ability to be assertive in communicating one's skills and abilities for the job market helps one to obtain better jobs, thus gaining higher salaries and more satisfaction.
>
> The responsibility for job seeking should be centered on the young job seeker and not on the formal network, thus helping to develop skill in taking responsibility for oneself and decreasing dependency on others.
>
> By obtaining job-seeking skills and going through the group process, young people improve their self-esteem and increase their level of motivation.
>
> Gaining job-seeking skills will carry over in finding a new job, should that become necessary in the future.

It is important to note that these principles go beyond the goal of obtaining employment and are significant in the context of general youth development. Thus it can be seen that work, crucial in so many ways to healthy, normal life, is also an excellent source of social support to individual workers. Unfortunately, however, those individuals who are most lacking a social support system seem to be those who face the greatest difficulty in finding work. It frequently becomes a vicious circle, since the individual's social support system is one of his or her major resources for finding competitive employment.

Regarded in this light, the youth worker's job can be viewed as enabling young people to break this vicious circle by learning both how to develop a social support network and how to use it to find a job. Presumably, the development and maintenance of a network can have consequences for a young person extending a good deal beyond the simple fact of his being employed. In other words, this approach can be seen as taking one aspect of a treatment plan—job-finding—and using it as a learning ground for skills that can be extremely useful in many other areas of daily life as well: independent living, social activities in the community, using leisure time, and, in general, taking responsibility for one's own life.

This leads to another major advantage of job-finding methods that emphasize the acquisition and use of the skills needed to develop and use a social support network over traditional approaches to placement: they emphasize independence and teach individuals to develop and use their resources actively. Perhaps unintentionally, more traditional methods tend to promote passivity and dependence: the young clients are taught to expect a social worker and/or placement counselor—the formal system—to assess their abilities and to find them an appropriate job; they, in turn, tend simply to wait until the help is forthcoming. In sharp contrast, a method emphasizing the use of social support networks expects clients to be extremely active in seeking out and developing contacts that will lead them to possible places of employment. Moreover, in contrast to seeking assessment information from the clients, this method would teach clients the skills necessary to develop and use their own resources.

It would seem, then, to be most appropriate for youth care workers to redefine their task as helping clients to learn and develop the skills necessary to build up and make appropriate use of their informal social support systems, both to obtain jobs and to maintain good, independent social and vocational functioning. In this connection, it should be noted, the job club has been shown to be so effective: it not only makes use of social reinforcement, but also provides a real, if temporary, social support network and trains individuals to make use of it and, by extension, of their own individual network. It seems apparent that such a broadening of the youth care worker's role would greatly increase both the efficiency of treatment plans for youths and the success of their outcome. Beyond the effect of this approach on individual clients, it can influence both the program and the ecology of the setting toward a normalizing orientation rather than reinforcing the traditional medical model.

Finally, one could hypothesize that youngsters who are institutionalized for longer periods of time without attention being given to the development of informal social networks would rely on and use formal job placement services. Yet research clearly shows the relative ineffectiveness of these formalized approaches to job finding, with implications for other life skills as well. Taken together, these observations emphasize the crucial importance of the role of the youth care worker in the vocational as well as the broader social development of institutionalized young people while they are in the institution and during aftercare.

REFERENCES

Ainsworth, F., and Fulcher, L.C. (eds.). 1981. *Group Care for Children: Concept and Issues*. London, England: Tavistock.

Akabas, S.H., and Kurzman, P.A. 1982. *Work, Workers, and Work Organizations: A View from Social Work*. Englewood Cliffs, NJ: Prentice-Hall Inc.

Akabas, S.H., Medevere, L., and Victor, J. 1979. Pounding pavements: A study of the job hunt of disabled people. *American Rehabilitation* 4(4): 9–15.

Anderson, J.A. 1968. The disadvantaged seek work—Through their efforts or ours? *Rehabilitation Record* 9(3): 5–10.

Azrin, N.H., Flores, T., and Kaplan, S.J. 1975. Job-finding club: A group-assisted program for obtaining employment. *Behavior Research and Therapy* 13(1): 17–27.

Azrin, N.H., and Philip, A.R. 1979. The job club method for the job handicapped: A comparative outcome study. *Rehabilitation Counseling Bulletin* 23: 144–155.

Azrin, N.H., Philip, A.R., Thienes-Hentos, P., and Besalel, V.A. 1980. Comparative evaluation of the job club program with welfare recipients. *Journal of Vocational Behavior* 16: 133–145.

Bradshaw, T.F. 1973. Job-seeking methods used by unemployed workers. *Monthly Labor Review* 96(2): 35–45.

Caplan, G. 1974. *Support Systems and Community Mental Health: Lectures on Concept Development*. New York: Behavioral Publications.

Corcoran, M., Patcher, L., and Duncan, G.J. 1980. Most workers find jobs through word of mouth. *Monthly Labor Review* 103(8): 43–45.

Farnel, J.E., and Pitzalis, E. 1978. How welfare recipients find jobs: A case study in New Jersey. *Monthly Labor Review* 101(2): 43–45.

Granovetter, M.S. 1974. *Getting a Job: A Study of Contracts and Careers*. Cambridge, MA: Harvard University Press.

Jaffe, A.J., Day, L.H., and Adams, W. 1964. *Disabled Workers in an Urban Labor Market*. Totowa, NJ: Bedminster Press.

Jones, R.L., and Azrin, N.H. 1973. An experimental application of a social reinforcement approach to the problem of job-finding. *Journal of Applied Behavior Analysis* 6(37): 345–353.

Jorgensen, G.Z., Janean, F.V., Samuelson, C.O., and McPhee, W.H. 1968. *Interpersonal Relationships: Factors in Job Placement (Regional Rehabilitation Research Institution Bulletin 3)*. Salt Lake City, UT: University of Utah.

McCleve, P. 1972. Placement through improvement of clients' job-seeking skills. *Journal of Applied Rehabilitation Counseling* 3(3): 188–196.

Meoney, W.T. 1966. *An Experiment in the Use of Two Vocational Placement Techniques with a Population of Hard-to-Place Clients*. Grant Number RD 807 P-63, NTIS-PB-197525, Final Report.

Neff, W.S. 1985 *Work and Human Behavior*. New York: Aldine.

Nirje, B. 1980. The normalization principle. In Flynn, R.J., and Nitsch, K.E. (eds.), *Normalization, Social Integration, and Community Services*. Baltimore, MD: University Park Press.

Parkes, H.S. 1954. *Research of Labor Mobility*. New York: Social Science Research Council.

Pinto, R.P. 1979. An evaluation of job interview training in a rehabilitation setting. *Journal of Rehabilitation* 45(2): 71–76.

The President's Commission on Mental Health. 1978. *Report to the President* (Vol. 1). Washington, DC: The Commission.

Purro, B., Sehl, R., and Cogan, T. 1966. Job readiness: Key to placement. *Journal of Rehabilitation* 32(5): 18–19.

Rees, A.E., and Schulty, G. 1970. *Workers and Wages in an Urban Labor Market*. Chicago, IL: University of Chicago Press.

Rosenberg, B. 1956. Counseling in a rehabilitation center. *Journal of Rehabilitation* 22(1): 4–6.

Rosenfield, C. 1975. Job-seeking methods used by American workers. *Monthly Labor Review* 98(8): 39–43.

Ruck, H.A. 1963. *Specialized Placement of Quadriplegics and Other Severely Disabled*. A Final Report of the Vocational Administration. Washington, DC: U.S. Department of HEW, RD 509, April.

Stione, C.I., and Geppert, C.G. 1979. Job interviewing skills training: An empirical investigation of two methods. *Rehabilitation Counseling Bulletin* 22(5): 396–401.

Taylor, H., Averbeck, D., and Hubert, M. 1976. Job Placement and Job Development Research Utilization Laboratory. No. 7. Chicago, IL: Jewish Vocational Service.

U.S. Department of Labor. 1975. *Manpower Research*. Washington, DC: U.S. Department of Labor.

Veglahn, P.A. 1975. Job-search patterns of paraplegics. *Rehabilitation Counseling Bulletin* 20(5): 129–136.

Whittaker, J.K. 1979. *Caring for Troubled Children*. San Francisco, CA: Jossey-Bass.

Whittaker, J.K., and Garbarino, J. 1983. *Social Support Networks: Informal Helping in the Human Services*. New York: Aldine.

Wolfensberger, W. 1980. The definition of normalization, update, problems, and misunderstandings. In Flynn, R.J., and Nitsch, K.E. (eds.), *Normalization, Social Integration and Community Services*. Baltimore, MD: University Park Press.

9

Working with Families of Children and Youths

in Residential Settings

KAREN VANDER VEN

John and Elaine, 1985

It's the end of a busy shift, and John and Elaine, child-care workers in a residential treatment center, breathing sighs and rolling their eyes heavenward, reflect on the events of the day as they sip coffee in the staff room.

"Well, can you believe it?" says John. "Jimmy wants to go home! Have you ever seen his mother? Always complaining about how hard everything is, and looking like a tired old dishrag. I'm glad my mother doesn't look like that. Weird! Knowing how lousy these kids' parents are at least gives me energy to put up with some of their tricks—certainly Jimmy's. And, I'll tell you—if it weren't for those parents, I could really make progress with that kid! After all—I'm just like a parent to him myself."

"Oh, listen, John," chimes in Elaine, "you're going to love this! It was announced at that staff meeting when you were out sick. We child-care workers are going to be expected to start making home visits to our kids.

171

And not only that, the muzzle's off! We're going to be allowed to talk to the parents about their kid's behavior now when they come here to Edgehaven. No more of that 'refer it to the case worker' jazz."

"Good grief!" exclaims John. "What's the world—and this agency—coming to? Next thing you know, I'll be on my way back to school the way you are—learning more not just about kids but families as well."

John and Elaine, 1988

"You know, Elaine, all that business we learned in graduate school about the child and the family being part of a system, and about not sending kids back to homes that are the same as they were when they began treatment, doesn't seem to apply here at Stonecrest. We should have asked more about it when we were interviewed here. This place is still rooted in the past. They make all this noise about child-care workers being part of the treatment team, but they don't even let us use what we know. If we had a chance to bring parents in, find out what they're like, and work with them on the ways we use to manage the kids and involve them in activities, we'd really be using our skills."

"Well, John, why don't you quit complaining about it and do something? Don't be one of those child-care workers who spends all his time telling war stories without going into battle!"

"OK, I'll plan something but I can't do it alone. Will you help?"

John and Elaine, 1991

"Hello, Mr. and Mrs. Moore. I'm John Cohane, the child-care family worker here at Stonecrest. You and I, and Gary, will be working together as part of his program here. We know how hard it is to be a parent of a difficult child, and we find that if we work together, it's easier all around. Sometimes we'll be joined by Elaine Regis, a child and family specialist who leads our parent groups. Let me tell you a little about what we do, and then we can see what concerns you have."

"I know that you've already been told about our parent involvement program and the activities that the kids and their families share together on our units. Before Gary is admitted, I'll be visiting you at home so we can find out a bit more about Gary and his interests and concerns and get more of a picture from you about what it's been like to live with him. Since his main problem seems to be his refusal to stay in school, I'll be working with his school to coordinate what we'll be doing with him here. After he's been with us a few weeks, you'll be coming in, and we'll all meet to set goals together. There's more, but why don't we see what your questions are at this point?"

These vignettes encompass an array of issues representative of the current emergence of concern with the families of children in care as a major focus in child and youth care practice. In this approach, the focus of child-care practitioners is still primarily on meeting the needs of the children, but in a way that enhances the practitioners' effectiveness by bringing families, both directly and indirectly, within their scope of activity. This approach has been referred to as "family-oriented" or "community" child-care practice [Seidl 1974].

This chapter describes issues related to family-oriented practice in a conceptual framework that identifies the varied kinds of knowledge child and youth care practitioners need in order to deal with them and thereby to enhance their practice. These knowledge areas include the historical evolution of family work in residential treatment, the growing professionalization of child care, the personal and professional characteristics of child and youth care practitioners, special issues for child-care practitioners in family work, and roles and functions of child-care practitioners in an expanded model of child-care practice with families.

Knowledge Area 1: Historical Evolution of Child and Youth Care Practitioners' Work with Families

To understand best how current child-care practice with children's families has evolved into its present form, it is useful to examine its historical evolution.

The Family Etiology Hypothesis

Families and child-care workers were once excluded from active participation in residential child treatment, an interesting and paradoxical phenomenon, given that both child-care workers and parents are those who traditionally spend the most time directly with children. Given the then-prevailing theories, however, it is easy to understand why. The most prominent theoretical models of human development for a major part of this century conveyed the notion that parents are specifically and directly the cause of the mental health and developmental outcomes of their children. This notion has been effectively termed "the family etiology hypothesis" [Whittaker 1979], or, less formally, "blame and shame" [De Salvatore and Rosenman 1986].

The result of translating this thinking into residential treatment was the casual removal of children from the noxious influence of their families so that they could thus be rehabilitated by benign caregivers and an authoritative clinical staff. The families were either excluded from involvement altogether or, possibly, were provided a modicum of therapy or case work so as to make them "better." Visits between parents and children were carefully rationed, and parents had little if any direct contact with their children's daily program and the staff members who provided their care. Those elements in the family that might justifiably have been changed to provide a sounder environment in which to receive the child back were not dealt with. If anything, parental guilt and isolation were reinforced, and breaches were widened. None of this boded well, of course, for the post-discharge adjustment of either children or family.

The Bottom of the Totem Pole

Although the children who were removed from their families spent the most time with child-care workers, the function of caregiving received little respect among the clinical disciplines. Child-care workers were not only excluded from active participation in treatment planning and implementation, but they also were often forbidden any direct contact with parents. As was frequently lamented, child-care workers occupied "the bottom of the totem pole" in the clinical hierarchy. That at this time many child-care workers were poorly prepared for their work, and that administrators held only minimal requirements for hiring them (common sense was often felt to be sufficient), tended to justify that position.

Recognition and Change

Both of these circumstances—practice based on the family etiology hypothesis and the low status of child-care workers—contributed to isolating children from their families and to isolation among the disciplines that served them. As the years went on and inevitable advances took place, this fragmentation fortunately changed. It became increasingly recognized that "trying 'to fix' the child apart from the context of his [sic] family [was] an impossible undertaking" [Ayres et al. 1987]. Although the reasons have already been alluded to, it is important to specify them.

Parents of various groups of exceptional children have often been even more successful than professionals in achieving passage of crucial legislation allocating much-needed services. For example, parents succeeded in having Public Law 94-142, requiring the delivery of appropriately mainstreamed schooling to exceptional children, enacted and put into effect. The result has been the recognition by professionals working with such children that they might be more effective in the political and legislative front if they were closely aligned with parents.

Within the family itself, the placement of a child out of the home for a period of time inevitably alters the pattern of relationships among the remaining members. They reconfigure themselves around the former influence of the absent person, making it difficult for the child to reenter the family following a period of treatment. If the families are integrally involved in the activities of the children in care, the likelihood of the child's place in the family system being maintained increases.

Just because the child still has a place, however, does not mean that the family structure is ideal. The content and pattern of relationships, including the handling of the child in care, frequently have to change in order to provide a more healthy situation for the child to return to. Excluding families from the treatment process of their children does not necessarily improve their ability to manage their lives in general, or to be more helpful to their children in managing theirs. When parents have participated in the activities that can lead to both learning opportunities and better conditions for their own lives, they become much more able to provide the kind of situation that will sustain children's gains when they return home. This belief accords with that of Garbarino [1982], who states that because "families that produce troubled children appear to be socially isolated from key support systems, they are acutely in need of a family support system." Participation in properly designed family involvement programs is obviously one way of providing a significant support system.

Theoretical Advances and Research

Relevant theoretical breakthroughs on developmental issues occurred, and, in keeping with the overall trend in human services toward evaluation, research began to be conducted on the relationship between family contact variables and outcomes for children in care. For example, it was documented as early as the 1970s [Seidl 1974] that studies showed children who had contact with their families throughout placement made better post-placement adjustments. As a result, parental involvement and the development of a family-oriented perspective were encouraged.

Basic Temperament

Basic temperament [Chess and Thomas 1986; Mohar 1988] refers to the "behavior style" of an individual; that is, the characteristic way in which he or she approaches life's tasks and, in these well-researched formulations, to such characteristics as activity level, persistence, attention span, biological regularity, predominant mood, approach/avoidance in new situations, and others. Such constitutional, or inborn, characteristics, imply that children themselves contribute to the course of their development; they are not just blank slates written upon by all-powerful parents.

Furthermore, certain configurations of temperament (for example, high activity level, biological irregularity, or predominantly negative mood) can result in difficult behavior, posing problems for even the most well-meaning parents.

Recognition of constitutional differences in children has contributed to a change in the way clinicians think about parental cause and effect, and a lessening of dedication to the family etiology hypothesis.

Ecology

The concept of ecology has become increasingly recognized as a theoretical construct with implications for the child and youth care field [Bronfenbrenner 1977; Garbarino 1982; Anglin and Glossop 1987]. This means that influences on the developing child come not only from parents, but also from various levels of the social environment that incisively affect the content and quality of children's and families' lives. A major implication for child and family practice is that successful intervention for the child must be targeted to the child and the family, as well as to the community and the economic, political, educational, and other variables that affect their lives. The adoption of an ecological perspective through-out human services is reflected in the growing emphasis on social networks that aid people in helping each other [Whittaker and Garbarino 1983; Anglin and Glossop 1987].

Systems Theory

In systems theory, stated simply, every individual is viewed as part of a system in which change in one variable affects all the others that are part of it. This perspective has, like ecology, been a pervasive influence in the design of interventions for children and families. Systems theory applied to family work suggested the concept that there is no identified patient, for example, the child, who is the locus and source of all the problems; instead, for one person to get better, everyone in the system has to change in a favorable way. In a systems model of intervention with children, therefore, families play a fundamental role.

Competence Models

Residential treatment philosophy has shifted from the traditional medical model, in which children have been seen as sick and interventions have been targeted at psychiatric symptoms and pathological syndromes, to a competency-based model in which the therapeutic goals became the development of social, emotional, and cognitive competence in children; one of the earliest programs actually implementing this was Hobbs' well known Project Re-ED [Whittaker 1979]. The trend toward competence models in residential treatment is reflected also in the current emphasis on social skills training, that is, promotion of social competence, in residential treatment [Fox and Krueger 1987].

Diffusion of Innovative Approaches

Historically, parent involvement in children's therapeutic and developmental programs was most noticeable in the early child-care sector of the field, with the advent of Head Start and other intervention programs in the 1960s, in which guidelines mandated parent participation as part of a move to strengthen families.

Gradually it became apparent that similar activities were taking place in the residential care sector of the child-care field. Among the first forms were models allowing more frequent visits and contact between parents and their children in care. The infusion of new ways of thinking about children and families, along with the suggestion that increased parental contact was linked to successful outcomes, resulted gradually but steadily in expansion into family-oriented service models in residential treatment.

Second, but less pervasively, the roles of child-care workers in many settings were upgraded to contribute their special skills, because the ecological and social competence approaches are particularly suited to the milieu-and-activities orientation of the child-care practitioner.

Today, as a result of the growing professionalization of child care, economic pressures, and other factors, the opportunities for child-care practitioners to work with families are indeed increasing. Interestingly, as economic cutbacks have forced the elimination of more highly paid clinical staff members, the recognition that the growing ranks of educated child-care workers might successfully assume some of their functions has encouraged the elevation of child-care practitioners to greater levels of responsibility and status (e.g., "the domino effect" [Vander Ven 1985]), including unlocking doors previously closed to parents.

Knowledge Area 2: The Field of Child and Youth Care Today—Specialized Skills and Expanded Practice Opportunities

"All agencies need to recognize and make a commitment to the field of child care as a separate treatment methodology" [Strategies for Serving . . . 1985]. This statement implies an important principle: that child care has a unique function to contribute to family work. The components of this function must be well understood by aspiring child-care family workers. Fortunately, professionalization activities in recent years have identified special functions of child care that tend to differentiate it from other human services [Ainsworth and Fulcher 1981; Conference-Research Sequence in Child Care Education 1982; Vander Ven 1986; Collins 1987]. These points can be summarized as follows:

Use of the self as a role model for positive behavior and growth strivings, particularly through interpersonal, relationship building, and communication skills

Hygienic management of both individual and group behavior so as to maintain a comfortable and growth-producing environment for all

Creation of a developmental/therapeutic life space or milieu, including using group process and helping children to experience their various experiences and relationships as an integrated whole

Handling the activities of daily living in a way that supports children's psychological growth and development

Employment of creative, recreational, and educational activities in the milieu as treatment rather than busy work

Use of community resources to expand the content and richness of the children's lives and to work toward their return to the community

The growing trend toward a family involvement-participation paradigm brought the recognition that these skills could also be applied to parents and families. It is important for child-care practitioners contemplating moving into expanded practice with families to recognize and to "own" this particular compendium of functions and its transferability from children to their families as well.

Knowledge Area 3: Personal and Professional Development of Child-Care Practitioners

It is now understood that human development does not end in childhood; adults follow a course of cognitive and affective development in both their personal and professional lives. For child-care practitioners, the ability to undertake work with parents and families is related to their own personal and professional growth.

Beginning child-care practitioners are often young adults who choose the work because of their own identification with childhood and a well-developed rescue fantasy, in which they see themselves as saving the children from the negative influences of their families and society. This fantasy actually provides the workers with the energy that fuels their work [Vander Ven 1980]. Workers at this stage in their own development, however, often have negative feelings about families rooted in still unresolved family issues with which they are dealing in their own lives, such as independence and authority. These workers, closely identifying with children, may feel that the parents are indeed to blame for their children's problems and even impede their efforts as child-care workers to help them. They may say, "If it weren't for those parents, this kid, with my help, could really go places."

This attitude is in accordance with the general tendency of younger, or less educated, less experienced workers, to engage in simplistic, linear thinking, to see one variable as directly causing another [Vander Ven 1984]. With guidance, structure, and supervision, such workers can interact with parents at this stage, but this task is best done in a manner that is closely related to their direct work with children.

Child-care workers' further growth and development as adults occur during a period that often includes becoming parents themselves. This frequently triggers a major shift in perspective, as they come to recognize the tremendous difficulties under which many families labor. The resulting empathy helps them to expand the identification in their work to include both children and families.

At this stage, rescue fantasies often change to a more objective motivation: to help children *and* families deal with the problems in the larger society that affect them—a change in practitioners' thinking from a linear to a systems mode. Rather than thinking that there is one cause for every outcome or effect, they are able to see how a number of variables may interact to bring about a particular phenomenon and how a systems intervention may modify it. These workers are now in a better position to transfer their child-care skills to constructive work with families and are less likely to fall into the conceptual trap of viewing parents unilaterally as the sole cause of their children's problems. As the workers continue to grow personally and professionally, they may further expand their repertoire of family-related skills, becoming able to work as advocates for conditions that promote positive family life, or directly with children and families, and to use advanced clinical applications of child-care skills [Vander Ven 1988b].

Knowledge Area 4: Special Issues in Child-Care Work with Families

That much of the work of the frontline child-care practitioner involves direct caregiving, which is a common enterprise of parents and child-care workers, poses special issues for the workers.

The Substitute Parent Issue

Whether child-care workers are indeed substitute parents is the first question. That some settings still use such terms as "cottage parents" compounds the problem. Although both child-care workers and parents provide daily care, *child-care workers do not replace parents*. As Garland [1987] puts it, "The major function of residential care has . . . shifted from family substitution to family intervention." To elaborate further, the role, function, and particularly the meaning of child-care workers in the lives of children is different from that of their parents. Parents have the ultimate responsibility for their children over a lengthy period of time, while the workers' contact, no matter how positive, is less intense and is intentionally time-limited [Katz 1984].

Furthermore, even in the worst families, children have a bonding or tie to their parents that is not duplicated even in the warmest external relationships. This fact is the reason behind the careful warning to child-care workers that they avoid insulting children by demeaning their families, no matter how abusive and neglectful the workers think the families may be [Trieschman et al. 1969].

Despite the clear differences between the functions of child-care workers and those of biological parents, the roles of child-care workers, more than those of any other human service discipline, parallel and overlap those of parents. A primary function of child-care workers, in addition to that of delivering appropriate therapeutic interventions, is to provide basic care, dealing with non-medical physical and psychosocial needs, within the daily living milieu. The similarity of the activity of the child-care worker to what is ordinarily provided by a parent can be called the parental approximation phenomenon; the closer the approximation, the more salient the issues regarding substitute parenting become.

One factor contributing to the significance of these issues is the fact that many children in residential care are physically distant from their own families. The families may live too far away for frequent contact, particularly in these days of interstate placements; they may be too fragmented or too poorly functioning to be active participants in a treatment process, or they may not exist at all. Although there are fewer orphans today, there are still some children with no immediate relatives.

In the earlier days of the field, the tendency was to deny both the approximation phenomenon and the surrounding issues. The current trend, however, is to conceptualize models for better understanding this function and for seeing its potential as a treatment modality, as well as a particular dynamic inherent in the role of the child-care worker in the daily milieu.

One example of a model with such a function is the Parenting and Reparenting paradigm of Soth [1986], which was developed in part to enable children in care, whose families were unable to be active collaborators in treatment, to experience parenting functions. Its theoretical base, as described by Soth, is the "corrective emotional experience" of Franz Alexander, which suggests that, "over a period of time emotionally charged attitudes developed in childhood . . . have to be corrected by reliving similar situations in the immediate present." The adult (therapist or child-care worker) "behaves very differently in the present situation as compared to parents in the past" [Soth 1986]. Within this general paradigm, "reparenting" refers to the process of making up for an actual lack of parenting (e.g., nurturing) experienced by children in earlier years and is intended to develop the healthy part of the personality. "Deparenting" refers to the process of correcting effects of earlier experiences of parenting, so as to extinguish those unhealthy responses the individual may have developed in response to them.

Serving in the capacity of "foster parent," "cottage parent," and so on obviously confronts child-care workers more directly with the need to understand the similarities and differences in their and the biological parents' roles, as well as how they can most effectively conduct their relationship with the child. Models such as Soth's can be very useful in providing a conceptual frame of reference for this task.

Child-Care Workers and Their Own Families

Recognizing the differences between child-care work and parenting can also help child-care workers to deal with the complexities of working professionally with chidren and, at the same time, dealing with personal issues regarding parenthood. As was previously mentioned, younger workers may still be in the process of separating from their own families and becoming independent adults, and these concerns can color their perceptions of parenthood in general. Older workers may be parents themselves, again raising important issues. In their capacity as biological parents, they are subject to the usual parental guilts and uncertainties, which may be exacerbated if their children have problems, or if workers feel that they are overinvolved with the children whom they serve to the point of investing less energy in their own [Vander Van 1988b].

Child-Care Workers and Parents: Partners, Not Competitors

Another issue, particularly for novice workers, is that of competition between child-care workers and parents. Parents, who already feel guilty, may covertly or even overtly resent the child-care worker, who may appear to be more successful with their children than they themselves have been. Conversely, child-care workers in the throes of their rescue fantasies may gain self-esteem from this very occurrence. Workers need first to recognize the differences between biological parenthood and child-care work. Then they need to use this sensitivity professionally so as to be able to acknowledge to parents the particular difficulties inherent in the role of biological parent. This reduces the perceived power disparity between the parents and the child-care workers. The two become collaborators in promoting the child's welfare, exchanging and using each other's talents, and recognizing each others' positions, rather than being adversaries.

At a more advanced level, competition may take another form: that of relating appropriately to the bond between child and parent if the practitioner is working with both together. For example, a child-care worker may actually come to be more strongly identified with a parent than with the child. In working with both together, the worker may subtly exclude the child, hardly serving a healing function for the family as a whole. The responsibility of the child-care worker with families is to facilitate the bonding between parent and child, rather than that of either to the worker, and then to relate to that joint bond, thereby strengthening the parent-child relationship [Anglin n.d.].

The worker's awareness of all these issues is the first step toward confronting them and then making sure that they do not interfere with whatever form and level of family-oriented work he or she may be undertaking. As the next section will show, there are increasingly many possibilities at hand.

Knowledge Area 5: Roles and Functions for Child-Care Practitioners with Families

Child-care practitioners' recognition of the historical evolution of both the role of parents and of child-care workers in residential care, their own potential for personal and professional development into expanded career functions and advanced ways of thinking about their work and their clients, their knowledge of the special skills offered by the field of child care, and, finally, their knowledge of the dynamics of the relationships between child-care workers, parents, and parental functions all come into play in conceptualizing and articulating the direct practice opportunities for child-care practitioners in working with families.

The formulation encompasses the roles of the child-care worker in both parental approximation and family intervention. Although some of the recent literature on child-care workers as family practitioners appropriately focuses on the interventionist role [Garland 1987; Peterson and Brown 1982], it is the premise of this chapter that the fundamental caregiving purpose—the commonality between child-care work and parenthood—of child-care work must be considered as well.

Level 1: The Primary Child-Care Worker

Primary child-care workers are the persons in the milieu who are responsible for providing the children with daily care and activities. In this function, they are approximating the parental role most closely. As their abilities expand, they will be able to assume more advanced parental approximation functions and/or to serve increasingly as interventionists, using identified and targeted modalities in working directly with families and with the wider systems that affect families. Primary workers, however, as mentioned before, are often beginning their careers and, at that stage, are still growing into the ability to become parent workers.

This corresponds to the *novice* and *initial* stages of professional development in a formulation of career stages [Vander Ven 1988a], in which workers may bring varied levels of formal education, experience, and commitment to the field. This does not mean, however, that they cannot assume responsibilities with parents and families appropriate to their position as direct caregivers, possessing the skill clusters of child care previously identified. Agencies with an articulated model of child-care worker involvement and participation in family work provide a structure that not only can engage this level of worker in a process of personal growth and learning but also can provide anticipatory socialization for more advanced and complex roles. In fact, careful supervision geared to experience and maturity can move them on to advanced developmental stages and levels of practice. Primary child-care workers, in this context, can appropriately perform the following functions with families.

Observation

Information on clients' responses in real life is an invaluable contribution to treatment planning and implementation. Child-care workers, particularly in agencies with established service models that include parents as active participants, have a wide range of opportunities for observation. They may see families, for example, as they call for, return, and visit children; as they participate in joint activities with their children and unit staff members; and as they accompany senior workers on home visits or in other conjoint family-staff functions.

Giving Information to Parents

These workers are often the ones on hand when parents come to the unit or cottage to pick up or return children. In the contemporary collaboration model, child-care workers would be permitted—even encouraged—to share information about issues within the appropriate purview of the child-care worker: for example, how the children are sleeping, how they participated in activities during the week, and how they like the new clothes they received. Child-care workers at this stage would not provide information on psychological test results, psychiatric diagnoses, and so on, referring the parent to the appropriate staff members.

Modeling

Whether contacts are incidental or part of a formally planned family program, primary child-care workers serve as models for child management, in particular.

They can informally—or formally, if such programs exist in their agencies—demonstrate to parents positive verbal techniques, various behavioral methods such as contingency management, and ways of handling the activities of daily living.

Teaching

Here again, whether or not workers are involved in a formal program of parent education, they may serve as teachers to parents by, for example, putting a child's behavior in developmental perspective or explaining the reasons for an agency policy.

Alliance Building and Empathy

Building alliances [Ayres et al. 1987] is a productive function for child-care workers. Encounters with parents that occur as a programmatic responsibility allow child-care workers to build positive alliances with the parents. Cordial greetings, support, information, and so forth can be imparted by the primary child-care worker, thus conveying empathy and helping self-conscious and guilt-ridden families to begin to trust.

Team Membership

In agencies with family-oriented programs, each family is assigned to a team; today it is a rare team that would not include child-care workers as members. Although the child-care worker may not be the leader, or even be assigned a primary responsibility for family work, the function of team membership allows for collaboration with other team members in setting goals and implementing programs for families [Ayres et al. 1987].

Participant in On-Unit or In-Home Family Activity

In general, novice primary child-care workers probably would not serve alone in such activities as assessment and follow-up home visits, family discussion and activity groups, and similar activities that are now part of agency family involvement programs. They might very well serve as supportive participants, however, accompanying and assisting more advanced workers.

Foster Parents

In line with the parental approximation concept, primary child-care workers may serve other functions than in-agency primary caregivers. They may, for example, be foster parents; since foster parents are not biological parents, foster care can be considered a child-care function even though not conducted in a group care setting. The quality of foster care provided depends, of course, on the experience, education, and maturity level of the practitioner. The recent advent of "therapeutic" or "clinical" foster care, in which home-based foster parents receive special training, ongoing supervision, and are actually considered to be therapeutic team members [Gabor and Kammerer 1982], is bringing the foster parent role closer to that of the professional child-care worker.

Level 2: The Child-Care Family Worker

These child-care workers are functioning on a higher level, corresponding to the *informed* stage [Vander Ven 1988a]. They bring to their work either formal education, such as an undergraduate degree in child care, extensive experience and personal maturity, or both. These workers are more likely to be identified with parental concerns and to be capable of thinking in systems terms. At this stage, the possible roles and functions with families increase, become more complex, and encompass greater responsibility; they include these types of service:

Parent Education

Child-care practitioners may participate in delivering formal parent education programs conducted in the agency. This duty usually involves their contributing knowledge on their specialties, such as discipline and child management, communicating with children, handling routines and activities of daily living, using community resources, facilitating play, and programming activity. Effective parent education requires that the workers not only use their knowledge, but also apply their programming and groupwork skills in presenting it in a manner that respects the parents as adult learners.

Parent Participation

Programs that actually bring parents to the unit—for visits, for interacting in various ways with their own and other children, for observing programming and child management, for engaging parents in constructive tasks such as painting furniture or repairing toys—may appropriately involve the informed child-care practitioner, who actively interacts with parents whatever the function may be.

Leader or Facilitator of Parent Discussions

This function is less formal than organized parent education, where the focus is on content: such work approaches the informality of incidental contacts. In these groups, parents sit down with the facilitator for open-ended discussion of problems and concerns and for the staff to bring parents up to date on agency program developments and policies. One example is the "Parents' Evenings" model of the Schweizer Kinderheim in Capetown [Davison 1987].

Family Activity Group Leader or Facilitator

Family activity groups [De Salvatore and Rosenman 1986] or family activity programming [Ainsworth and Hansen 1987], sometimes involving siblings and other relatives as well as parents and the child in residence, are an extremely promising way to use the best in child-care workers and in families. These sessions provide a facilitative arena that allows modeling, demonstration, and direct intervention into unproductive interactions. Family members also accrue the same benefits that children do from activity programming: ego-building skills, sense of mastery and achievement, and opportunities to demonstrate strengths.

Clinical Family Work Associate

The child-care worker as co-therapist with a family therapist—usually a member of another discipline—is an increasingly recognized model of practice [Collins 1987; Garland 1987]. Each member of the therapy team can contribute his or her particular perspective to serving the family. In the case of child-care workers, this contribution would include observations of the child in the daily living situation, including those instances when parents are participating, and suggestions for practical child management and programming.

Home Visitor from Pre-Treatment through Post-Discharge

Home visiting is an increasingly important child-care worker function, as is documented in many current writings (e.g., Balgopal et al. [1988]). These workers may make pre-enrollment home visits to orient the family to the residence and to gather information about family dynamics, the child's place in the family, and general interests; ongoing home visits to monitor family progress (which may include accompanying the child home); and post-discharge home visits to determine how well the child and family are managing and to serve as a liaison with schools and other community agencies. During any of these visits, the child-care practitioner may deliver an indicated mix of child-care skills: modeling and demonstration of behavior management, designing home environments, activity programming, handling of the activites of daily living, and helping the family to obtain community programs and resources.

Parental Approximation

Participation in clinical foster care and in reparenting and deparenting milieu programs such as those described by Soth [1986] represents role options in the parental approximation mode for informed workers. Rather than including families in their interventions with children, as previously described, they actually play the role of some form of substitute parent.

Clinical foster care may involve the practitioners taking into their homes highly complex and difficult cases, and working actively as collaborators on a clinical team. To perform these functions properly requires a theoretical and practice sophistication that is well beyond the novice stage of practice. Within the category of parental approximation functions probably belong those workers who have undertaken special training for a role combining primary caregiving and education—for example, the Teaching Family [Blase and Fixsen 1987].

Level 3: Child-Care Family Interventionist

This is a highly responsible and professional level of practice that corresponds to the *Complex* stage of worker development [Vander Ven 1988a]. Practitioners at this stage usually hold an advanced degree and have both personal maturity and a background of experience. They serve a truly interventive role with families, using an array of clinical and administrative skills to design family-oriented programs, to involve families in them, and to apply the most effective strategies to achieve significant change. These practitioners not only possess a broad knowledge and skill base, but also can think in terms of systems, both within families and within the wider community, that contain and influence the life of a particular family.

Program Designer

Advanced child-care practitioners conceptualize and design programs for children and families that use child-care skill areas. These include formal parent education programs dealing with child management, activities of daily living, recreational activities, use of community resources, and so forth, as well as participation programs that bring families directly to the living unit for observation, joint participation in activities, behavior management demonstrations, and the like. Also included are special programs that the agency may offer as an enrichment to or extension of its residential services, such as therapeutic day care, respite care, and/or intergenerational programs bringing children and elderly people together.

Systems Coordinator and Liaison

Practitioners at this level are able to serve as liaison among families, the agency, and community resources. This role is quite similar to that of the case manager, in which one person centralizes and coordinates all the separate services provided for a client so that these are experienced as a purposeful whole. It has been suggested [Krueger 1983] that the milieu-based child-care practitioner is the ideal person to serve in such a role. In the context of a family model, such service might entail work with a school and teachers to set up an appropriate program for a child ready to move from intramural to public school; accompanying a youth to a post-discharge group home; or helping to pave the way for a family to enter a community recreation program. The particular strengths that child-care practitioners bring to these activities include their direct knowledge of the children and families, their recognition of the significance of continuity in making transitions, and their knowledge of child management strategies that would be particularly helpful for new staff members working with the individuals involved.

Team Leader

The advanced child-care practitioner may serve as a clinical team leader, in keeping with the premise that the person most connected with the daily life space of the child is the one most appropriate to assume responsibility for coordinating the various supportive clinical services and family activities so that the child experiences all as a cohesive whole [Krueger 1983]. In this function, the advanced practitioner may be regarded as a systems integrator.

Clinical Work with Families

Advanced child-care practitioners with graduate clinical credentials may serve as clinicians to families, using requisite knowledge and skills in family systems and incorporating into this work their backgrounds in child development and areas of child care. Their work may be dynamically oriented, dealing with in-depth and historical variables, in contrast to the behavioral level and primarily educative orientation of work at previous stages. In the capacity of family clinician, the advanced practitioner's developmental knowledge is particularly useful, consonant with the previously stated point that traditional family therapy involving child members has often failed to take developmental variables into consideration, such as a child's ability to understand a particular level of communication patterns [McDermott and Char 1974]. Similarly, the child-care practitioner's knowledge of practical management of children through such interventions as activity programming and environmental design may be crucial in a clinical context, providing means for parents to apply concepts that are discussed in family sessions.

For example, conjoint play therapy, in which parents, children, and therapist meet together in a pre-planned play situation or other activity, uses child-care skills in a family context. Furthermore, this approach was found to be effective with resistant families, who perhaps were better able to respond to the more practical, hands-on approach [Griff 1983]. The advanced child-care practitioner with families might use a complete array of clinical skills: assessment through observation at home and in the agency; setting goals and family contracting; crisis intervention; post-discharge planning, and follow-up.

Advanced child-care practitioners can also pioneer the expansion of family-oriented practice into new settings, such as hospital-based child life programs [Ferguson and Larson 1987]. In these days of multi-generational families, and an increase in the number of families in which the mid-life parents are responsible for caring both for children and their own elderly parents, it should be pointed out that the growing recognition of the commonalities between child care and care of older adults should make the advanced child-care family practitioner helpful to families in dealing with this dual responsibility [Vander Ven 1986; 1990].

Toward Implementation

For those readers who feel that their practice would be enhanced by expansion into family work but whose agencies still cleave to older models of parent and/or child-care worker exclusion, the task of persuading their agencies to adopt the more contemporary and progressive models comes first. The following statement may set them on the way: "Agencies that utilize child care personnel to the fullest extent are finding that, when appropriately trained, they are capable of performing many functions usually performed by other disciplines" [Strategies for Serving . . . 1985]. Raising the economic and educational bases of child care are also important steps to be taken to move practitioners increasingly into the wider area of family work.

The precedent has already been set for child-care workers as family workers, as has been described here and in a number of the writings cited above. Although this chapter has offered an overview of major concepts and content in child-care practice with families, space limitations bar extensive detail. The interested practitioner might, in addition to obtaining formal education in such topics as family systems and therapy, adult education, counseling, and other helping skills, read in the works listed as references for in-depth elaboration of many of the points made. These works include, in particular, articles dealing with child-care workers as family practitioners, for example, Ainsworth and Hansen [1987], Collins [1987], Anglin and Glossop [1987], Garland [1987], Jenson and Whittaker [1987], Vander Ven [1988b], Peterson and Brown [1982], and Whittaker [1979].

It would also be useful for anyone working with families of exceptional children to read parents' direct accounts that describe life with, and the pursuit of services for, these children. Such writings include Turnbull and Turnbull [1978] and Featherstone [1980]; a list of several book-length accounts is included in

Vander Ven [1982]. These accounts can aid the workers greatly in developing empathy and respect for such families. Many of these readings themselves include extensive bibliographies as further instructional resources.

John and Elaine, 1985

"Well, Elaine, what a day!" exclaims John as he settles into the decrepit old stuffed chair in the Edgevale staff room. "I made my first solo home visit to Jimmy's family. And did that open my eyes. Sure, I thought his mother was weird, but when you look at what she actually does, you'd be amazed. She has five other kids and has somehow rearranged their space so each one has privacy. I made some more suggestions about some playthings and community groups for Jimmy, and she seemed pretty interested. She's a great cook, too. You should taste the apple pie she served me. At our team meeting, I'm going to see if we might bring her into one of those family cooking groups we've talked about starting."

"Yes, John," says Elaine, "you really do get a different perspective on parents when you see them in their homes. They have strengths as well as problems that we need to be aware of. It's certainly different for me, too, now that we're allowed to share information with parents. Remember how Johnny was having those toilet accidents? Well, when I explained that to his father, he suggested trying pants with elastic waists. I tried that, and it's really worked. Of course, it's not all sweetness and light. Mrs. Jones gave me a real ear-blistering when Jane's schoolbooks were misplaced. But still, I feel a lot more effective now that we're talking with parents. It seems that we're all working with each other for the kids, rather than against them, the way it used to be."

John and Elaine, 1988

"Well, Elaine, today was a banner day—the inauguration of this agency's first model for family involvement, and fully using child-care practitioners at that! Remember when we first thought up the idea of getting this agency into the last half of the twentieth century by putting a proposal together and going to the adminstration to convince them to try it? That was quite a job. Not only were families excluded, except for their periodic casework, but the job descriptions and organizational design here were so traditional. We got all the child-care workers together, did a literature review on how child-care workers were used with families in other programs, showed how our skills could be used to work with our families here, and made our pitch. Well, to make a long story short—as you recall—they bought it."

"What fights we had, though," she responds. "The social workers were afraid that we'd steal their turf. But when they could see that families could use the special skills of each of our fields, we finally got their support. Mrs. Aspen couldn't help but agree that the family she was doing systems therapy with communicated better after the child-care workers involved them all in an activity."

"Yes," John agrees, "when Mr. Cloherty found that the family he was working with couldn't understand what 'contingency management' meant and brought them up on the unit for us to demonstrate, he found that we could really help them achieve their goals. He also learned that the family actually respected him more when he introduced them to others here at Stonecrest. Well, I have to go now. It's time for me to get ready for my parent education group tonight. We'll be discussing discipline and home management. Who'd have thought that we'd ever be doing this? Catch you later!"

John and Elaine, 1991

"Well, Elaine, it's good to be back. I've been off grounds most of the day. I spent quite a lot of time with Gary Moore and his family, since this was Gary's first day at his new school. I went over early to have another meeting with the teachers, and we worked out a plan for them to let Gary call us here if he should have one of his panic attacks. Even though he's not all better yet, he certainly has made progress since he came here and wouldn't go to school at all. I remember how hard it was to find out why he was so adamant about that—even the psychiatrists said he was one of the most severe cases of school phobia they had ever seen. But my home visits began to help. For some reason, the family seemed to find having someone come there made it easier for them to open up. The day I finally had a breakthrough was when his mother told me about the day her mother, who was visiting, was found dead in bed by Gary."

"Anyway, as you know, all of us on the team worked on this together for several months. Gary was afraid to leave home for fear something would then happen to *his* mother, and we helped him recognize how this was connected to his fear of school. The family sessions you had here with the family and the social worker also helped us all understand what was going on. So we were able to work out the plan for Gary to gradually make it back to regular school. It's interesting that he feels he can stay for a good part of the day as long as he has his 'worry stone' in his pocket. We child-care workers make sure he has it before he goes!"

"Leave it to the child-care workers to know about 'transitional objects,' even for older kids"! laughs Elaine. "That reminds me of one of the families I'm working with—the mother seldom leaves the house, and I'm trying to encourage her to get out in the community. Maybe you have some ideas. I have to go now, but let's talk about that one later."

REFERENCES

Ainsworth, F., and Fulcher, L. (eds.).   1981.   *Group Care for Children: Concept and Issues.* London, England: Tavistock.

Ainsworth, F., and Hansen, P.   1987.   Incorporating natural family members into residential programs for children and youth. *The Child Care Worker* (Claremont, South Africa) 5(6): 3–5.

Anglin, J.   n.d.   Counselling a single parent and child: Functional and dysfunctional patterns of communication. Victoria, BC: School of Child and Youth Care, University of Victoria.

Anglin, J., and Glossop, R.   1987.   Parent education and support: An emerging field for child care work. In Denholm, C., Ferguson, R., and Pence, A. (eds.) *Professional Child and Youth Care: The Canadian Perspective.* Vancouver, BC: University of British Columbia Press.

Ayres, S., Colman, J., and DeSalvatore, G.   1987.   Parents: The critical yet overlooked component of effective inpatient/group care child treatment. Paper presented at the Albert E. Trieschman Conference, Cambridge, MA.

Balgopal, P., Patchner, M., and Henderson, C.   1988.   Home visits: An effective strategy for engaging the involuntary client. In Olson, D. (ed.), *Family Perspectives in Child and Youth Services.* New York: Haworth Press.

Blase, K., and Fixsen, D.   1987.   Integrated therapeutic interactions. *Journal of Child Care* 3(1): 59–72.

Bronfenbrenner, U.   1977.   Towards an experimental ecology of human development. *American Psychologist* 33(7): 513–532.

Chess, S., and Thomas, A.   1986.   *Temperament in Clinical Practice.* New York: The Guilford Press.

Collins, D.   1987.   Child care workers and family therapists: Getting connected. Paper presented at the Albert E. Trieschman Conference. Cambridge, MA.

Conference-Research Sequence in Child Care Education.   1982.   Principles and guidelines for child care personnel programs. *Child Care Quarterly* 11(3): 221–244.

Davison, M.   1987.   Parents' evenings. *The Child Care Worker* (Claremont, South Africa) 5(3): 8.

DeSalvatore, G., and Rosenman, D.   1986.   The parent-child activity group: Using activities to work with children and their families in residential treatment. *Child Care Quarterly* 15(4): 213–222.

Featherstone, H.   1980.   *A Difference in the Family: Life with a Disabled Child.* New York: Basic Books.

Ferguson, R., and Larsen, C.   1987.   Meeting developmental needs of children and families in medical settings. In Denholm, C., Ferguson, R., and Pence, A. (eds.), *Professional Child and Youth Care: The Canadian Perspective*. Vancouver, BC: University of British Columbia Press.

Fox, R., and Krueger, M.   1987.   Social skills training: Implications for child and youth care practice. *Journal of Child Care* 3(1): 1–8.

Gabor, P., and Kammerer, K.   1982.   A meeting point: Developing treatment-oriented foster care. *Journal of Child Care* 1(3): 87–97.

Garbarino, J.   1982.   *Children and Families in the Social Environment*. New York: Aldine.

Garland, D.S.R.   1987.   Residential child care workers as primary agents of family intervention. *Child and Youth Quarterly* 16: 21–34.

Griff, M.   1983.   Family play therapy. In Schaefer, C. (ed.), *The Handbook of Play Therapy*. New York: John Wiley.

Jenson, J., and Whittaker, J.   1987.   Parental involvement in children's residential treatment: From preplacement to aftercare. *Children and Youth Services Review* 9(2): 81–100.

Katz, L.   1984.   Contemporary perspectives on the roles of mothers and teachers. In Katz, L. *More Talks with Teachers*. Urbana, IL: ERIC Clearinghouse on Elementary and Early Childhood Education.

Krueger, M.   1983.   *Careless to Caring for Troubled Youth*. Milwaukee, WI: Tall Publishers.

McDermott, J., and Char, W.   1974.   The undeclared war between child and family therapy. *Journal of the American Academy of Child Psychiatry* 13: 422–436.

Mohar, C.J.   1988.   Applying the concept of temperament to child care. *Child and Youth Care Quarterly* 17: 221–238.

Peterson, R., and Brown, R.   1982.   The child care worker as treatment coordinator and parent trainer. *Child Care Quarterly* 11(3): 188–203.

Seidl, F.   1974.   Community oriented child care: The state of the art. *Child Care Quarterly* 3(3): 150–163.

Soth, N.   1986.   Reparenting and deparenting as a paradigm for psychiatric residential treatment. *Child Care Quarterly* 15(2): 110–123.

Strategies for Serving Families with Children in Residential Treatment.   1985.   Dobbs Ferry, NY: Symposium at the Children's Village.

Trieschman, A., Whittaker, J.K., and Brendtro, L.K.   1969.   *The Other 23 Hours*. Chicago, IL: Aldine.

Turnbull, A., and Turnbull, H.   1978.   *Parents Speak Out*. Columbus, OH: Charles E. Merrill.

Vander Ven, K.   1980.   A paradigm describing stages of personal and professional development of child care practitioners with characteristics associated with each stage. In *Proceedings of the Ninth International Congress of the International Association of Workers with Maladjusted Children*. Montreal, PQ: The Association.

Vander Ven, K.   1982.   Puzzling children: A challenge to the child care system. *Children in Contemporary Society* 14(4): 5–12.

Vander Ven, K.   1984.   How adults think about children: A significant variable in their development and potential well-being. Invited paper for Pittsburgh Association for the Education of Young Children, 20th Anniversary Monograph.

Vander Ven, K.   1985.   You've come a long way baby, and you have a ways to go. In Vander Ven, K., and Tittnich, E. (eds.), *Competent Caregivers: Competent Children*. New York: Haworth Press. Also published in *Children in Contemporary Society* 17(13): 1–34.

Vander Ven, K.   1986.   From child care to life cycle developmental caregiving: The numbered painting and the evolution (guest editorial). *Child Care Quarterly* 15(2): 75–76.

Vander Ven, K.   1988a.   Development of professionalism in early childhood educators: Pathways to professional effectiveness. In Spodek, B., Peters, D., and Saracho, O. (eds.), *Early Childhood Educators: Perspectives on Professionalism*. New York: Teachers' College Press.

Vander Ven, K.   1988b.   Working with familes: Expanded roles for child care professionals. In Olson, D., (ed.), *Family Perspectives in Child and Youth Services*. New York: Haworth Press.

Vander Ven, K.   1990.   From two years to two generations: Expanded career options in direct child and youth care practice. In Anglin, J., Denholm, C., Ferguson, R., and Pence, A., (eds.), *Issues in Professional Child and Youth Care*. New York: Haworth Press. Also published in *Child and Youth Services* 13(1/2): 331–345.

Whittaker, J.   1979.   *Caring for Troubled Children*. San Francisco, CA: Jossey-Bass.

Whittaker, J.K., and Garbarino, J.   1983.   *Social Support Networks: Informal Helping in the Human Services*. New York: Aldine.

10

Students' Response to Residential Schools and Their Staffs: Implications for Program Effectiveness and the Professional Development of the Field

MORDECAI ARIELI

YITZHAK KASHTI

Young people are not usually sent to residential facilities just because they have no other place to live. Placement in such settings is considered to be an educational or social intervention. Those responsible (parents, human service professionals, or legal agencies) wish to safeguard youths from the effect of damaging influences and/or to expose them to a re-educating or re-socializing experience that represents a culture different from the one in which they were living. The English public schools provide examples of the predominantly guarding or preserving type of facility, whereas corrective institutions for deliquents are examples of the re-socializing type. Although the former are designed to preserve and develop the elitist background and the cultural idiosyncrasies of their students, the latter are expected to help achieve the modification of the inmates' identities.

In both cases, the assumption, whether overt or covert, is that the facility separates its residents from certain hurtful environments, thus weakening or reducing the socializing effect of the environment while keeping the residents in a setting in which their exposure to pre-selected influences can be largely secured. The relative separation and closure as well as the controlled exposure turn the residential facility into a "powerful environment" [Bloom 1964].

At the same time, it is recognized that the residential facility incorporates within itself mechanisms and processes that may clash with the intended social-ization influences. Descriptions of the inmates' world in the "total institution" provide indications of the power of the peers' informal order, which, under certain circumstances, not only rejects the staff's formal order [Lambert el al. 1973], but also exerts pressure on the staff to assume the values and the norms of their charges rather than to mediate the values and norms of the institution to them [Polsky 1962].

As an elementary school teacher who attended a party with a group of students she had taught five years earlier observed.

> They have all definitely changed, but there are a few whose change is more emphatic . . . somewhat more profound . . . I can't tell whether these few changed for the better or the worse . . . I'm not so sure that I know in what way they've changed. I only know that they changed more than the others, and that, unlike the others, they all went to boarding schools for their secondary education.

In short, for better or worse, the residential setting is a powerful tool in the hands of the staff, and it is essential that its influence be understood if it is to be used effectively. This is the focus of the present chapter.

The Role of the Resident

What follows examines perspectives and responses of residents concerning the staff and the residential situation in general during the course of their place-ment and schooling within Israeli youth villages. The youths are introduced here as actors in a series of social scenes during which they perform a role—that of the residential school student.

Many classifications of the various components and complements of the young person's role can be made. In day schools, the main differentiation seems to be between scholastic or individual components and those that are connected with the organization of the school. Some of the students' tasks, the learning tasks, can be performed at home, outside school hours; others are connected directly with their membership in the school organization, such as "arriving on time," "listening to the teacher," and "being nice to friends." Authors such as Jackson [1968], Friedenberg [1965], and Calvert [1975] have claimed that the expectations that teachers have of day school students and the expectations of the students themselves often stress the organizational aspects of the student role.

The role of the student in residential schools contains more components than that of the day school student, especially those relating to membership in the organization, and residential school youths spend much more of their lives within the school organization than day school students. How do they perceive the relative weight of the scholastic or individual components and the various organizational components? The answer to this question is particularly important, because the relative weight of these role components indicates the relative importance they attribute to their role components—such role partners as teachers, residential care workers, and peers—and to the various school subsystems.

The grade level of the students is a variable that generally indicates both their ages and their seniority as performers of their role within the organization. It seems important to examine the relative weight the pupils attribute to the various components of their role at various stages of their careers (grade levels), including whether the status of the respective components changes and to what extent.

Therefore, we asked the following three questions with regard to ninth and

What do youths in residential schools think are the components of their role? How do they define these components?

What do they view as the relative importance of each of the components of their role?

What is the relative importance that beginning students and "old-timers" attribute to the various components of their roles? What are the similarities and the differences between these two groups?

The research was carried out in five coeducational residential schools in Israel.

The Schools Researched

Most Israeli residential schools are designed to serve educational and care functions at the same time. They act as integral parts of the Israeli regular school system, using the regular curriculum and teaching methods. Since their populations usually come from the weaker socioeconomic strata, often show various signs of educational disadvantage, and actually live in the setting, however, the residential schools apply care programs in addition to the regular educational ones.

The schools studied include three subsystems: the schooling, the occupational-agricultural, and the residential-social subsystems. Students move from one subsystem to another daily. The boundaries among these subsystems and between them and the students' informal system are not always marked.

The schooling subsystem functions very much like an ordinary day school and often caters also to day students from neighboring communities. The schools studied are agricultural schools, and all students are required to participate in the daily work of the on-grounds farm, within the framework of the occupational subsystem. The residential-social subsystem divides the students into social units of 25 to 40 students each, which are not identical with the classes within the schooling subsystem. Each such social unit has its own dorm and formally organized extracurricular activities, designed for their expressive and tension-releasing nature.

Each of the three subsystems has its own staff. The teachers (similar in background and training to day school teachers) act within the schooling subsystem. Agricultural instructors head the various aspects of the farm work (and sometimes serve also as teachers of the agricultural subjects within the schooling subsystem). The residential-social systems are headed by group care workers called (in the plural) "*madrichim*" (the male workers) and "*metaplot*" (the female workers). Most are not professionally educated but have some formal training in one of the educational or care professions. The formal role prescription of madrichim includes supportive and custodial, individual and group functions. The role prescription of metaplot is similar to that of the madrichim, with emphasis on hygiene and nutrition.[1]

Two samples from each of the five schools are represented in the research population: a ninth grade (first secondary school grade) and an eleventh grade (third of the four secondary school grades). Thus, in total, the research population included ten samples and 516 pupils, the majority in each coming from socially disadvantaged backgrounds, according to three major characteristics often selected in Israel as indicating disadvantage: non-Western ethnic background, father's relatively low formal education, and relatively large families.

Research Procedure

The research was carried out in two stages. In the first, which was treated as a pilot study, we looked into the question of role components as viewed by students. Seventy-two pupils in an agricultural school, not one of the schools studied but similar to them in several important respects including the curriculum and the socioeconomic background of the pupils, were asked to spend 30 minutes writing a composition describing what they viewed as a resident who is "OK." In analyzing the content of these compositions, we sought to obtain characteristic items describing "the role of the student [resident] in the residential school," in the students' own language, as the basis for developing a questionnaire on the student's role. In the second stage, we looked into the other questions raised above, the relative importance of role components in general and as viewed differentially by beginning students and by "old-timers."

Twenty items were selected for the questionnaire and were classified in two ways. The first classification was on the basis of the "content of the predicate," with ten items considered to be "action" items, and the other ten to be "attitude" items. The second classification was on the basis of the "object of reference" of the item: ten items (five "action," five "attitude") contained mention of a "role partner" as an object of reference, while the other ten (also five in each category) contained an "organizational aspect" as an object of reference. (The 20 role items are listed according to these categories in Table 1.)

This Pupil Role Questionnaire was then presented to the research population. Respondents at both research samples were asked to rank these items according to their view of the importance of each item in describing the OK resident.[2]

TABLE 1

Student Rankings of Components of the Student Role

		Rank	
		Ninth Grade	Eleventh Grade
Object of Reference	Content of Role Item		
Role of Partners			
Friends (action)	Gets on well with friends	3	1
Friends (attitude)	Respects friends	11	4
Madrichim (action)	Obeys madrichim's instructions	1	12
Madrichim (attitude)	Respects madrichim	2	11
Teachers (action)	Does homework as teachers require	10	16
Teachers (attitude)	Respects teachers	4	14
Agri instructions (action)	Works as agricultural instructors demonstrate	19	17

(Continued on next page)

TABLE 1 (Continued)
Student Rankings of Components of the Student Role

		Rank	
Object of Reference	Content of Role Item	Ninth Grade	Eleventh Grade
Agri instructors (attitude)	Takes instructions of agricultural instructors seriously	9	14
Metaplot (action)	Obeys the metaplot	15	19
Metaplot (attitude)	Respects the metaplot	16.5	18
Organizational Aspects			
Orderliness (action)	Is clean and tidy	7	5
Orderliness (attitude)	Respects the discipline rules in the institution	8	6
The setting (action)	Takes care of the institution's property	5	3
The setting (attitude)	Regards setting as home	20	20
Work (action)	Pursues work assignments	13	7
Work (attitude)	Responsible at work	18	10
Group (action)	Takes part in organized social activities in the group	16.5	15
Group (attitude)	Cares about what goes on in the group	12	2
Schooling (action)	Attends all the lessons at schools	6	8
Schooling (attitude)	Appreciates results from schoolwork	9	13

Results: The Students' Perspectives

"Gaining" or "losing" importance refers here to the tendency for the ranking of an item by the eleventh grade sample to exceed its ranking by the ninth grade sample, or the reverse, respectively. For discussion purposes, the items have been classified into three groups:

1. *High importance and importance-gaining role components*: This group includes items that were ranked in relatively high and stable positions in the

rank orders of the ninth and the eleventh grade samples, as well as items that were ranked higher by the eleventh graders than by the ninth graders.[3]

2. *Low importance and importance-losing role components*: This group includes items that were ranked in relatively low and stable positions as well as items that were ranked lower by the eleventh grade sample than by the ninth graders.

3. *Middle position ranked role components*: These were included in neither of the categories just described. (Item rankings are presented in Table 1.)

High Importance

Residents imply that the most valued components of their role as students are linked to their attitudes toward their peers. A student who is OK first and foremost "gets on well with friends." This trait is something residents report is true throughout, starting from the beginning of their lives at the residential school, if not earlier. After they have gained experience as residents, they also understand that "respecting friends" and "caring about whatever goes on in the group" are almost equally characteristic of the student who is OK.

If, at the age of 14 to 15, members of peer groups are content with "getting along" with each other, at the age of 16 to 17 the peers require the more profound relationships of social solidarity, involvement, and cohesion. This need is particularly stressed, and probably often gratified, in a total life situation such as that of the residential facility.

Getting along well with friends also reflects an opportunity that the residential school gives its students to experience a known and already shared norm. It is always important that one's contacts with one's peers be as smooth and conflict-free as possible. This norm is particularly important in a residential setting, however, where one has to get along with one's friends for longer stretches of time during the day and in complicated and spatially compressed life situations. Disharmonious life with those with whom one has to share a room can be particularly agonizing.

In a total life situation, the resident's peers offer not only some refuge from the daily constraints imposed by the staff members, who always function, at least to some degree, as controlling custodians, but also the only opportunity for relationships based on symmetric reciprocity and equality.[4] Thus, being friendly and committed to one's peers is perceived by residents as more vital than other tasks, such as learning well or taking part in the organization of social activities.

The relatively low ranking of the component "takes part in the organization of social activities with the group," particularly by the ninth grade sample, suggests that the students do not attribute much value to formal social activities, which are usually initiated and controlled by the staff. A joint consideration of the group findings (importance attributed to informal peer interaction and relative rejection of formal social activities), together with the generally poor rankings of items that relate to staff members, seems to support previous suggestions concerning the tendency of peers within residential facilities to become supportive of each other while functioning as a counterculture through the formation of cohesive informal orders that tend to reject the facility's formal one.[5]

Of the three subsystems within the residential facility—schooling, residential, and occupational—residents select the third as the most meaningful for the performance of their role as students. The higher status of the items "work (action)," "work (attitude)," and "instructors (attitude)" among the eleventh grade samples in comparison to their status among ninth grade samples probably indicates that the residential school has been instrumental in assisting the pupils to discover meaning in their agricultural work.

The prestige of manual work in general and that of the agricultural worker ("farmhand") in particular has been increasingly shattered in the Israeli society (as well as in many other western societies) in the course of the last three decades. Joining an agricultural school is often perceived by the students and by their parents as acceptable only because the students have not been admitted for secondary schooling to the relatively more prestigious academic day schools, as a result of their low scholastic achievement upon completing elementary schooling. This fact probably accounts for the low status of the work items in the rank order of the ninth grade samples.

In the course of the students' stay in the residential school, however, two parallel processes frequently occur. On the one hand, the students often become increasingly disappointed with their prospects for significant progress in the purely academic domain (which is perhaps implied in their descending respect for and conformity toward teachers). On the other hand, after a period of specialization in one of the agricultural branches that they have chosen, students often discover that the occupational subsystem provides opportunities to prove oneself competent and capable of taking responsibility in a field other than the schooling one and thereby to experience success. This realization is, perhaps, why the students have an ambivalent attitude toward the agricultural instructors. The students are reluctant to look up to a staff member whose position in the power structure of the residential school is low, yet they treat respectfully and seriously the person who has been instrumental in helping them to develop feelings of competence.

Many observers of social realities within residential facilities, especially within custody-oriented settings for deviant adolescents, and many group care workers expect residents to try to vandalize the facility's campus, equipment, and furniture, or at least to be careless with them. This expectation is based on the assumption that many adolescents in placement need to "act out," "act rebelliously," and so on. Therefore, the fact that (in an anonymous questionnaire) students chose to rank the item "take care of the setting's property" in high positions is indeed somewhat of a surprise, particularly since residents generally showed little identification with the facility. One way to explain this finding is to suggest that residents may have been pre-socialized by parents and other social agencies, long before joining the facility, toward treating public property with respect. This value is culturally broadly based, coherent, and does not characterize residential facilities and their particular ethos alone.

To sum up, the student who is OK as his peers view him is first and foremost one who identifies with the peer group and is committed to it, who respects work and works properly, and who takes care of the facility's property. The residents do not perceive students' attitudes toward the facility, its ethos, and its staff as highly important components of their role.

Low Importance

Placing a youth away from home is sometimes necessary when the family has been undergoing a crisis such as death or illness, particularly mental illness, of a parent. Agencies then attempt to select a facility with a particularly warm climate, appropriate rehabilitative programs, and a warm staff. Under such circumstances, it seems to be widely assumed, youths require a "home away from home." It also seems quite common, however, for group care workers who treat youths whose homes have remained essentially intact to assume that the residential facility should serve as a home to its residents, and to relate successful rehabilitation to the ability of the resident to view the facility as a home. In our study, however, the item "regards the setting as his home" was ranked in the lowest position (20) by the ninth graders in most samples. Furthermore, this evaluation does not change in the course of the students' stay in the settings. The main significance of this result is that the traditional ethos concerning the youth village being a home to its charges—sometimes the "first and only home"—is not internalized, to say the least, by current students.

In the past, the initiators of the children's communities in Israel believed that they assisted the pioneer youths of the 1930s and the orphaned young refugees of the 1940s to feel "at home." Whether the inmates of these communities (youth groups in kibbutzim and youth villages) indeed viewed the settings as their homes and, if so, to what extent, has not been investigated. It seems clear, however, that the disadvantaged residents of the youth villages in the 1970s—who usually have a family and a home outside—seem reluctant to view the setting as a home away from home.

The status of this role item seems indirectly to imply that the students do not view the expressive aspect of the residential school as its strongest or most important quality. A similar evaluation, it will be remembered, was found concerning the item "takes part in organizing social activities in the group," its ranking by the ninth graders being so low that it calls into question one of the central components of the educational socialization philosophy of the Israeli residential school over almost half a century. The responses of the eleventh grade samples on this item are less unanimous, but not to the extent that they remove the doubts concerning the success of the implementation of the idea of group life as one of the three pillars of residential education in Israel.

Once they have been distanced from their parents and placed in a residential setting, residents are expected to relate to their care workers as their "significant adults." A consistently low evaluation, however, or one that decreases in the course of the stay of the residents in the setting, characterizes the students' attitude toward the residential care workers, those members of the staff whose roles are idiosyncratic to the residential school: the metaplot (housemothers) and the madrichim (housefathers).

It is felt that the low position of the metaplot is related to their role in the setting. Although they are officially defined as group care workers, their role has generally been reduced to that of workers in charge of cleanliness and orderliness, either as supervisors of inmates' work in these areas or, in some cases, as supervisors of adult workers. In four of the five schools, the metaplot do not usually join the madrichim in leading or supervising educative evening activities.

It is the status of the madrichim, however, that represents the most acute problem. Although the ninth graders ranked the madrichim as most esteemed role complements, this high evaluation descends dramatically in the eyes of the eleventh graders, who view the madrichim as emphatically less important.

It seems quite understandable why the newer, younger students attribute much esteem to the madrichim, who often both choose and are constrained to present themselves as sympathetic and empathic substitute fathers. The expectations that the madrichim arouse within the residents and the subsequent admiration that the residents show for them are both high. This may reflect the fact that the madrichim are expected to function as personal counselors, social leaders, and academic tutors and are often perceived by the pupils as the staff members who are both entitled to and capable of making crucial decisions concerning the residents' careers in the institution.

Reasons for the dramatically lower status of the madrichim among the older youths, however, are somewhat less clear. Is the change a reflection of decreasing dependency on significant adults among growing adolescents? Is it an indication that, in the course of time, students have become increasingly aware of the effect that role conflicts have had on the madrich? Have the students discovered that these conflicts limit the madrich's capacity to support his charges? Are the students becoming gradually aware that the madrichim's actual share in the power structure of the entire system is rather small? Is it an outcome of the discovery that the madrichim are not fully professional and do not enjoy a high status in the wider social and occupational stratification?

Middle Position Role Components: The Realm of Schooling

The residents are viewed primarily as students who live in a residential facility that is defined primarily as a school. Although the provision of education through schooling is generally considered by outsiders to be a school's main objective, the findings suggest that the residents do not consider this aspect of their life at school to be the major component of their roles. This perception exists even though being schooled is the only activity that the students perform in much the same way as they would have had they been attending a day school. Similarly, teachers form the only group of staff members with whom the residential students usually interact in the same manner as they would have had they been in a day school.

The two schooling items were ranked in middle positions by both the ninth and the eleventh grade samples. In other words, the students seemed to attribute neither particularly high nor particularly low importance to school throughout their stay in the residential setting. Their readiness to comply with the rule that requires regular attendance at school is, however, somewhat higher than their appreciation of what schooling does for them.

Many of the students were, perhaps, sent to the residential school because of difficulties they were facing during their elementary school studies—difficulties that were particularly manifest in the academic field. They were aware of the norm that attributes prestige to formal education and, therefore, showed considerable readiness "to attend school regularly." Their experience in the schooling subsystem, however, often consistent with previous failures at the elementary school, does not raise their appreciation of what schooling can do for them to a particularly high level.

The students' attitude toward their teachers is somewhat different. As juniors, they rank the component "respects the teachers" in a high position. This ranking perhaps expresses, among other things, their hope that the teachers will serve as important agents in changing their life careers and their status as students. (The residential school is sometimes introduced as a place where those who have failed elsewhere may have a second chance to succeed in the academic field.) In the course of time, however, the students seem to discover that the differentiated and universalistic attitude that the teachers at the elementary day school may have had toward them also characterizes the attitude of the teachers at the residential school. Perhaps the students seem to feel somewhat abandoned by teachers as such. Consequently, the readiness to prepare homework "as the teachers require" also decreases.[6]

Implications: A Framework for a Second Chance?

The disadvantaged residential school students, to judge by their report of their role priorities, do not, on coming to the school, stand trembling with awe at the gates, nor is their identity as adolescents shattered by the effect of a powerful environment. They tend to reject the totality of the institution, to the extent that this exists. They are not easy objects to be swallowed up in the culture of the setting; they are not easy targets for acts of cultural colonization or co-optation. They do not regard the setting as their home, nor the metaplot and madrichim as substitute parents, nor do they expect the teachers to bring about sweeping changes in their schooling career or their social standing. Is this attitude a mistrust of, or disappointment with, adults and their possible influence? Is it perhaps an accumulation of disappointments from past experience with the socialization organizations in the depriving home environment? Or is it, possibly, a combination of the two?

The residential school students do not wish for highly structured relationships, organizational formalities, and authority, particularly when these are associated with adult figures. They understand and appreciate order and discipline, but they do not want these to be forced on them in a patronizing manner. With the passage of time, they tend to open up to the members of their peer group. The formal "youth society" does not tend to arouse them to the anticipated levels of involvement and identification. Thus, it seems that the students' school careers lead in the direction of instrumental goals: they know that they have to be orderly and to observe the rules; they know the value of good friends and informal involvement in their peers' lives; they know they have to study and to be active in the classroom; they learn in the course of their time at the residential school that work can be a thing of value and even interesting and satisfying.

It is clear, therefore, that we do not have here the subdued inmates of a total institution, nor young members of the elite being co-opted to their school culture, leading them (smoothly or roughly), as in years gone by, to the status of prominent civil servants and pioneers. We have here a setting that is largely a reflection of daily life outside as it is perceived by its disadvantaged students.

But the residential school emerges as a framework for a second chance for those whose chances tend to be limited, and they seem to make use of it for their needs in the way that they themselves, not their educators, understand and define these needs.

Can the way the residents of residential schools in Israel perceive their role as students and attribute value to different components of the program help us to understand how youths elsewhere relate to the residential facility in which they live?

We must begin with three fundamental factors that limit the generalizability of the present findings.

Traditional and Cultural Idiosyncrasies

For many generations, residential schooling was considered as a means of entry into the Jewish (religious schools or yeshivot) and Israeli (youth societies in kibbutzim) elites. Thus, Israeli residential schools developed an ethos of pioneering, avant-garde collectives.[7] Much of this tradition has changed during the four decades of independent statehood: the student population now comes mostly from the weaker social strata, and the school curricula aim toward widely prevalent or normative educational objectives.[8] Residential schools have retained prestige, however, to the extent that it seems that they are not yet stigmatized as are many similar settings in western Europe and North America; in that sense, they are unique.

Care or Education versus Care and Education Settings

In most countries, one can make a coherent differentiation between care-oriented and education-oriented residential settings for adolescents. Care-oriented settings usually cater to deviant populations (homeless, maladjusted, delinquent), while education-oriented settings are generally elitist schools. Care-oriented settings, unlike the education-oriented, often do not include a schooling subsystem, and their resident population is sent to neighboring day schools. Most Israeli residential schools, it will be recalled, are simultaneously care- and education-oriented, striving to provide education to children whose social disadvantage is perceived as requiring "special" care in addition to "normative" education.

Nonprofessional versus Professional Group Care Workers

Although most Israeli group care workers (madrichim and metaplot) have no formal education qualifying them for their roles, group care workers in many other countries often have some kind of relevant diploma. In spite of these differences between the Israeli and non-Israeli social realities, however, the total life situation within the residential setting is fundamentally similar and seems to justify a careful treatment of the Israeli case as at least partially generalizable.

The residents' rejection of the suggestion that the setting is a home, on the one hand, and their reluctance to take part in organized social activities while considering informal social interaction most important, on the other, combine to suggest their collective definition of the situation: an institution cannot be a place one can identify with to the extent that one would consider it as one's home. (In the authors' opinion, the fact that it is often called a home in different languages and in various organizational contexts seems to intensify alienation from, rather than identification with, the place one has been more or less coerced to live in.) Once youths have been placed in an institution, however, they would prefer to view it as their own territory. Taking part in organized social activities is probably perceived as the expectation of controlling caregivers who wish to manage and regulate residents' time. Social life, as the residents themselves would have it, means "caring about whatever goes on in the group," "respecting friends," and "getting along" with them; it has relatively little to do with organized activities.

Caregivers sometimes seem to try to create social life for residents. Israeli madrichim, for example, often insist on introducing "positive, constructive, and educational" social activities for their charges, but students tend to reject such efforts. Caregivers are thus perhaps better advised that residents' social life should be respected and supported rather than molded for them.

Residential settings are multi-dimensional socializing organizations [Kahane 1981]. Unlike day schools, which usually offer but one major, formal track for experiencing achievement and success, residential settings, through their schooling, occupational, and residential subsystems, offer students a variety of means to achieve self-actualization and social success. As a result, disadvantaged populations have often valued work and informal social contacts with peers more than schooling, because in these pursuits they could experience achievement that—due to accumulating educational deficits—schooling often could not provide.

If this is indeed the case, one could use the implications of this finding also in residential settings that have no schools (schooling subsystems) of their own: youths who feel unsuccessful or rejected at school may experience success and improve their self-esteem in more "hospitable" territory—among their friends and at work. The introduction of work linked with meaningful vocational training seems particularly suitable for residential settings, which may either develop their own occupational subsystems, like Israeli residential schools, or refer the residents to work and occupational training within the neighboring community as the Job Corps often did in the United States [Smilansky et al. 1982].

One advantage of introducing work in residential settings relates to the possibility that a positive self-esteem-as-worker may serve to enhance a youth's self-esteem-as-learner, subsequently influencing actual school performance. Group care workers and teachers in residential settings should, however, also alert themselves to possible hazards that relate to success at work. In spite of its instrumental aspects in preparing residents for the occupational world, work at the residential school is usually part of the expressive curriculum; that is, it leads mostly toward expressive gains, such as self-fulfillment. Work is not a characteristic part of most residential schools' instrumental curriculum, and its contribution to the preparation of the residents to improving their position along the mobility ladder in the future adult society is usually less significant than that of academic studies. Success at work within the residential setting is thus less important in itself than as a means to motivate residents to renew academic efforts and to experience success according to criteria set by the instrumental curriculum.

Since one expects group care workers to function not merely as service-providing agents but as significant adults providing models for imitation and identification by their charges, the low and declining positions of the madrichim and metaplot in the residents' view seem rather disappointing, although this state of affairs does not come as a complete surprise. It seems unrealistic to expect adolescents to select models for their future lives from among adults whose social status (as in most western countries) tends to be rather low.

In Israel, one sometimes serves as a group care worker without possessing the governmental certificate of completion of high school education—a document that many of one's charges will attain upon completing the residential school's program. In several western European countries as well as in the United States and Canada, educational qualifications for residential group care work, if any, are among the least required for work in the welfare, care, and educational professions. In many cases, group care workers are paid less than many other professional caregivers. Daily unresolved conflicts embedded in their multifaceted and diffuse roles (for example, support and custody, individual counseling and group activities), day-long exposure to clients, and often actual living with clients result in various burnout phenomena and, consequently, in short-term careers. Group care workers traditionally do not specialize in any discipline or field of expertise and have typically had no monopoly over any aspect of the professional knowledge that they apply at work.

Many of these problems seem to be inherent in the structure of the occupation. Group care work apparently cannot be highly specialized, nor should it be, if group care workers are expected to relate to the total situation of their charges' lives rather than to a particular aspect of their education or development. Herein lies the major challenge to the professional development of the field.

Policy makers of residential networks will also need to realize that, for group care work to be constructively purposeful to its clients, workers must be recruited from among graduates of prestigious programs in the behavioral disciplines and must assume those social traits that would make them attractive models for imitation and identification. Workers proficient in all these respects will not join the profession to serve as competent child and youth care generalists unless they are adequately rewarded.

NOTES

[1] Detailed descriptions of Israeli residential schools, their structure and staff are included in Arieli et al. [1983], Kashti [1979], Shlasky [1986], and Smilansky et al. [1982].

[2] The methodological considerations and procedures in this process are described in Arieli [1980].

[3] It was decided to consider a difference of four or fewer ranks between the rank orders of the ninth grade and eleventh grade samples as a relatively stable position.

[4] Symmetric reciprocity in the relationships of peers in informal social situations has been discussed by Kahane [1981].

[5] See, for example, Sykes [1958], Polsky [1962], Ward and Kasselbaum [1965], Giallombardo [1966], Street et al. [1966], Polsky and Claster [1968], Lambert et al. [1975], Millham et al. [1975], and Kashti and Arieli [1986].

[6] Consider also the parallels between the rankings for madrichim and for teachers, and in the explanations that have been suggested for each.

[7] For a discussion of the traditional functions of Jewish and Israeli residential settings, see Arieli et al. [1983].

[8] Changes in Israeli residential schools since the early 1950s are discussed by Kashti [1979].

REFERENCES

Arieli, M.   1980.   *The Role of Disadvantaged Pupils in Israeli Residential Schools.* Unpublished Ph.D. thesis, University of Sussex.

Arieli, M., Kashti, Y., and Shlasky, S.   1983.   *Living at School: Israeli Residential Schools as People-Processing Organizations.* Tel Aviv, Israel: Ramot.

Bloom, B.S.   1964.   *Stability and Change in Human Characteristics.* New York: Wiley.

Calvert, B.   1975.   *The Role of the Pupil.* London, England: Routledge and Kegan Paul.

Friedenberg, E.A.   1965.   *Coming of Age in America.* New York: Random House.

Giallombardo, R.   1966.   *Society of Women.* New York: Wiley.

Jackson, P.W.   1968.   *Life in Classrooms.* New York: Holt, Rinehart and Winston.

Kahane, R.   1981.   Multi-model institutions: A conceptual framework for the analysis of residential education centers. *Alim* 3–15. (Hebrew).

Kashti, Y.   1979.   *The Socializing Community.* Tel Aviv, Israel: Tel Aviv University.

Kashti, Y., and Arieli, M.   1986.   Social conditions and pupils' responses in Israeli residential schools. In Eisikovits, Z., and Beker, J. (eds.), *Residential Group Care in Community Context: Insights from the Israeli Experience.* New York: Haworth Press; also published as *Child and Youth Services* 7(3/4): 51–70.

Lambert, R., Bullock, R., and Millham, S.   1973.   The informal social system: An example of the limitations of organizational analysis. In Brown, R. (ed.). *Knowledge, Education and Culture.* London, England: Tavistock.

Lambert, R., Bullock, R., and Millham, S.   1975.   *The Chance of a Lifetime? A Study of Boys and Coeducational Boarding Schools in England and Wales.* London, England: Weidenfeld and Nicholson.

Millham, S., Bullock, R., and Cherrett, P.   1975.   *After Grace—Teeth: A Comparative Study of Residential Experience in Approved Schools.* London, England: Human Context.

Polsky, H.W.   1962.   *Cottage Six.* New York: Russell Sage Foundation.

Polsky, H.W., and Claster, D.S.   1968.   *The Dynamics of Residential Treatment.* Chapel Hill, NC: University of North Carolina Press.

Shlasky, S.   1986.   *Residential Care Workers.* Unpublished Ph.D. thesis, University of Sussex.

Smilansky, M., Kashti, Y., and Arieli, M.   1982.   *The Residential Education Alternative.* East Orange, NJ: The Institute for Humanist Studies.

Street, D., Vinter, R.D., and Perrow, C.   1966.   *Organization for Treatment.* New York: Free Press.

Sykes, G.   1958.   *Society of Captives.* Princeton, NJ: Princeton University Press.

Ward, D.A., and Kassebaum, G.G.   1965.   *Women's Program.* London, England: Weidenfeld and Nicholson.

PART 3

Doing Residential Child and Youth Care

Work in an Organizational Setting

11

Teamwork in Residential Care

LEON C. FULCHER

From a practical point of view, the problems of teamwork in residential care call to mind a poster hanging in the office of a 24-hour emergency care center in Montreal. It illustrated a group of workers caught in the middle of a marsh-like terrain, surrounded by large reptiles. A feverish warning appeared at the bottom: "When you're up to your neck in alligators, it's hard to remember that the original aim was to drain the swamp!"

So numerous and powerful are the influences that can make teams function at less than their potential that, all too frequently, the task of providing effective care for children is neglected.[1] Although substantial demands are made on residential care workers, both as individuals and as a team, children in care should still be given at least this minimal guarantee: their level of social functioning should not deteriorate at a rate faster than it would have, had they not entered a residential care center [Billis 1980].

It has been a prevalent assumption in residential care work that some level of cooperation and collaboration between workers is required if "good-enough" services are to be provided for children in care.[2] This assumption is critically evaluated in the course of this chapter. First, the need for teamwork is identified through practical illustration and reference to the occupational focus of work in residential care settings. Next, attention is given to the "enacted environment" of residential care in order to highlight ways in which teamwork influences the delivery of services in this field. Finally, consideration is given to several contextual influences on teamwork that have been identified in a study of residential and day care workers from Great Britain and North America.

"Who's on This Weekend?"

Most child and youth care workers can recall a particular kind of conversation overheard among children near the office door of a residential group care unit on a Friday afternoon. One of the children just in from school will ask "Who's on this weekend?" Someone looks at the staffing schedule and answers the question, thereby prompting a loud "Hooray!" or a dismal "Oh no, not her!" Another child may ask, "Who's on with her?" and the response is likely to elicit more grumbles or excitement. If the expected worker has called in sick and a relief worker will be covering for the weekend, curiosity or muttered obscenities may result. "Who is the relief worker?" "Does anyone know him?" "What's she like?" Conversation may then turn to "What are we doing tonight?" Almost always, children in residential care are found to discriminate precisely among the caregivers in their environment. Even slight alterations in the normal rhythm are noted and incorporated into the events and the experience of daily living.

Most workers will also have participated in another dialogue that takes place inside the office, involving members of the staff team. A supervisor going off duty is likely to say, "Be sure to take a good look at today's log; it's been quite a day!" One of the line workers might be shaking his head: "Whew, I really need this weekend off after covering for Helen on the night shift Wednesday." Another might ask, "Have we got a replacement for Tom yet?" On receiving the answer, her rejoinder might be, "Why does it take so long to get someone?" or "It's about time!" A third worker might pose the question: "Which children are going home this weekend?" And next, "What are the transportation arrangements?" Annoyance might be expressed over the late arrival of a fourth worker, well known for his frequent tardiness. Contingency plans may be required to cover for the worker who has called in sick. If, for some reason, the work schedule has been reorganized, then staff conversation is likely to be dominated by shift arrangements and the extent to which these will influence plans that workers have made for their social lives outside work. Conversation may finally get around to the new youngster who was admitted during the morning shift, or to the social worker who called in with some important information about a girl whose home visit had gone poorly the weekend before.

Teamwork Is Inherent in This Work

In reviewing this illustration from residential practice, one cannot escape the fact that the job responsibilities of child and youth care workers and other residential staff members require the attention of more than one individual. The task must be shared, requiring at least a minimum level of cooperation and teamwork. Team members may be treated as replaceable or expendable objects, as might have been the case in an infantry platoon during World War I, or as highly valued and skilled participants in a complex task. From the latter perspective, the contributions of individual workers are very important, as are the unique life histories and work styles in which they are rooted. A distinguishing feature of residential care teams is that they are continuously engaged, in one way or another, with the production of services. Normally, residential settings, primarily through their direct care workers, are expected to supply a 168-hour-per-week service, 52 weeks a year, like hospitals, police or fire departments, or large airlines, to cite parallel work examples.

Thus, the concept of a relay team can be used metaphorically to describe how personnel on one shift hand over the "baton" of responsibility to those on the next, who take responsibility for running or swimming the next lap. Some residential care teams may be functioning with individual residents in "sprint" or "middle-distance" events, as in an observation and assessment center. One must note, however, that such programs operate in a sustained manner since periods of residence overlap for different individual residents. Other teams may function in "marathon" events that present team members with different demands and varied stimulation. Members of a residential care team providing for children with profound mental handicaps or working in a long-term secure unit might at times feel like participants in an endurance test.

Whatever the event—being on duty, during the handover of duty, or while on call—some level of cooperation and transfer of responsibility in the work is implicit. Residential workers frequently carry, pass on, and receive their own baton of responsibility, whether symbolized in keys or the daily log. At other times, responsibility rests simply in the particular role that each worker assumes when he or she goes on duty. In all cases, responsibility is transferred from one team member to another and then back again, throughout the course of the working week.

Toward Effective Teamwork

In her classic study on the functioning of care staff in a hospital setting, Menzies [1970: 8] described the development of a number of interacting factors within social care organizations. Crucial among these were "the primary task of assignment, including such environmental relationships and pressures as that involves; the technologies available for performing the task; and the needs of the members of the organization for social and psychological satisfaction." Later work extended these formulations to an analysis of "task" and "anti-task" dynamics in the functioning of personnel in institutions for adolescents. "Task" was interpreted generally to incorporate "activities that an enterprise must perform in order to survive" [Menzies 1977: 13]. This work identified "a danger of primary task being implicitly redefined when the task, as originally and perhaps more realistically defined, becomes too difficult, or when societal pressures against task definition are too great. In other words, task may implicitly slip over into anti-task" [Menzies 1977: 16]. Conclusions drawn from this study stress the importance of staff support systems that can sustain positive task performance among residential care teams.

The Limited Role of the Individual

A fundamental question involves the extent to which individual influences shape team activity and outcomes in residential care. Pfeffer and Salancik [1978: 9–10] have noted several reasons based in theory for expecting that individuals will have less effect on service outcomes than would otherwise be expected. First, both individual and organizational selection processes tend to result in similarity among an agency's staff members. This result restricts the range of skills, characteristics, and behaviors found among those who achieve such positions. Second, even when a relatively prominent position has been achieved in an organization, the discretion permitted to a given individual is limited. Decisions may require the approval of others in the organization or outside; discretion may be limited by legal or contractual provisions; information used in formulating decisions comes from others; and some persons invariably seek to influence or put pressure on others in their work roles. All these factors further constrain the degree of latitude available to individuals. Beyond this, many of the things that affect individuals and teams are, for a variety of reasons, simply outside the control of the immediate participants in a residential care task. What is required is an orientation that takes account not only of individual performance, but also of the ways in which residential care depends upon external influences.

The Role of the Leader

The tendency to attribute great effect to individual actions, particularly actions taken by persons in designated positions of authority, may be partly accounted for by the desire for a feeling of personal effectiveness and control over one's social environment. In this light, it is a major function of the team leader or manager to serve as a symbol or focal point for a team's successes and failures. In this way, a leader may come to personify a team, its activities, and its outcomes, as did Albert Trieschman at the Walker School, A.S. Neill at Summerhill, and so on. Endowing leaders with an aura of power enhances individual feelings of predictability and control, giving observers an identifiable target for emotion and action. People want to believe in the effectiveness of leadership and personal action, and to say that managers serve as symbols is not to deny their importance. The sacking of an unsuccessful football coach, a supervisor, or an agency executive provides an emotional release that is too marked to dismiss as unimportant. Those who remain in the organization are left with the hope that things will be improved, thus reaffirming their belief in the importance of individual action.

The Role of Other Staff Members

Any evaluation of teamwork in residential care requires an analysis of ways in which individual staff members contribute to a collective task. It can be argued that the integrity of a residential care service virtually depends upon the ability of individual workers to collaborate in a shared enterprise. It also depends on the extent to which staff members are supported in that enterprise over the course of weeks, months, and sometimes years.

The events encountered by a collection of workers in a residential center are rarely accompanied by tidy explanations that readily inform staff members of the responses required of them. Rather, workers and children in a center give meaning to the events they encounter there. Thus, it is a prevalent view of staff members and administrators alike that residential environments are created by the staff members and children who interact in them. This view holds that as residential environments are created, used, and defined, so the network of referring agents and agencies adapts to them and endorses them as providing good-enough care and treatment for children [Winnicott 1960]. Experience would suggest that this view is grossly simplistic.

The Enacted Environment

Weick's [1969] notion of "the enacted environment" clarifies a number of features about teamwork in residential care. As human actors, the staff members and children who inhabit a residential center do not just react to their physical and social environment. In many ways they can be said to enact or create their environment. The term enactment has two meanings, both of which involve action. The first meaning is "to decree by legislation or policy directive"; the second is "to re-create or represent something as by staging a play." Both types of action can be found in the analysis of events in any residential care center. Staff members are directed to a particular workplace with a specific mandate—to engage children, along with other staff members, and through more or less prescribed roles, be engaged by children in activities that encompass work, leisure, and the entirety of their daily lives.

Weick [1969: 65] identified several properties of the enacted environment, each of which influences the quality of teamwork in residential care. First, in the process of enactment, the creation of personal and social meaning comes from remembering, and thereby paying attention to, events that have already occurred. Reference to what is written in the daily log and discussion at change-of-shift meetings can be said to incorporate this first property of the enacted environment in a residential care center.

Second, since attention is directed backward from a particular moment in time, whatever events are occurring at that time will unavoidably influence what persons recall from their past experiences. These memories establish the basis for further actions in the present and, as such, become mental cues for enactment. The experienced worker, faced with a difficult situation, is likely to recall previous situations that resemble that encounter. Hence, even if through an instantaneous mental process, memories become cues for enacting the next act of the drama. Goffman [1974] explained this mechanism as a process of "framing" one's experience in such a way that it makes sense to the person and, thereby, informs his or her behavior. Maier [1978] analyzed the same process through the application of Piaget's principles of sensorimotor learning in professional helping.

An example of a residential care worker facing a difficult situation clarifies the third property that Weick postulated as central to the process of enactment. Here one sees how memory influences the meanings or interpretations that workers give to experiences. A middle-aged woman, herself a single parent of adolescent boys, was hired to work as a group-life counselor in a residential school for delinquent girls. She reported for her first day of work wearing a skirt and high-heeled shoes, which seemed to befit the professional status accorded to counselors there. She was directed to one of the cottage living units and soon found herself locked into one of the first secure treatment units for delinquent girls in the United States. Within minutes of her entering this work environment, a riot broke out, injuring the supervisor. The new worker lost her high-heeled shoes and barely managed to alert security in time to avert a mass breakout. This experience had a telling effect on the woman's subsequent performance. Some years later, while she was working again in the same secure unit, tension and increased authoritarian responses were aroused in her at the slightest indication of rowdiness.

Only after this staff member's authoritarian responses occurred in the center did the sources of her behavior become known. Here one finds illustration of Weick's fourth property of enactment. Weick claimed that "an action can become an object of attention only after it has occurred" [1969: 65]. Although the staff member was acting in an authoritarian manner and thereby changing the tone of the environment, the reasons for this behavior were not entirely clear. Thus, in the early days of her return to working in the secure unit, it was not unusual for people to wonder what was bothering this woman and to question why she was acting as she did. Later, through the aid of supportive supervision, this staff member was able to develop other responses for dealing with tense situations at work.

Collective Structure

But the question here is how one can better understand teamwork and the influence of coalitions whose actions shape the group canon or pattern of normative functioning in a team. Weick's discussion of the social psychology of organizing is helpful in this regard. Whenever there is a group event where, for an individual to perform some act it is necessary for other persons to perform other acts (whether similar, different, or complementary to the actions of the first team member), so it is possible to identify a "collective structure" of teamwork. Weick argues that this collective structure emerges not only to produce order and regularity, but also for other reasons. If other persons are around, for example, it may be rewarding to them and to us to have our presences acknowledged. Reciprocal acknowledgment actually constitutes an elementary form of teamwork, although this is of limited significance. One must look further "for instances in which with regularity worker A emits an act which is followed predictably by an act from worker B, and B's act then determines A's subsequent act" [Weick 1969: 46]. It is this model of collective structure that is pertinent to our teamwork concerns.

It is important to note that behaviors, not people, are what become inter-structured in teams to create a collective structure. It is also the case that a person does not invest all of his or her behavior in a single group; instead, commitments and interlocking behaviors are dispersed among several groups. Once this point is recognized, one can move closer to understanding why team-work problems are such common phenomena in residential care services. Workers are frequently heard to say, "If I had to be concerned only with the residents (instead of the staff) around here, my job would be a whole lot easier!" There are many instances when team members are required (or choose) to interlock their behaviors with other members of the team, while on different occasions they vary their involvement considerably. Furthermore, once a particular pattern of teamwork is established, team members tend to invest a great deal of energy in preserving it [Allport 1962].

The important point about this notion of collective structure is that it is assumed to be a basic property of groups from which other properties of teamwork derive. Collective structure incorporates the idea that teams are made up of individual workers, that teamwork is defined in terms of observable behaviors, and that teams are in many respects unique. The uniqueness of collective structure is anchored in a property not found in isolated individuals, namely that teamwork is defined by repetitive, interstructured behaviors over a given period.

The Experience of Time

To appreciate fully the notion of an enacted environment, it is essential to understand certain characteristics about time, which is experienced in two distinct forms. The first involves pure duration, perhaps best described as being a stream of experience, in which coming-to-be and passing-away remain undifferentiated. It is the second form of time, wherein discrete time segments are experienced as having distinct spatiotemporal properties, that most accurately describes the sense of time experienced by most residential care workers. As we know it, experience of work in residential care has a quality of discreteness and separateness. The only way we get this impression is by stepping outside the stream of experience and directing attention to it. In this respect, Weick asserted, "It is only possible to direct attention to what has already passed; it is impossible to direct attention to what is yet to come. All knowing and meaning arise from reflection, from a backward glance" [1969: 64]. Thus, it is the meaning that is given to events by individuals and coalitions of workers in a team that shapes their collective structure or pattern of teamwork with children. This also helps to account for the importance of reflective thinking in consultation or supervision with teams and individual workers.[3]

One can see, then, how the human actors in a residential center are immersed in an ongoing flow of experience. Once lived, this experience is potentially available for attention, even though most of it remains unnoticed. If the actors are able to step out of their stream of experience to gaze reflectively at that which has recently passed, it then becomes possible for experience to be viewed as well-defined, distinguishable experiences. Meaning is ascribed to these experiences, depending on the attitudes prevailing at that moment in time. Prevailing attitudes in the workplace help to determine the kind of attention that will be directed backward and, in so doing, frame the meaning that given experiences are likely to have [Weick 1969: 68–69]. It is in this sense that a regular staff meeting or a house meeting with residents can give collective meaning to the weekly events in a residential care center.

Enactment of Teamwork

Enactment as a process in any residential center is only loosely structured, suggesting that the diversity of its outputs can be substantial. Decision making in teams must sift through areas of ambiguity with the aim of trying to make them less ambiguous. For this reason, the enactment process is less concerned with questions such as "Why are we doing this?" or "What are the implications for the wider system?"; it is more concerned with "doing something." Any endeavor that seeks to improve teamwork is likely to require an overlap of both processes, calling attention to both "What is happening in this team?" and "Is this what the team wants to happen?" The organizational nature of residential care means that yet a third question must be asked, namely, "Is the overall performance of this team good enough?" It was Weick's claim that the major constraint associated with assessing and influencing the enactment process is that of making it possible for all team members to give meaning to the events that have already occurred and may be influencing their performance [1969: 71]. The failure to hold regular staff meetings can be said to impose this very constraint on teamwork in a residential care service.

Political Considerations

Child [1972] clarified some of the political dynamics that accompany team activity in a residential care center. The notion of a "dominant coalition" identifies those who collectively hold the most power and influence in a team over a particular period of time. Dominant coalitions are able to make strategic choices, involving a wide range of decisions, which influence future courses of action taken by a team. In some instances, it is possible to find situations where more than one coalition is operating and where one faction constrains or challenges another.

The idea of a dominant coalition does not imply that other members of a team do not have some power to modify or undermine any plans that have been formulated. Information reaching the dominant coalition is open to reinterpretation at the hands of anyone who has to pass it on. Those in boundary roles can screen information coming from the external environment, and those in workroles lower down in the hierarchy can restrict information being passed up or down or restrict its use. A social worker who fails to pass on important information illustrates the first point; a night staff member who fails to report an incident or who disregards an agreed practice illustrates the second. Overall, the idea of a dominant coalition in teams opens up such issues as the distribution of power and the processes of strategic decision making, which are an integral part of teamwork in residential care.

Problems in Teamwork

Problems that arise in the enactment of residential care services may adversely affect workers' prospects for continued employment and success. Such problems may also affect their capacity to adapt to the changing social environment that surrounds them [Pfeffer and Salancik 1978: 79–83]. One type of problem is evident when workers do not correctly perceive all the external groups and individuals on which they depend, or the relative importance and power of each. A second type arises when an individual, group, or organization is recognized as being influential, but the residential care team misreads the evaluation criteria being used or the type of demands being made; such a misunderstanding may be the result of selective perception or the filtering of information. Thus it is that workers may attend only to that which they have been trained to notice, or to those factors that are relevant to their own particular work situation.

Residential care workers are confronted with a paradox, however, in that if they attend to everything, they will be swamped with information and be unable to function. If insufficient information is forthcoming, however, then important changes that occur outside a center may leave workers unprepared to face ensuing threats to continuing performance. The industrial action taken by members of Britain's National Association of Local Government Officers (NALGO) in 1983 offers a useful illustration of this point. The ban introduced on new admissions and overtime by residential workers in social services departments actually helped to further public spending policies of the Thatcher government, which favored voluntary and private sector services at the expense of those sponsored by local government. Residential workers in the trade union clearly overestimated their own importance when thinking that a ban on new admissions would put pressure on management and force agreement on a new pay offer. Instead of negotiating with the trade union, managers simply arranged for alternative placements in private and voluntary centers, which had been under threat of closure due to a lack of referrals from local government departments. Had local government trade unionists noted the surplus capacity or empty residential beds available in their local communities, rather than focusing only on those within their own agencies, it is likely that the outcome of this dispute would have been substantially different.

Another dilemma associated with the enacted environment in residential care occurs when staff members are committed to doing things in a certain way, irrespective of new approaches with proven value or changes of policy that require different methods of working. The misuse of isolation or time-out facilities offers one common example. The uncertainty and confusion that often follow the introduction of new legislation is another good example. Finally, there is the problem of balancing the competing demands of many individuals and groups. Calls for "consistency in approach" may disregard the underlying fact that different people and groups may have quite different needs. Thus, under the not-so-secure blanket of superficial explanations for complex questions, solutions to one set of teamwork problems frequently create the conditions for new difficulties. It is in this sense that a contextual analysis of teamwork is important.

Teamwork in Context

It is to Bronfenbrenner [1979] that one turns for a consideration of contextual influences that shape teamwork in residential care over time. Practitioners may find that some features of the Bronfenbrenner model will require modification if they are to be readily used. There seems to be good justification for referring to "contextual influences" instead of the more technical "systems" terminology employed in Bronfenbrenner's original formulations. The well-known Russian toy made up of several nested dolls forms the conceptual basis for this social ecology schema. The smallest doll, Valecchi, can be viewed metaphorically as the *immediate setting* of a residential care center.[4] The second doll, Vemoni, can be used to illustrate the *network of relationships* that people in the immediate setting have with others outside that setting. The third doll, Malenki, can be used to represent the *organizational context* that sponsors and administers a residential care service. The fourth and largest doll, Matruska, can be said to highlight the *social policy environment* in which practice is embedded. It is essential to distinguish between two spheres of social policy environment if comparative research is to be carried out between centers in different states or countries. Both the *territorial/cultural context*, specific to a particular state, and the *international/cross-cultural context* require consideration. If one places the cluster of Russian dolls inside a dollhouse, it is possible to illustrate the five social contexts that influence teamwork in residential care.

In a comparative study of residential and day care teams working with children [Fulcher 1983], several contextual influences were identified that were found to have a significant bearing on the function of residential care teams. Quality of working-life assessments were obtained from workers in 63 different teams from 13 separate agencies in Great Britain and North America between 1977 and 1982. These assessments were subjected to a log-linear analysis to obtain a statistical measure of causal relationships between team functioning and several contextual features of practice. The major findings are summarized below, emphasizing a number of factors that are likely to require attention by those wishing to support and encourage teamwork in residential care.

Context I: The Immediate Setting

Special issues are associated with the siting and physical design of a center. Teams working in rural settings, where accessibility is restricted, would seem to be particularly vulnerable to isolation and, therefore, potential neglect. Teamwork is inevitably plagued with travel problems. Ensuring that workers get to and from work, providing children with recreational activities, and organizing family visits are all aspects of practice that demand special attention by workers who are required to make detailed travel arrangements in the course of any working day in rural settings. Since workers in rural settings are generally farthest away geographically from the major agency decision makers, extra travel time is required by all concerned in order to avoid isolation of each from the other. Furthermore, one finds that the residential workers rather than the managers do most of the traveling! Travel time inevitably also takes its toll in the form of increased operating costs and vacancies in the shift rotation. This, in turn, places extra demands on workers who remain in the center, who work on in the absence of ready support.

Teams working in suburban settings, or on the periphery of a population area, would seem to be in a better position. As with all units, however, regular involvement with someone who maintains liaison between the center and decision makers in the broader organizational context is essential. Emergency support during periods of special stress is also clearly indicated. This study found that the teams working in urban settings were much less predictable than teams in rural and suburban settings. Fatigue and overinvolvement in work would seem to be issues that require careful monitoring among urban teams, particularly when younger staff members are a dominant feature of the team.

With regard to the personnel complement of teams and team deployment, it would seem that recruitment practices should strive for a relative balance between men and women in teams. Teams with a wider age range between youngest and oldest workers appear to be more adaptive and capable of providing a greater variety of role models and a wider range of responses to children. Teams with a high proportion of young, single, and more highly educated workers would seem to be particularly susceptible to frustration, team intrigue, and turnover. The worst possible recruitment axiom seems to be, "If we only had more people like me/us around here we could really make this place work properly." That view promotes the principle of sameness and a narrowing of available role models, which is likely to stimulate rivalry among workers. It also assumes that team members are little more than replaceable parts.

When considering recruitment, it is far more important to assess what skills, interests, and attributes are missing in a team at the time of a vacancy. In so doing, the principle of "interchangeable parts" is built into team recruitment, where the contributions of each worker provide something that others in the team cannot provide. Teamwork is then more likely to produce a service that is greater than the sum of the individual parts. Careful attention is also required in the design of staff work schedules to ensure that the service needs of children are not consistently given second place to staff priorities for time off at particular periods of the week or for particular friendship patterns.

Patterns in the use of time and activity are influenced directly by the staffing roster that is used to deploy workers over the 168 hours of a residential care week. Ironically, little research information is available on the effects of different work schedules in a variety of residential settings. This lack seems strangely paradoxical, given the importance that residential workers place on their position in the duty roster. Few events can rival the significance of a change in duty roster at a residential care center, or the potential for irritation it generates for staff members and residents alike.

Diverse patterns in the use of time and activity are especially important in settings where physical restrictions are imposed on the movements of staff members and children. Whether because of a requirement for physical security, sight surveillance, or other reasons, teams working in the most restrictive environments require special attention if anti-task responses and potential burnout are to be avoided. Careful consideration should be given to means whereby staff members can enact close, personal relationships with children in restrictive settings. The use of planned activities, work with small groups, and carefully monitored house group meetings may all offer opportunities for such relationships to develop. In overtly restrictive environments—such as secure units—and sometimes in nominally more open settings, interpersonal relations can easily deteriorate to the point where all interactions revolve around issues of power and control. When this happens, staff teamwork and service production become extremely vulnerable.

Specific patterns of team functioning were found to be closely linked with admission and discharge of residents in a case study of 11 Canadian residential programs during the late 1970s [Burford and Fulcher 1985]. In-depth assessments of all children referred to the agency between 1978 and 1980 were carried out and allowed consideration of how different types of children affected team functioning over time. Diversity of individual capabilities in a resident group, the amount of structure children require in their learning environment, the interpersonal maturity of residents, and the particular patterns of learned behavior presented were all found to be important considerations when admitting new children into a particular resident group. Conflicted children and power-oriented children were found to place particular strain on the capacity of staff teams to perform. Not surprisingly, conforming children were found to generate the greatest amount of satisfaction among the small sample of teams, even though questions were raised whether these children were actually "helped" during their time in care, even though they made the staff feel good. The findings of this study highlighted the need for continuing research into the relationship between resident group influences and team functioning in residential care.

Context II: The Network of Relationships
with Others Outside

One social custom or practice highlighted in this study—the practice of employing live-in residential workers—requires careful consideration. No matter what the rationale used, such as the "special relationship" fostered between children and live-in staff members, the evidence supplied by this study tends to call such a practice into question. The strain that such arrangements place on the personal lives and families of residential workers should not be underestimated. Many problems associated with teamwork in centers with live-in houseparents may be attributed to this source. It would seem that unless there are compelling reasons for establishing a total community experience for staff members and residents, problems associated with shift work and workers living off the premises except for sleep-in duty are preferable in the long run to live-in staff members. For residential workers who do live in, very careful attention must be given to the use of off-duty time for relaxation and changes of routine that involve activities outside the immediate work setting.

More generally, workers' home lives and social relationships outside work cannot be taken for granted if residential care teams are consistently to produce good-enough services for young people. At least one close personal relationship with someone outside work who does not have direct involvement in residential group care would seem to be indicated.[5] One should not underestimate the strain that residential practice can impose on marriage relationships, particularly through the requisite intensity of close emotional involvements with colleagues and children. Erratic patterns of off-duty time, built into the duty roster, can easily lead to emotional attachments forming between work colleagues, resulting in less time being invested in home or family activities. The intimate affairs that develop between team members in residential care work frequently become part of the team folklore that is rarely talked about, except after a late shift and a few drinks at the pub. Such personal involvements are invariably the source of significant levels of intrigue in residential care teams, and such intrigue requires careful monitoring by all concerned. Those concerned with maintaining a good-enough level of services in residential care may need to give special attention to the means whereby staff members can maintain ongoing links with family and community life, while at the same time developing close working relationships with children and staff members at work.

In the absence of agreed criteria for reviewing and evaluating performance, residential workers in many settings have sought support from trade unions in their dealings with employers. This would seem to be especially the case in Europe, where there is a longer tradition of trade union activity. Elsewhere

[Fulcher 1979], the writer has asserted that residential workers have a right to collective bargaining in a number of matters concerning work in this field, so as to ensure that individual workers at the "coal face" of practice are not exploited. Evidence from this comparative study suggests that union membership does help residential care workers to be more self-sufficient in their work and to avoid being placed in a totally dependent position by their employers. Through involvement in a trade union, however, the special work demands of residential workers may become obscured in a union's negotiations for whole classes of workers. This point was highlighted in the industrial action taken by residential workers in Great Britain during 1983. Labor-management issues in many residential centers became deflected from immediate issues and working relationships associated with the residential care task. Instead, the issues were translated into broad union demands that ranged across a variety of organizational roles. In the process, both union members and managers lost sight of their original grievances or the professional concerns underlying them. The baby was all too frequently thrown out with the bathwater, with the best of intentions!

Unless employing organizations and trade unions attend to the particular needs of the direct caregivers in residential care work in ways that are also responsive to the needs of the children, then maladaptive and conflicted patterns of teamwork are likely to result. Sensitive but realistic negotiations are required at all stages in the relationship between an employing organization and residential workers. Where possible, the negotiations should involve workers directly in the clarification of agreed performance criteria that can be used to evaluate their practice. Unless such matters are carefully addressed in union-management relations, anti-task performance is a likely outcome in the provision of services for children.

Context III: The Organizational Context

Special attention should be given to the social policy brief or the mandate for services in a residential care center. Teams working in imposed care and control settings, such as secure units, institutional living units, or security assessment centers, would appear to be especially vulnerable to stress and fatigue. The workers in these kinds of settings appear to require direct emotional support and clearly defined periods of off-duty time, as recommended for all residential workers, if adaptive teamwork is to be sustained. An erratic pattern of scheduling and long shifts would seem to be particularly wearing on workers in imposed care settings. Teams working in community-based services, such as group homes, would seem to require different kinds of support. These teams are likely to be more isolated from decision makers and are prone to restricted and inhibited teamwork responses with children. The maintenance of team self-confidence and morale through the sensitive involvement of a trusted outsider who has links with external decision makers is clearly indicated.

The external organizational environment surrounding a residential care service is one of the most diffuse features of practice that teams must address if they are to sustain the production of good-enough services for children. Such an environment is diffuse in that the organizational context is largely an abstraction, a social construction of reality. In day-to-day practice, the organizational context is made up of people who sit behind desks, speak over telephones, and make visits to a center. It is the sum total of these involvements, however, along with the policies and procedures that frame their actions, that constitute the external organizational environment. If relationships in this environment are predictable and cooperative among specific people and settings, then team functioning is likely to be adaptive and task-oriented. In these instances, the organization is less complicated and the ground rules for interaction are known to all parties involved.

If the external environment becomes more competitive and survival-oriented, however, then team functioning is likely to become more prone to factionalism and maladaptation. Teams working in such environments require special kinds of support. During periods of rapid change associated with the reallocation of resources or legislative change, teams must be encouraged to find a new sense of direction in their approach to service production with children and families. Otherwise, their capacity for providing good-enough services in the immediate and longer term will be left open to question.

Teams working in turbulent environments are apparently the most vulnerable of all. Unpredictability of referrals and discharges, along with uncertainties associated with policy and decision making, make work in such environments especially problematic. Without the support of people who can advocate in behalf of a center and its team of workers, low morale, disinclination, fragmentation, and conflict become increasingly likely.

Context IV: The Social Policy Environment— Territorial/Cultural Sphere

A complex set of cost input-output relationships are a feature of every residential care program [Davies and Knapp 1981]. Of all the costs, those associated with human resources represent the largest single source of recurring expenditure. Thirty-eight of the 63 teams in our comparative study of residential and day care workers (roughly 60 percent) were found to have been working together for less than two years. For several of these teams, such a pattern persisted over the four years they participated in the study. When the three longest-serving teams were excluded from the analysis—7.5, 8.2, and 10.3 years together, respectively—it was found that only six other teams had been working together for more than five years. The overall picture to emerge was that of a highly mobile work force, with relatively high rates of reported changes in both work life and personal life [Holmes and Rahe 1967]. There seems to be little reason to assume that this pattern is atypical for many residential care teams or that the pattern has changed significantly since the late 1970s.

Most would agree that it takes at least six months of orientation and supervisory investment during the initial probationary period to help a new residential care worker develop into a fully productive team member. Many claim that this process actually takes closer to a year. If one accepts this claim, then approximately 12 to 18 months of good-enough service production can be anticipated from the initial training investment with new residential care workers before they move on to another post. It is not surprising, therefore, to find that many care teams are preoccupied with orienting new workers to the demands of their respective programs. Attention is rarely able to extend into advanced practice planning and development. In short, residential care teams are (necessarily, under the circumstances) adept at re-creating the wheel.

The lost opportunities in such a scenario are self-evident. It should be obvious, therefore, that a strategic goal aimed at reducing staff turnover from less than two years to roughly three or four years would result in a significant saving in human as well as fiscal resources. It does not follow, however, that just because workers stay longer, teamwork will automatically improve. Continued support and investment in team development are prerequisites. Futhermore, regional variations in the pattern of staff recruitment, training, and turnover are to be expected. Each region of a given country needs to develop its strategic plan to address these potential problems; through, it is hoped, close collaboration among service agencies and educational institutions in the area. The development of distance education technologies may offer further scope for such education and training initiatives. It is clear, however, that special attention must be given to recruiting, training, and retaining good residential care workers.

Context V: The Social Policy Environment— International/Cross-Cultural Sphere

Given the complexity of practice in this field, the high rate of staff turnover, and the resulting emphasis on early developmental patterns of teamwork, there can be little wonder that so many writers have developed theoretical and ideological models to explain the "production of welfare" process in residential care. Most of these efforts can be said to have failed to acknowledge at least three ideological influences that have shaped residential care services since the late 1960s, especially in North America and Great Britain. First, the post-Vietnam economic recession in the United States, which extended to Canada and Britain by the 1980s, was paralleled by a major thrust toward deinstitutionalization. Second, the principle of normalization has been used increasingly as moral justification for providing services in local communities, even though at times this practice results in a poorer standard of service due to funding restrictions. Third, evaluation research has been used to monitor expenditure and to provide organizational decision makers with elaborate justifications for their actions, always within the context of stringent cutbacks in public expenditure on social programs.

The analysis of cost per unit of service delivered has become a continuing exercise for most residential care centers in North America, just as defense spending was spiraling beyond all comprehension. Similar pressures have been encountered by residential care workers in the British context, as parallel developments in fiscal accountability become increasingly evident in the scrutiny of health, education, and welfare services at the central government level.

The economic orientation that currently shapes the practice of many North American teams is frequently accepted as an underlying social policy assumption. In this sense, North American teams in our study tended to reinforce the cultural stereotype of being "superficial idealists" in their approach to policy matters. These teams were capable of developing a sophisticated plan of action but often failed to take account of important contextual variables that consistently thwarted their residential care efforts. By contrast, the British teams tended to give far greater attention to policy matters, frequently at the expense of direct practice concerns. In this respect, the British teams tended to reinforce the cultural stereotype of being "conflicted pragmatists" who acknowledged a range of contextual influences but found difficulty in developing a strategic plan of action at the direct practice level.

The irony in all this is that, in striving for more technically sound and economical means of service production, social planners seem to have moved further away from the historical and cultural traditions that have shaped child and youth care work on both sides of the Atlantic. Those traditions have emphasized close interpersonal relations and the expectation that care would be provided in a personalized manner by elders and caregivers—to the extent humanly possible—for each new generation of children. Now, without clearly agreed outcome measures by which to evaluate residential care services in cultural terms as well as through economic calculation, evaluation research is more open to abuse than at any other time in history. The potential remains for evaluation research to be used (sometimes with the best of intentions) by those with the most power and influence who pursue their ideals at the expense of the poor, the handicapped, and the disadvantaged, who are still overrepresented in the residential care services of most western countries.

Conclusion

It has been argued that the collective structure of teamwork requires careful consideration in any attempt to define and evaluate residential care programs. Workers are employed to operate in teams to "enact" a care environment for children and young people. In creating and maintaining a care environment, residential care teams are required to offer the minimum guarantee that good-enough services will be consistently available. Teamwork has been shown to represent the enactment potential of a residential care service and should receive close attention in all efforts to evaluate practice.

Some residential care teams tend to approach their work in a comparatively superficial way. They seem to be concerned with variables A, B, and C, but do not want to be disturbed by a wider range of concerns. It is extremely important for teams such as these to seek clarity about their goals and methods of work and to acknowledge the emotional issues that frequently arise in their direct care work. Such teams are especially prone to making simplistic assessments of complex social issues. They tend to ignore a number of contextual influences that shape their practice and resist efforts to bring such matters to their attention. Directive styles of supervision are likely to be most effective with this type of team.

Other teams tend naturally to have a wider appreciation of problems and prospects, taking much greater account of the complexities of practice. For teams of this type, it is important to ensure that interpersonal and emotional concerns do not deflect attention from their primary tasks. Indeed, sometimes the attention these teams give to consideration of complex issues only delays their taking action. Such teams are especially prone to dissociation and factionalism, where staff intrigue can all too easily get in the way of team performance. Supervision that seeks clarity of purpose and task accountability is likely to be most successful with this type of team.

It is the persistence of residential care teams to continue functioning as they have operated previously when members change and when tasks or assignments are reallocated that encourages further study of teamwork in this field. In general, the functioning of staff teams and the functioning of children and young people in their care are interrelated parts of a whole. One feature of practice cannot be explored in isolation from others. Yet, ironically, much of the research carried out in this field over the past 40 years seems to have taken little account of how teamwork influences practice in residential care.

NOTES

[1]The writer is indebted to several people for helping to clarify some of the ideas presented in this chapter. Among these, I would like to thank particularly Frank Ainsworth, Richard Bland, Gale Burford, Helen Kinloch, Henry Maier, and Chris Turner.

[2]The concept of good-enough services recognizes that we are rarely, it seems, able to realize the full potential of residential or other human service programs. It refers to that level of quality that we consider to be acceptable or worthwhile in this less-than-perfect world.

[3]The ideas presented in this paragraph and the one following are elaborated by Guttmann elsewhere in this volume.

[4]I am indebted to Michael Holosko for giving me names for the Matruska dolls.

[5]For this reason as well as the live-in problem just mentioned, the practice of involving married couples as cottage parents or group home parents should be considered very carefully.

REFERENCES

Allport, F.H.   1962.   A structural conception of behavior: Individual and collective. *Journal of Abnormal and Social Psychology* 6: 3–30.

Billis, D.   1980.   Managing to care. In Billis, D., Bromley, G., Hey, A., and Rowbottom, R. (eds.), *Organising Social Services Departments*. London, England: Heinemann.

Bronfenbrenner, U.   1979.   *The Ecology of Human Development*. Cambridge, MA: Harvard University Press.

Burford, G.E., and Fulcher, L.C.   1985.   Resident group influences on team functioning. In Fulcher, L.C. and Ainsworth, F. (eds.), *Group Care Practice with Children*. London, England: Tavistock: pp 187–214.

Child, J.   1972.   Organizational structure, environment and performance—the role of strategic choice. *Sociology* 6(1): 2–22.

Davies, B., and Knapp, M.   1981.   *Old People's Homes and the Production of Welfare*. London, England: Routledge and Kegan Paul.

Fulcher, L.C.   1979.   Keeping staff sane to accomplish treatment. *Residential and Community Child Care Administration* 1(1): 69–85.

Fulcher, L.C.   1983.   *Who Cares for the Caregivers? A Comparative Study of Residential and Day Care Teams Working with Children*. Stirling, Scotland: University of Stirling, Ph.D. thesis.

Goffman, E.   1974.   *Frame Analysis: An Essay on the Organization of Experience*. Cambridge, MA: Harvard University Press.

Holmes, T.H., and Rahe, R.H.   1967.   The social readjustment rating scale. *Journal of Psychosomatic Research 11*: 213–218.

Maier, H.W.   1978.   Sensori-motor phase knowledge applied to beginnings in professional helping. In Magary, J.F., Poulsen, M.K., Levinson, P.J., and Taylor, P.A., (eds.), *Piagetian Theory and the Helping Professions*. Los Angeles, CA: University Publishers.

Menzies, I.E.P.   1970.   *The Functioning of Social Systems as Defense Against Anxiety*. London, England: Tavistock Institute of Human Relations.

Menzies, I.E.P.   1977.   *Staff Support Systems: Task and Anti-Task in Adolescent Institutions*. London, England: Tavistock Institute of Human Relations.

Pfeffer, J., and Salancik, G.R.   1978.   *The External Control of Organizations: A Resource-Dependence Perspective*. New York: Harper and Row.

Weick, K.E.   1969.   *The Social Psychology of Organizing*. Reading, MA: Addison-Wesley.

Winnicott, D.W.   1960.   *The Maturational Processes and the Facilitating Environment*. London, England: Hogarth Press.

12

The Child and Youth Care Worker

and the Organization

ROBERT R. FRIEDMANN

David, a 12-year-old boy in a semi-secure residential boarding school for delinquent children, has been sitting near the gate crying loudly for half an hour. Finally, one of the child-care workers notices and asks the boy what is troubling him. "I want to go home," replies David, begging the worker to let him go because he suffers at the school and misses his mother.

In a full-security detention center, a group of detainees are closing in on Michael, a new counselor, and are trying to influence him to help them break out that night. "The guy before you helped us. He was cool!"

John, a young patient in a chronic illness ward, is complaining of being denied information about his illness. He demands from workers to know what exactly is wrong with him, how he is going to be treated, when the tests will be over, and why he is refused the information.

Dinah, a youth worker in a correctional facility, is trying to organize her co-workers to demand the improvement of food and hygiene standards. She meets strong resistance from management on the grounds of insufficient money.

Rita, a youth worker in a detention center, observes what she views as abusive staff treatment of juveniles, such as beating them up and denying food; she wants to report it and to make sure that it will not happen again.

These examples demonstrate why it is a major task of residential direct care workers to help the clients adjust to the residence and to improve the setting from within. The adjustment depends, among other things, on the setting's orientation, or ideology, which determines its goals, objectives, and means; these, in turn, circumscribe its mode of operation. It is in this context that the worker has to adapt expectations and behavior and try to exert an influence.

Yet, beyond the orientation of the setting, actual everyday work in child and youth care is dictated to a large extent by organizational factors. Furthermore, preparation or training of workers for their roles usually occurs in an organization as well. Thus, the workers' overall roles and modes of operation are molded both by the educational or training organization involved and by the employing residential setting. The organization defines and sets the roles and, through its structure and goals, specifies modes of operation in the residence. The workers therefore need to be aware of the existence of organizational influences on their work.

Incidents such as those given above might be handled in a variety of ways, depending on one's intuition, experience, work orientation, philosophy, skills, practice methods, and the like. In each case, however, more efficient and effective solutions can be offered when workers take into account the organization in which they do their work as an additional component in their interaction with clients [Hacon 1972]. In other words, workers must be organization-conscious in order to maximize the effectiveness of their work by using the organization in a positive way.[1]

Why Is Knowledge about Organizations Important?

The direct care worker may ask, "Why should I know about organizations and how they function? I am here for the clients, not the organization!" The answer lies in the nature of organizations: since the worker is an organizational resource that produces by interacting with clients and others, organizational factors such as staff cohesion, the prescribed role of the worker in relation to other roles, the organization's definition of clients and their rights, staff conflict, staff turnover, and the type of control the organization exerts over its members will all in some way pose limitations on or provide avenues for success in direct work [Abrahamson 1967; Etzioni 1969; Johnson 1981; Maier 1971; Martin and Wilson 1978; Ohlin 1958; Portnoy 1973; Rosenhan 1973; Skipton et al. 1981; Vander Ven 1979; Zald 1962, 1971]. Workers who lack an understanding of organizational influences and how to use them will be weakened in their ability to serve clients effectively.[2]

For example, one danger for the direct care worker lies in missing organizational knowledge that directly pertains to the selection of clients. Studies show that when organizations face reduction of clientele, they react by minimizing their administrative barriers to access to the services they provide; when facing a surplus of applicants, they tend to serve smaller and more homogeneous populations. Organizations can do so when they wield strong boundary control, thus sending potential clients to other organizations with weaker boundaries [Greenley and Kirk 1973; Kirk and Greenley 1974]. One possible consequence for the direct care worker is the range of children and youths who constitute the clientele.

This chapter provides an organizational framework for the understanding of residential child and youth care work and maps out major organizational variables and theories to be considered by the worker in planning and decision making. Using this knowledge base, the chapter ends with suggestions for organizational solutions to the case examples. In this context, the author's perspective is that the direct care worker's role links the impositions, requirements, and specifications of the organization with the professional skills and individual idiosyncrasies of the worker and other individuals in the cause of providing effective service to clients.

The Conceptual Framework of the Organization in Residential Programs

A number of studies have dealt with organizational aspects of welfare agencies [Greenley and Kirk 1973; Kirk and Greenley 1974], mental health settings [Goffman 1961; Strauss 1964], and correctional institutions [Street et al. 1966; Zald 1962], but there is little evidence in the current literature of a systematic organizational approach to the analysis of residential care.[3]

With the current trend in residential care away from custody and treatment to acquisition of skills for living in the community, Toigo's [1972] call to shift our focus to a more systemic one should be acknowledged and reinforced. The position taken here follows Toigo's ideas. It does not imply the wishing away of the concepts of treatment, psyche, or individual care; rather, it suggests that an additional unit of analysis be employed; namely, that of the organization.

The Nature of the Organization

Although debate has continued between individualists [Brodbeck 1958], who believe that groups or organizations are merely the sum of the individuals comprising them, and holists [Wagner 1964; Webster 1973], who maintain that the organization is an entity different from the statistical sum of its members, the holistic approach has gained prominence in both theory and research over the past 30 years [e.g., Azumi and Hage 1972; Etzioni 1975; Hage 1965; Hall 1982; Hasenfeld 1972; Hausser 1980; Lawler et al. 1980; Leavitt et al. 1975; Olsen 1968; Price 1972]. Briefly, the holistic approach claims that we should focus on the characteristics of the social relationships that produce the organization as a whole. For residential workers, it is their professional as well as their social relations that constitute the organization. This holistic orientation is used throughout this chapter.

Interestingly enough, organizations are so pervasive that we take them for granted as the means through which we achieve our objectives. It is only when we realize their pervasiveness that they acquire ends of their own, that we seek to cope with them, to reduce their influence, or simply to find alternatives [Hall 1982; Townsend 1970]. It has been suggested, however, that the alternatives to organizations are other organizations, in essence because the populations of industrialized nations have grown so large and their problems so complex as to preclude non-organizational modes of operation. In residential care, this process is most observable in the trend of deinstitutionalization, which has not eliminated organizations or residential settings but, has, in fact, added some new ones, largely community-based. Irrespective of the shape and character of a residential setting, it remains an organization and is here to stay as such. The nature of organizations frames the residential program environment.

Intensive theorizing and empirical research have advanced the field to greater sophistication that, in turn, has been utilized to increase organizational efficiency and effectiveness [Lawler et al. 1980; Nadler 1980]. Most of our knowledge about organizations stems directly from work done in industrial settings with regard to worker behavior, attitude, motivation, and worker-management relations in production.

Within this domain of knowledge, many definitions of organizations have been proposed. This chapter uses Hall's [1982] integrated definition: "An organization is a collectivity with a relatively identifiable boundary, a normative order, ranks of authority, communication systems, and membership-coordinating systems; this collectivity exists on a relatively continuous basis in an environment and engages in activities that are usually related to a goal or a set of goals."

Implications for the Child and Youth Care Worker

The immediate tendency of the worker may be to ask, "What's in it for me?" ("Why should I know more about organizations?" "How can I and my work benefit from my knowing more about organizations?"). "What's in it" is the potentiality for better performance, effectiveness, promotion, and interpersonal relationships—all components of satisfaction in the job and with oneself.

The direct care worker does not need to dedicate time and energy required for daily tasks to seeking organization-related information. By becoming more sensitive to these factors, however, the worker becomes able to discern information pertinent to clientele, the worker's own daily performance, and the residential setting's climate.

Acquiring Organizational Understanding

As in clinical case assessment, acquiring organizational knowledge is done through planning, data collection, analysis, feedback, and follow-up of organizations. What this chapter offers is essentially a sort of road map to walk an individual through the important and germane components of the organization. In other words, what is it that is worth paying attention to rather than simply taking for granted or ignoring?

Mapping the Residential Organization

Many business, industrial, and public organizations distribute to their employees an organization chart that delineates the structure of roles and the hierarchy of positions and may include names and photographs of individuals. After a while, workers learn about internal dynamics that do not necessarily reflect the formal chart. The following paragraphs describe the process by which the direct care worker can chart or map the organizational environment in the context of theories of organizations and their relations to environments.

The *first rule* in mapping the residential organization, following the definition above, is to identify the key dimensions: organizational boundaries (geographical, physical, social, professional); the normative order (culture, rituals, accepted forms of behavior between service providers and clients, among clients, and among workers); organizational compliance (why, how, and with whom; for instance, is compliance derived from the power of administrators or from the power of the workers' professional training); how communication is conducted, regulated, and facilitated or hindered (in other words, who knows what, when, and under what circumstances); how new members (staff members, volunteers, clients, and so on) are admitted, accepted, and oriented; the organization's status over time (history, plans); the environment that surrounds the organization (quality of the community, characteristics of human resources, type of clients, type of interaction with the community); and the organization's goals and the means available to achieve them.

The *second rule* has to do with Thompson's [1967] distinction between organizations as closed systems for achieving specific goals and as open systems responding to external and internal pressures. The intent of the second rule is not to resolve any dispute between the two perspectives but rather to understand that some organizations function as closed systems and others as open ones; frequently, these two elements are mixed. It is important for the worker to identify ways in which the organization operates as a closed system and as an open one, so that resources can be better utilized, pressures handled, and accountability established.

The *third rule* concerns the formal and informal aspects of the organization (in particular, see the summary in Tausky [1970]). The formal aspects include such organizational dimensions as structure (role relations, statuses), process (working to achieve goals), and official rules and regulations. The informal aspects deal with setting norms, social relations, power structure, and means of informal communication—which may, in turn, affect organizational performance and formal structure. The worker should therefore consider both formal and informal aspects. To delineate the formal structure, it would help to chart the official roles and positions from the director through teachers, nurses, cooks, clinical staff, vocational staff, secretaries, janitors, and so on (see examples in Street et al. [1966]). Then observe the rules they follow, when they play by the book, when not, and why.

The *fourth rule* in mapping the residential setting as an organization is to determine what type of human service organization it is. The two major types of human service organizations to which residential centers belong (with most arrayed between these extremes) are (*1*) people-processing organizations, and (*2*) people-changing organizations.[4] When the goal is processing, the organization is structured so as to produce people with an altered status, a status different from the one they held before entering, such as from sick to well (e.g., prisons, general hospitals, some schools). When the goal is change, the organization focuses on producing certain desired behavior by socializing or resocializing its clientele (e.g., other schools, residential treatment centers, mental hospitals).

Most interesting is the difference between these two types of organizations in terms of the relative duration of staff-client encounters, normally short-term in the processing organization and long-term in the changing one (see particularly Hasenfeld [1972]; also Street et al. [1966]). It is important for the worker, then, to identify the processing and changing features of the residential setting, in order to understand the organization's and the clients' situations and needs and to what extent they may be made more compatible.

In residential settings, both personnel and clients are members of the organization, although in different statuses, roles, lengths of stay, and so forth. The organizational production process, it is important to note, is performed directly on the clients, who are also the product, and not through marketing intermediaries or outlets (see Maier [1972]; Whittaker [1971, 1979]; Whittaker and Trieschman [1972]). Thus, if you do not like a piece of merchandise you may return it or buy another; receiving bad service from teachers, families, or hospitals is of a different nature altogether.

Organizations are differentiated as predominantly *coercive* (prisons, correctional facilities, relocation centers, P.O.W. camps, coercive unions); *utilitarian* (industries, peacetime volunteer armed forces, businesses, unions); or *normative* (religious organizations, hospitals, colleges, social unions, voluntary associations, professional organizations, and therapeutic mental hospitals) (see Etzioni [1975]). There are, of course, combinations of these types as well, such as ships or company towns, which are examples of the normative-coercive orientation [Etzioni 1975], or working farms operated by residents of a treatment institution.

Thus, the *fifth rule* or task is mapping residential organizations along this coercive-normative continuum. The organizational orientation will determine the basis of compliance by organizational members, be they staff members or clients. In coercive organizations, members comply because of power relationships; in utilitarian organizations, because of remunerative relationships; and in normative ones, compliance is due to the values and norms under which performance takes place. This delineation can be exceedingly helpful to the worker, and it poses problems if it is ignored in the process of attempting to achieve compliance [Watkins 1979]. Most residential settings, although clearly coercive and non-voluntary in nature, exhibit characteristics of normativeness and utilitarianism as well.[5] In the mapping process, the worker should notice these three elements as characterizing routine activities, the program rationale, and professional exchanges. This may facilitate a better understanding of residential life, including possible built-in contradictions and conflicts, such as those between the nominal program rationale or ideology and the reality [Montalvo and Pavlin 1966].

The *sixth rule* deals with identifying organizational ends and the means to achieve them [Gross 1965]. Although it may seem that the major end of the organization is the realization of the set goals for which it was established, the literature distinguishes between a number of organizational ends that are related to the declared or manifest ones. Thus, correctional facilities or residential facilities are there to detain, punish, rehabilitate, and train juveniles, but they also have in common the fact that, as organizations, they simply want to survive. In many cases, they are important to the economy and social structure of the local community, which may influence the behavior of many of the staff members who live in that community.

Adaptation to its environment is a major organizational end. Changes in policy, practice, or structure of the organization are possible indicators of its flexibility in response to external conditions (i.e., its adaptability). Production is a second objective, as indicated by the organization's effectiveness: how many juveniles are processed in a residential setting, how many will not be recidivists, how many will return to school after discharge, and so forth. A third goal is efficiency: when cost per unit of production is lowest, the organization is using its resources well rather than wasting them. In not-for-profit organizations (including many residential settings), in which it is difficult to evaluate the quality of the product clearly, acceptable cost is determined on a normative basis; that is, standards are developed to define reasonable expenses and what will exceed them. A fourth goal is employee job satisfaction, without which it is difficult to maintain efficient and effective organizations. This is indicated by such factors as the rate of turnover, which tends to be inversely related to job satisfaction or employee morale.

The goals that the organization seeks to accomplish are contingent on a set of means that are also devised and supplied by the organization. For the direct care worker, the identification of organizational means (explicit and implicit) is of key importance for better functioning and development. Goals tend to be remote; they are usually not discussed daily, and they may not influence or change the worker's work-related behavior on a continuing basis. Means, however, continually shape the worker's organizational life.

Organizational means include complexity, centralization, formalization, and stratification [Hage 1965]. *Complexity* is indicated by the level of specialization of workers, how many specialized positions there are, and the training level required. *Centralization* is the way the organization establishes its ranks of authority—who and how many are making decisions, who reports to whom, who is responsible for the performance of a task, and so on. Some of these decisions are extremely important when they concern such matters as treatment or care ideologies and how staff members and clients comply with those. *Formalization* deals with how positions are standardized or routinized. Thus, the work of a warden is more routinized than that of a teacher, and the teacher's more than that of a treatment worker in a mental facility or correctional institution. Also, within a particular job role there may be more or less variability and discretion in terms of the

content of tasks, nature of treatment, or cases treated. Finally, residential organizations allocate rewards to members according to some formally and informally
established criteria, and thus a status, or *stratification*, system (a pecking order) is
created, which is expressed by income, seniority, prestige, professional esteem,
mobility between positions, and the like.

The Rules in Summary, and Additional Concepts

Let us summarize, then, the rules or tasks we face when mapping the
organization.

Rule 1. Identify the organizational dimensions (elements of organizational definition).

Rule 2. Locate the organization along the closed/open continuum.

Rule 3. Identify the organization's formal/informal aspects.

Rule 4. Locate the organization along the people-processing or people-
changing continuum.

Rule 5. Locate the organization along the coercive/normative continuum.

Rule 6. Identify the organization's goals and means.

Some aspects of organizational life that direct care workers might choose
to focus on for further study are suggested by Tichy and Hornstein [1980] and
include such items as informal groupings; span of organizational control, resources,
and leadership; formal and informal reward systems, technology, and tasks; staff
selection and training; fiscal characterization; employee job satisfaction; authority
structure; goals (organizational, individual-private); information channels; organizational culture, norms and values of members, relations with environment
(government, citizens, other organizations); job performance and its appraisal; and
employee turnover. Other lists include institutional arrangements, organizational
size, organizational autonomy, internal division of labor, conflict, alienation [Azumi
and Hage 1972], power distribution, and aspects of the organization as a change
agent [Hall 1982]. In the empirical literature, attention has been given to these
organizational aspects and to such others as absenteeism, distributive justice,
innovation, mechanization, routinization, and succession [Price 1972].

In addition to defining the organization and delineating the components of
the definition in mapping organizations in which one works, there is a broader
factor related to these rules, having to do with a whole set of organizational
theories that should be considered. These theories explicate the nature of relationships between the organization's environment and resources, between authority and production, or any other set of components included in the definition.
Several such theories deal with those relations that impede or enhance goal

achievement or influence organizational behavior [Azumi and Hage 1972; Brodbeck 1958; Bronfenbrenner 1979; Etzioni 1975; Hall 1982; Lawler et al. 1980; Magnusen 1973; Olsen 1968; Perrow 1972; Price 1972; Scott 1974; Strauss 1963; Thompson 1967; Turner 1972; Wagner 1964; Webster 1973]. This wide body of knowledge has not been sufficiently utilized in residential settings.

Explaining Organizational Functioning

The major theoretical and empirical breakthrough with regard to organizational contexts relates to how we want to explain why and how organizations function. Most theories explain organizational functioning either in individual, group, or organizational terms. *Individual* explanations focus on the motivation, perceptions, and learning of individuals in organizations. *Group* explanations focus on group membership of individuals in organizations and group dynamics, using data from small groups research. *Organizational* explanations focus on organizations as distinct entities in terms of their structure, process, and important characteristics discussed earlier. As modern organizational phenomena became too complex to be explained unidimensionally, however, integrative models emerged that comprehensively synthesize the three (see Hausser [1980]). This is of particular relevance to the direct care worker because only rarely will an example of a single, theoretically pure model be found in real life. As was previously suggested, the ideal types are constructs that help us to understand things, but reality does not necessarily appear as such. Thus, workers will be able to identify individual, group, and organizational elements in their settings.

Systems Theory

The synthesis of the organizational literature, including the kinds of variables that have been presented here, has led to the application and wide popularity of the systems approach. Generally, a system is defined as a "complex of interrelated parts surrounded by a boundary and existing in an environment" [Hall 1982; Turner 1972]. This definition is complementary to the open organization described earlier. In fact, the residential care literature exemplifies the use of this organization-in-the-environment approach [Polsky 1962; Polsky et al. 1970; Rosenhan 1973; Strauss 1964; Street et al. 1966; Thomas 1980; Toigo 1972, 1975; Tutt 1975; Weber 1962; Zald 1962]. Moreover, residential settings are not merely organizations; they also display the characteristics of communities, such as culture, lifestyle, and formal and informal power bases, as well as internal dynamics that may or may not be influenced by external considerations. It may be helpful for the direct care worker to consider residential settings as communities with special organizational features [Goffman 1961; Polsky 1962].[6]

Practice Implications

When exploring their organizational surroundings, direct care workers can read the organizational map and use the information as a guide in decision making and action. They are advised to adopt the participant observer perspective of the exploring social scientist;[7] by doing so, they are already one step ahead. When, in addition to the desire to help, workers also have the desire to familiarize themselves with the abstract realities of organizational life, more effective practice can result.

Observation should be continual since, even after one becomes familiar with the organization, it continues to change. Observing the organization is to be done simultaneously with the performance of one's tasks. Soon the gathered data will aid in task performance by providing a more comprehensive perspective on the work reality. Figure 1 illustrates in a systematic way how to become better acquainted with the residential setting as an organization.

Toward Problem Resolution Using
the Organizational Component

Let us examine now how the organizational map discussed earlier adds to the skills of the direct care worker, skills that can improve the performance of the organization and help the worker to function more effectively in it.

The Incident with David: "I want
to go home!"

Intuitively, a number of options are open to the worker. He or she could sit down to talk with David, or locate the worker who regularly works with him (or even take him to the bus). Utilizing organizational knowledge, however, the worker might first gather information (which could have been obtained before the incident) about the way such incidents are usually treated there; that is, could any worker handle the situation, or should it be referred to David's worker? What are the established task priorities of direct care workers? If the worker decides to deal with David, what should be done about the situation? In addition to the attempt to examine David's perceptions of the crisis, should not information be obtained about his peers in the residence or his relations with other workers, not to mention a history of his previous behaviors? Without such information,

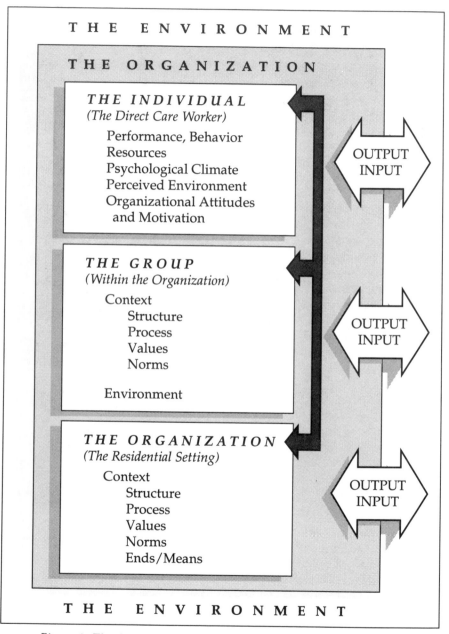

Figure 1. The direct care worker and the organization: An illustration.

the worker might find himself or herself repeating a destructive pattern, being manipulated, and so on. In other words, the worker should systematically gather organizational information and act upon knowledge of division of labor, norms, values, regulations, and staff-client relations.

The Incident with Michael: "Are you our friend?"

This incident is one of those typical crisis situations that are created to test the new adult on the scene. For the new direct care worker, the dilemma is between being nice to the young people so as to obtain their trust (which is so needed at this stage of entree)—and perhaps to lose that of the residence staff—or to risk their trust by refusing to cooperate. From an organizational perspective, however, the worker might seek to examine roles and role expectations in the residential setting. The worker is in a role different from that of the clients/inmates, and, paradoxically, responding positively to their request will not necessarily make the worker more likeable, because they do expect the worker to behave as an organizational power broker. Therefore, if the worker is there to execute the institution's goals, there is no expectation that he or she would do otherwise. This knowledge could help initiate a worker's entree into a group of clients, as well as, at the right time, helping him or her to facilitate clients' growth in understanding of such situations.

The Incident with John: The "Right" to Know?

Though John clearly understands that something is very wrong with him, he suspects that exact information with respect to his illness is being withheld from him. After the worker promises to "see what can be done," he or she might first try to verify John's suspicions by discussing his situation with other qualified staff members. If his story is not true, then the next step would be to deal with John and his perceptions; otherwise, the worker should explore with other staff members the reasons for denying information. Whether the information is being denied because of similar previous practices or because of John's particular situation, the worker faces an organizational ethical practice dilemma: Should John's request be fulfilled or not? What are the worker's chances of convincing the staff to reveal the information? What will be the results (for John and the worker) if the worker reveals the information despite organizational objections?

The Incident with Dinah: Workers
Matter, Too!

Workers experience efforts at unionizing or organizing around a specific issue, and some tend more than others to lead such events. In addition to the questions of what, who, and how workers will benefit from it, special consideration should be given to sources of resistance, to the efforts to be invested to influence the administration's policies, to other staff members and their possible support or resistance, and, last but not least, to the effect of such efforts on the clients. The answers to the following questions should guide the worker: (1) How long will it take to organize and mobilize the needed support? (2) Is it possible to achieve an end by some indirect means without going through all this effort in the first place? (3) Who and what are the organizational resources that might aid in this process? (4) What is the workers' relative power position in the residence? (5) If the organizing effort succeeds, which positions might be alienated, which will cooperate?

The Incident with Rita: Responding to
Observations of Abuse

Abuse of an inmate is one of the most difficult situations in organizational or institutional life. The role of the caring staff member is particularly stressful, because trying to change the situation places one in conflict with colleagues and often in a power struggle with anxious and threatened administrators. Recent reports about whistle-blowers show that they are the ones who pay the price: threats, demotion, and even loss of their jobs (e.g., Durkin [1982]). There are many routes for action that may result in cessation of abuse of the specific residents or of that behavior altogether. This problem is one of the most complex of ethical and professional dilemmas and, because the worker is at a disadvantage to begin with, the organizational situation should be assessed very carefully (in terms of consequences for inmates and staff) before proceeding. History of the organization, background of the abuse, knowledge of the individuals, and possible support in and outside the residence are key elements in planning for action. Such forethought may provide an edge over unconsidered whistle-blowing in which various approaches and their consequences were not thought out in advance.

Conclusions

For direct child and youth care workers, ignoring organizational considerations is likely to have detrimental effects on their job performance as well as job satisfaction. Reading this chapter, however, child and youth care workers might feel a bit overwhelmed: "If this is what I have to do just to pay attention to the organization, when will I have the time to dedicate to my clients, with whom my primary responsibility lies?" The worker is not expected to research organizations but to operate in them.[8] The ideas provided here should be viewed as pointers that, when used, can actually ease the worker's performance and make it more successful and fulfilling.

The worker may evince another reaction: "After reading all these pointers about the organization, I feel so small and helpless. Nothing I can do will matter anyway!" This impression is unwarranted, not because organizations are not pervasive or powerful, but because the workers *can* significantly influence residential life, particularly when they bring organizational factors to bear on it. It is really up to the worker to place this knowledge in the proper perspective. With such awareness, it will become more possible to influence the residence as an organization in the service of clients rather than to be controlled by it.

Finally, workers equipped with sensitivity to the importance of organizational factors in the performance of their tasks will tend to have an advantage over workers who are not. Of course, one can argue that, as more workers acquire such knowledge, that advantage will be lost, or it will become less significant. Rather than promoting competition among workers, however, this chapter seeks to promote their skills and to enhance the level of service that they provide to their clientele. It is hoped that this advantage will be welcomed.

NOTES

[1] Residential settings in the fields of health and mental health care, education, social welfare, and justice are evident in their organizational forms, such as hospitals, schools, detention centers, orphanages, community homes, and the like (see Ainsworth and Fulcher [1981]).

[2] A growing realization of the importance of organizations is evident in the supervision literature, which reports on efforts to increase the organization's awareness of staff members' needs for supervision that will develop their professional potential [Fant and Ross 1979].

[3] Treatment professions have emerged on the basis of providing individual-oriented therapy; it is not surprising that, despite enormous progress made in the last two decades in community work and the sociology of organizations, most practitioners are psychology-oriented. They are somehow either fascinated with the concept of the psyche or believe it is more understandable, identifiable, accessible, and, therefore, treatable. A real difficulty is encountered when the concept of organization is introduced; it seems more abstract and less humane, understandable, identifiable, accessible, and treatable. At the same time, practitioners want more power or control over their work and over the organization's policies and administration.

[4] Again, a word of caution: it is not implied that people-processing organizations do not change their clients or that people-changing organizations do not process them; the position taken here concerns the manifest orientation or goal of the organization—what it wants to achieve— and recognizes this dimension as a continuum.

[5]In all the rules suggested here, one should observe the delineation of ideal types and then note how they are mixed in everyday life.

[6]See also the discussion by Wozner elsewhere in this volume.

[7]The scientist lives with the group or society under study and practically becomes a member. At the same time, the scientist gives careful attention to collecting the relevant data.

[8]Obviously, the primary function of the direct care worker is to provide direct service. For those direct care workers who are interested in carrying out research or in cooperating with outside researchers, however, one should not preclude the possibility.

REFERENCES

Abrahamson, M. (ed.).   1967.   The Professional in the Organization. Chicago, IL: Rand McNally.

Ainsworth, F., and Fulcher, L.C. (eds.).   1981.   Group Care for Children: Concept and Issues. London, England: Tavistock.

Azumi, K., and Hage, J.   1972.   Organizational Systems. London, England: D.C. Heath.

Brodbeck, M.   1958.   Methodological individualism: Definition and reduction. Philosophy of Science 25: 1–22.

Bronfenbrenner, U.   1979.   The Ecology of Human Development. Cambridge, MA: Harvard University Press.

Durkin, R.   1982.   No one will thank you: First thoughts on reporting institutional abuse. In Hanson, R. (ed.), Institutional Abuse of Children and Youth. New York: Haworth Press.   Also in Child & Youth Services 4(1/2): 109–113.

Etzioni, A. (ed.).   1969.   The Semi-Professions and Their Organization. New York: The Free Press.

Etzioni, A.   1975.   A Comparative Analysis of Complex Organizations. New York: The Free Press: pp 3–67.

Fant, R.S., and Ross, A.L.   1979.   Supervision of child care staff. Child Welfare 58: 627–641.

Goffman, E.   1961.   Asylums: Essays on the Social Situation of Mental Patients and Other Institutions. New York: Doubleday.

Greenley, J.R., and Kirk, S.   1973.   Organizational characteristics of agencies and the distribution of services to applicants. Journal of Health and Social Behavior 14: 70–79.

Gross, B.M.   1965.   What are your organization's objectives? Human Relations 18: 195–215.

Hacon, R. (ed.).   1972.   Personal and Organizational Effectiveness. London, England: McGraw-Hill.

Hage, J.   1965.   An axiomatic theory of organizations. Administrative Science Quarterly 10: 289–320.

Hall, R.H.   1982.   Organizations: Structure and Process. 3rd Edition. Englewood Cliffs, NJ: Prentice Hall: pp 28–33.

Hasenfeld, Y.   1972.   People processing organizations: An exchange approach. American Sociological Review 37: 256–263.

Hausser, D.L.   1980.   Comparison of different models for organizational analysis. In Lawler, E.E. III, Nadler, D.A., and Cortland, C. (eds.). Organizational Assessment. New York: Wiley: pp 132–161.

Johnson, S.M.   1981.   Staff cohesion in residential treatment. *Journal of Youth and Adolescence* 10: 221–232.

Kirk, S.A., and Greenley, J.   1974.   Denying or delivering services? *Social Work* 19: 439–447.

Lawler, E.E. III, Nadler, D.A., and Cortland, C. (eds.).   1980.   *Organizational Assessment*. New York: Wiley: pp 1–20.

Leavitt, H., Pinfield, L., and Web, E.   1975.   *Organizations of the Future*. New York: Praeger.

Magnusen, K.O.   1973.   A comparative analysis of organizations: A critical review. In *Organizational Dynamics*. New York: AMACOM, a division of American Management Association.

Maier, H.W.   1971.   The child care worker. In *Encyclopedia of Social Work*. New York: National Association of Social Workers: pp 130–134.

Maier, H.W.   1972.   The social group work method and residential treatment. In Whittaker, J., and Trieschman, E. (eds.), *Children Away From Home*. Chicago, IL: Aldine: pp 153–167.

Martin, P.Y., and Wilson, A.A.   1978.   The conceptualization and measurement of organizational size in residential treatment organizations. *Journal of Social Service Research* 2: 177–198.

Montalvo, B., and Pavlin, S.   1966.   Faulty staff communications in a residential treatment center. *American Journal of Orthopsychiatry* 36: 706–711.

Nadler, D.A.   1980.   Using organizational assessment data for planned organizational change. In Lawler, E.E. III, Nadler, D.A., and Cortland, C. (eds.), *Organizational Assessment*. New York: Wiley: pp 72–90.

Ohlin, L.   1958.   The reduction of role conflict in institutional staff. *Children* 5: 65–69.

Olsen, M.E.   1968.   *The Process of Social Organization*. New York: Holt, Rinehart and Winston.

Perrow, C.   1972.   *Complex Organizations*. Glenview, IL: Scott Foresman.

Polsky, H.W.   1962.   *Cottage Six*. New York: Russell Sage Foundation.

Polsky, H.W., Claster, D.S., and Goldberg, C. (eds.).   1970.   *Social System Perspectives in Residential Institutions*. East Lansing, MI: Michigan University Press.

Portnoy, S.M.   1973.   Power of child care worker and therapist figures and their effectiveness as models for emotionally disturbed children in residential treatment. *Journal of Consulting and Clinical Psychology* 40: 15–19.

Price, J.L.   1972.   *Handbook of Organizational Measurement*. London, England: D.C. Heath.

Rosenhan, D.L.   1973.   On being sane in insane places. *Science* 179: 250–258.

Scott, W.G.   1974.   Organizational theory: A reassessment. *Academy of Management Journal* 17: 242–254.

Skipton, L.H., Margolis, H., and Keating, D.J.   1981.   Salient factors influencing resident advisor turnover. *Child Care Quarterly* 10(4): 329–333.

Strauss, A.L.   1964.   *Psychiatric Ideologies and Institutions*. New York: The Free Press: pp 184–187; 190–195; 297–298.

Strauss, G.   1963.   Some notes on power equalization. In Leavitt, H.J. (ed.), *The Social Science of Organizations*. Englewood Cliffs, NJ: Prentice-Hall: pp 39–84.

Street, D., Vinter, R.D., and Perrow, C.   1966.   *Organization for Treatment*. New York: The Free Press: pp 115–121.

Tausky, C.   1970.   *Work Organizations: Major Theoretical Perspectives*. Itasca, IL: F.E. Peacock.

Thomas, E.J.   1980.   Beyond knowledge utilization in generating human service technology. In Fanshel, D. (ed.), *Future of Social Work Research*. Washington, DC: NASW: pp 91–103.

Thompson, J.D.   1967.   *Organizations in Action*. New York: McGraw-Hill.

Tichy, N.M., and Hornstein, H.A.   1980.   Collaborative organization model building. In Lawler, E.E. III, Nadler, D.A., and Cortland, C. (eds.), *Organizational Assessment*. New York: Wiley: pp 300–316.

Toigo, R.   1972.   The dynamics of the juvenile institution: A systems theory approach. *Child Care Quarterly 1*: 252–263.

Toigo, R.   1975.   Child care manpower development: A literature review. *Child Care Quarterly 4*: 6–17.

Townsend, R.   1970.   *Up the Organization*. New York: Knopf.

Turner, J.A.   1972.   *Patterns of Social Organization*. New York: McGraw-Hill.

Tutt, N.   1975.   *Care or Custody*. New York: Agathon Press.

Vander Ven, K.   1979.   Towards maximizing effectiveness of the unit team approach in residential care. *Residential and Community Child Care Administration 1*: 287–298.

Wagner, H.   1964.   Displacement of scope. *American Journal of Sociology 69*: 571–584.

Watkins, T.R.   1979.   Staff conflicts over use of authority in residential settings. *Child Welfare 58*: 205–215.

Weber, G.H.   1962.   *A Theoretical Study of the Cottage Parent Position and Cottage Work Situations*. Washington, DC: U.S. Department of Health, Education and Welfare.

Webster, M.T.   1973.   Psychological reductionism, methodological individualism and large scale problems. *American Sociological Review 38*: 258–273.

Whittaker, J.K.   1971.   Residential treatment. In *Encyclopedia of Social Work*. New York: National Association of Social Workers: pp 169–175.

Whittaker, J.K.   1979.   *Caring for Troubled Children*. San Francisco, CA: Jossey-Bass.

Whittaker, J.K., and Trieschman, A.E. (eds.)   1972.   *Children Away From Home*. Chicago, IL: Aldine: pp 3–35.

Zald, M.A.   1962.   Organizational control structures in five correctional institutions. *American Journal of Sociology 68*: 451–465.

Zald, M.A.   1971.   *Occupations and Organizations in American Society: The Organization Dominated Man?* Chicago, IL: Markham.

13

Program Integration in Residential Care:

The Residential Center as the

Instrument of Care Delivery

YOCHANAN WOZNER

Verbatim comments by youths in various group care settings in England [Lambert and Milham 1974]:

> I am proud to be part of an institution as well-founded and successful as [X]. I like the freedom to develop my own philosophy and to think and discuss my religion, which I would be unable to do in Anglican schools of this sort.

> Before I came to this school, I did not realize what a wonderful life and what a real home away from home it was. The privileges are so good that you are happier doing work and learning things, knowing what wonderful things you can do in your spare time such as swimming, football, netball,

rugby, table tennis, billiards, snooker, cricket, and many other things .... I am proud of my school, and I've longed to come to boarding school for years. The atmosphere is wonderful, the teachers are nice, the school is marvelous ....

"Ben," our dormitory teacher, is better than I thought even though he does punish severely. This school is a real comforting home away from home.

When I first came here three years ago, I was told I may be able to take two or three "O" levels and am taking three "A" levels. This would have been impossible had I stayed with my parents. Being a new, modern school with a tremendous drive, there is a never ending series of things one can do. The opportunities are tremendous due primarily to the size of the school. Yet the boarding houses are not large and institutional but small and friendly. There is a distinctly friendly atmosphere. One is respected as a person and as such gets a certain amount of freedom. If this were not the case, I would have left by now. I also have a room to myself and therefore privacy. I like this place.

This school is a rotten old dump. You get rotten old bloody food. You get maggots in your spuds. The boys swipe all your stuff. Windows get smashed. The bog rolls are all down in the bogs and in the slash 'oles. The beds come from the junkyards. They can't even afford two bog rolls. Our House Master is a fat-gutted rotter.

I hate the staff. I could kill them for all the misery and cruelty they inflicted on me in the early years when this place was very strict. Teachers snoop—they crawl on all fours to the back of the bunkers to pounce on smokers. They're always at people, enforcing petty rules and inspections and they hit you without questioning. You should see how they smile before they cane you. They ask questions afterwards but most don't ask any. They delight in making life a "physical hell" for the offenders of the pettiest rules.

The system does not agree with me—it causes me much unhappiness. It is outdated in the modern world today, even in my two-and-a-half years here I have seen ideas change and boys revolt against the dictatorial authority of the Victorian age. The "Public School" boy is now as "with it" as anyone— yet any attempt at this is banned. No smoking, no drinking, I cannot see my family very often—they [my parents] won't be alive forever—would it really hurt my education to be at a school for day boys? I do not like the place or

the way it is run as a whole. It is high time for changes—it is 1966 not
1866.

We are treated like children, we are locked up and never see a girl.
There's too much fucking religion. The priests aren't priests; they wear
cassocks and that's about all, apart from being bloody hypocrites. They lecture
about how bad homosexuality is, but what do they do to prevent it? Lock
us away from girls. The rules are petty. . . . Our lockers are searched, the
dirty sneaky slimy priests spy on us and enjoy giving us the cane for no
reason at all. This is not an exaggeration. These are the raw facts of a borstal
(British residential training school) which costs £500 a year. Also, the six
head prefects were expelled last term. Shows how good their choice is.

Mr. Tomkins is a dirty master. He is a horrible master. This school is
horrible. This school is the worst I have been to. This school is full of smokers.
This school should get rid of the cane. I hate a boarding school. The school
food is rotten. They should have decent meals. Too many boys are food
poisoned. There are too many monitors. The food is not very good, especially
sausages; they are always the worst. You hardly get the things you like. The
desks are always broken and windows. Everyone takes everyone else's things.
I have had ten pens pinched and a watch.

I hate the place—being spied on and one's life being pried into by
housemasters and others.

Why is it that residential group care settings, here called internats,[1] are not
always effective instruments of constructive change? For many years, we have
known the what, the why, and the how, and still we have dehumanizing and
destructive residential settings. We hear many loud advocates of deinstitutionalization—not just removing those residents who can be served better elsewhere,
but closing the institutions themselves—and few proponents of revitalization. I
suggest that this attitude exists, among other reasons, because child-care workers,
social workers, and other members of the helping professions are too rarely
interested in organization. They focus their attention on person-to-person contact,
therapeutic interaction, and caring, while organization is left to planners, managers,
and bureaucrats who tend to think and work according to different assumptions
and principles.

This chapter presents some organizational considerations with regard to the
services offered by internats that are important for direct child and youth care
workers as well as administrators and other professionals who work in such
settings.

Who Is the Client?

One can approach the issue of residential treatment from two complementary points of view: its social mandate, that is, whether it meets the expectations formulated by society, or the extent to which residential treatment meets the needs of individuals who are in its care and/or custody. The first perspective pays most attention to the outcomes of residential treatment and little to the process; the second relates to both the process and the outcomes. This chapter postulates that both society's and the individual resident's expectations should be considered and that the intervention process must be conducive to the attainment of satisfactory results at both levels.

The Influence of the Organization

The principal and most influential characteristic of internat care is the encounter between the organization and the resident, because the resident's entire life space is encompassed by the organization, in contrast to other organizations, such as schools and offices, where only a part of a person's life space is affected. Detrimental effects of internat care on the residents are more often attributed to organizational impediments, physical and social, than to maltreatment by individual personnel. To be sure, maltreatment occurs from time to time, but individual maltreatment would not lead to the widely accepted condemnation of internat care as such, except in internats with clearly injurious goals and practices.

Thus, classical studies of internat care usually point to organizational features as the damaging factors [e.g., Spitz 1945, 1946; Polsky 1962; Street et al. 1966]. When the organization of the internat has been subjugated to the requirements of an ideologically or theoretically formulated change program, however, the results have been much more promising and even outright positive [Jones 1953; Redl and Wineman 1951, 1952; Bettelheim 1950; Makarenko 1953, 1955]. The internat's success in orchestrating service delivery is the crucial variable that decides whether life within it will be detrimental or constructive for the residents.

The foregoing is not to say that the interpersonal interaction of staff members and residents is of no consequence or importance. Surely it is, but the interaction must be viewed in the context of internat life. It is not the skills of child-care workers within or outside the internat that are different. In both environments, they must have empathy, tolerance, knowledge, sensitivity, a theoretical framework, practice skills, and so on. Within the internat, however, their activities must be integrated with the internat's environment. They are part of the system, and only if the whole system is well integrated will the outcome be that which is desired.

The Integrated Internat

Integration is defined by *The American College Dictionary* [1969] as "to bring together [parts] into a whole." Thus, an integrated internat is one in which the component parts fit together so as to create a system evolving in a given and planned direction. Perhaps the first image that comes to mind is of a monolithic monster that overwhelms the people who are within its reach. It seems to be more total than the most horrible asylum dreamed about by Goffman [1961], mortifying the soul, devastating the body, and oppressing the spirit. I state clearly and loudly that *this is not what I mean*! What I do mean is that the component parts of the internat are functionally integrated around the needs and capacities of the members—residents and staff.

What Is to Be Integrated?

A well-working hospital is integrated, but its integration is along technical and bureaucratic dimensions. It is a smoothly running, complex organization that may in one sense be very efficient. It may use the most modern equipment and be managed according to the newest ideas of management science. As such, it is probably well suited to render services to a willing clientele who do not need special means of persuasion. Administrators love these internats. So do lay members of society who like to see their money spent "efficiently." Alas, many actual and prospective residents of internats are not voluntary, willing, and ready clients, and for them such an organization may be devastating precisely because of the prevalence of managerial integration.

The four following *organizational* subsystems have been defined as areas within which integration should take place [Shye and Wozner 1978]:

Interaction among various parts of the internat, compatibility of members and procedures

Interaction among various physical components of the internat

Compatibility of roles in the internat

Consonance of values adopted by the internat with those of society at large

Integration in these four areas was suggested as the basis for increasing the internat's quality as an organization. Because the internat is an organization that works *with* people *on* people, however, *personal* subsystems must be considered as well. The four where integration should take place are as follows [Wozner 1982]:

Mental health and mental balance

Physical health

Grasp of the social environment and congruence among social roles

Grasp of values and feeling of morality

In an integrated internat, the two sets of subsystems are brought together to form one system, which becomes the instrument for living. Thus, an integrated internat enables members to practice problem solving, experience novel situations, facilitate learning, learn and exercise skill, and demand gradual responsibility and independence of the members. The intervention techniques are well balanced, the goals are compatible, and a relative consensus exists among staff members regarding policy. The physical components are planned to fit the members' needs and capacities. It is organized so as to promote health and to facilitate physical and esthetic development.

An integrated internat enables its members to enact various roles, prepares them to fit into various social settings, and enables the residents to meet social expectations to gain a sense of belonging. There is a good balance among members' values and belief systems, the effort to develop personal value systems and behaviors fitting them, and the clarification of members' cultural heritage and pride in its behavioral implications [Wozner 1982].

One must not confuse integration with totalitarianism. Integration is a negotiated order by which members agree to act in harmony and objects are fitted together to create an agreed-upon life setting. Integrated internats are not identical; they do not have to be similar to each other any more than families are, for example.

Parameters of Integration

There are four interrelated criteria by which the relative success of integration can be assessed; they are presented here without reference to the order of their importance.

Mastery

Mastery is defined as "the capabilities of an internat's residents, both those helped and the helpers—traditionally called inmates and staff" [Wolins and Wozner 1982: 37]. Organizers of an internat must assess the mastery level of entering residents and establish hypothetically the desired mastery level of residents for discharge. The mastery level of the staff must also be considered. An approximation of the best fit between the two mastery levels is necessary to ensure the constructive functioning of the internat; thus, both undereducated and overeducated staff members may be a hindrance to integration.

Activity

Activity is defined as "the presence and behavior of individuals and objects composing the internat, and includes all objects and actions with their psychological values" [Wolins and Wozner 1982: 37]. The internat is an ecosystem consisting of the integration of buildings, vegetation, staff members and residents, ideas, and things. This system of activity includes the program, the facilities, the social roles, and the cultural matrix, each of which is linked to all the others by feedback loops conveying either positive (OK, Go!) or negative (Wrong, Modify!) communications. The communicators are the staff members and inmates, each of whom acts according to his or her mastery level.

The analysis of each subset reveals additional components that can be seen as the subsets of the subsets. The analysis may be continued to microscopic levels, depending on the nature of the tasks to be accomplished by the internat. Bettelheim, for example, analyzed the significance of "from dreams to waking":

> In the morning particularly, he insisted that the counselor lay out his clothes, but each piece she brought him he rejected angrily. After she had gone through every one of his shirts (some six or seven, or more) and he was convinced she had brought out all he owned, he would condescend to accept one of the ones he had just finished rejecting. The same process repeated itself for his socks, pants, shoes, and so on [Bettelheim 1950: 100–101].

This activity is a part of the program: it is taking place within a physical environment, formalized by role expectations according to certain values. If the theory on which the internat's program was based did not require such minute attention, then dressing in the morning would become an unmentioned action within a larger sub-subset, such as "getting ready for breakfast."

The interactions described by Bettelheim are not only the actual behaviors taking place between the child-care worker and the child, they are the result of an integrated program that (a) allows the worker to spend a long time with one child, (b) provides enough shirts to choose from, (c) allows some flexibility as to when one can eat breakfast, and (d) accepts the value "self-determination" (autonomy) as a part of the child's progress.

Goals

As we have seen, activity is not only related to mastery, but is also strongly influenced by the goals of the members. There are four goal subsystems—resident, staff, organization, community—and two goal categories—overt and covert—within each. Examples of each appear in Table 1.

Each goal set may have an overt and a covert variation. In a well-integrated internat, the goals of each group and in both categories will be similar if not identical.

TABLE 1
Goal System and Categories

Goal categories (by subsystems)	Overt (formal)	Covert (informal)
Goals of the individual residents	To learn, become good citizens	To run away, to get revenge
Goals of individual staff members	To care, teach, help	To get ahead, to get back at colleagues
Goals of the organization	To supply, nourish, rehabilitate	To seclude, to save, to succeed politically
Goals of the community regarding the internat	To reclaim	To punish, to isolate

Deviation of any subsystem causes disintegration or hinders integration. The goals of the individual resident (G1) are often different from those of the other three subsystems, but this may be the very reason for the individual's residence in the internat. Actually, therefore, the other three subsystems (G2, G3, G4) must create a dynamic system that, so to speak, embraces the incoming resident and incorporates him or her into the overall system of goals. In less abstract terms, this means, for example, that rebellious youngsters (whose goals may be to run away, to upset their parents, to subdue their peers, to satisfy their immediate needs) are accepted by the staff members (whose goals are to support, guide, give help to, and direct the youngsters toward learning, working, playing, and developing as creative, self-expressive, and self-reliant persons) in an organization that is planned to carry out such a program and is supported in this endeavor by the community. We shall see further on how complications within the goal systems may interfere with the integration of an internat.

Consequences

Each activity (action) is followed by either a positive (rewarding) or negative (punishing) consequence for those who are acting. The consequence's valence (positive or negative) is always as it is experienced by the actor, not as it is evaluated by an observer or a bystander. Consequences play a major role in controlling behavior, and thus activity. As consequences are evaluated by the experience of the actor, obviously the actor's mastery level is highly relevant. Goals come into this configuration because activity can be either goal-oriented or opposed to a goal and will be rewarded or punished accordingly. Thus, consequences must be integrated with mastery, activity, and goals in a way that ensures that an action on a given mastery level will be rewarded only if it fits the internat's goal system and will be punished (or at least not rewarded) if it does not fit the goal system. Bettelheim's words underline this assertion:

> We also try to organize the child's total life activities so that gradually he becomes able to master more and more difficult tasks .... But this we can do only by creating a general setting in which all experiences are so dosed as to remain manageable by the child .... We retain the dimensions of reality, but we present tasks implied in successful living so that their mastery will strengthen [Bettelheim 1950: 33].

> What is therefore most characteristic of the school is the fact that we try to create a total setting that includes all important activities of the children and permits them to concentrate on unifying their lives. In order to be able to do so, we have to try to eliminate or to control certain other activities or experiences that we consider less important, or even a hindrance [Bettelheim 1950: 31].

Obstacles to Integration

Two general sources of obstacles to integration will be discussed: those that are indigenous to the internat and those that are external to it.

Indigenous Obstacles to Integration

Of the four goal subsystems described above, three are internal and one is external; all are potential obstacles to integration. As long as these are separate goal subsystems, the internal obstacles can be contradictory and conflictual. For instance, the management wants to keep costs down, the child-care workers want to give the children opportunities to express themselves, which is often expensive, and the children want to go about their own business, which is not necessarily parallel to either of the above-mentioned goals. The situation becomes even more complex and potentially difficult when we think about individual goal divergence. In this case, the many individuals who make up the internat's membership go about their own business, creating *anomie*, a feeling of normlessness.

Goal divergence is not necessarily the outcome of willful rebellion; it is often the by-product of different mastery levels, which is actually the usual *raison d'etre* of the internat, at least with regard to the residents. Different mastery levels are expressed in varied and often conflicting activity, which can, of course, be colorful and interesting but also disintegrative. Staff members with different ideas and habits of behavior may relate to each other and to the residents with widely differing approaches, thus adding more confusion to the disintegrating situation. The organization's response to this *anomie* is often repressive. Rules and regulations are invented and enforced (in the name of an ideology of keeping order) to minimize interaction and to bring uniformity to the little interaction that is there as the essential by-product of existence. Thus we have the dehumanizing internat, and, instead of creative integration, we find ourselves moving toward submissive conformity.

Divergent goals, different mastery levels, and conflicting activity—all three together but especially the first—may set the stage for inconsistent consequences, which will probably completely eradicate the possibility of integration.

External Obstacles to Integration

The internat is to a greater or lesser extent an open system. That is, there is a constant, mutual flow of communication and material to and from the internat and its environment. This transaction is the lifeline of the internat, but some of what is transmitted may obstruct its integrative functions. Four categories of potentially obstructing external sources can be depicted.

Clients [Krause 1969]: Persons whose complaints may be alleviated by treatment. These persons can include the families of the residents, who may want to interfere with the internat's policies. Referring agencies may wish to take part in the programming of the internat. The general public often has contradictory expectations and ideas about the allocation of consequences (sanctions) within the internat.

Competitors [Thompson 1967]: Persons or organization who have (or presume to have) a claim on what the internat purports to do. These may be professional organizations and, of course, the families.

Sponsors [Krause 1969]: Persons whose planning and material support are responsible for the provision of treatment.

Regulatory Groups [Thompson 1967]: Those makers of laws and regulations who have the power to interfere with the activity within the internat.

These four sources can generate input in a variety of forms that may severely interfere with the internat's integrative efforts. It is not, of course, possible, nor would it be desirable to eliminate such influences, but it is important to keep them at a level that leaves the internat enough autonomy to go about its business; that is, to plan and carry out its activity.

Suggestions for Integration

The major attribute that is necessary for integration is a unifying theme or ideology [Wozner 1972; Wolins and Wozner 1977, 1982]. The concept of a unifying theme means that the people who share it have common goals and also agree about the means by which these goals can and are to be achieved; that is, a consensus on goals and means exists. A unifying theme can be religious, scientific, political, or pragmatic; the content is not important to the present discussion, except that it should not be anti-people. What is of interest here is that the members of the internat, and especially the staff, should have a set of criteria by which goal-appropriate activity can be judged and sanctions (consequences) can be allocated [Wozner 1979].

Apprehension concerning the idea of a unifying theme is understandable. What comes to mind is a strict, doctrinaire approach, a strong totalitarian regime, which obviously is contrary to a democratic and liberal belief system. A unifying theme need not be totalitarian, however. It can be pluralistic. It can prescribe that people may do, read, write, eat whatever they choose, and that disagreements must be settled by consent, or by voting, arbitration, and so on. The main issue is that whatever modus operandi is decided upon in the internat, it should be accepted and observed by the members.

The two main barriers to the formulation of a unifying theme are differing goals and differing beliefs about means. Both can most easily be alleviated by controlling the size of the internat. The larger the internat, the more difficult it is to have people with common goals and means, and the more power will be needed to obtain consensus, perhaps more accurately termed compliance. Some degree of compliance is needed, but let that be the task of new residents, who will have to pass the compliance phase while adapting to the internat's integrated system.

The second important attribute expediting integration is autonomy; that is, the internat needs the power to make decisions for itself on such matters as intake and discharge policy; the kinds of staff members to be employed (e.g., professional versus non-professional, male versus female, young versus old); program (schooling, work, vocational training); building; and, in general, expenditures. The more the decision-making process in these areas is in outside hands, the less will the internat be integrated [Wolins and Wozner 1982: 57–67].

The degree of autonomy of an organization is connected with the amount of power attributed to it. In non-people-changing organizations, an often-sought avenue to amassing power is to increase size. Organizers of internats may try to increase the internat's power by making it larger as well, not realizing that by this very effort they undermine the effectiveness of the internat as a people-changing and/or people-serving instrument. I believe that the power source of the internat is closely connected with its unifying theme. An internat that stands for something gains power because it is also able to achieve its goals; that is, it delivers. Such an internat cannot, of course, be contradictory to society's norms and values. Thus, an autonomous internat can exist only within a society that allows it to be an internat and regards it as a legitimate, normative framework for people-changing.

Who Integrates?

Internats are run by their members. Obviously, certain members have more formal authority than others, but everybody in the internat has his or her own share in running the show, formally or informally. Thus, to have an integrated internat, all members have to contribute their shares.

Paradoxically, the role of the inmate is relatively simple. The hoped-for path of wards who enter the internat is to reach the stage when they can be bona fide integrators. That is, after they have gone through the changes, transformations, growth, or learning processes that the internat's staff has intended for them, then they are at least figuratively ready to become members of the staff. In most internats, this is when they leave. Therefore, inmates have to be considered as actors whose integrating activity is selective, restricted, or even nonexistent. This does not, of course, mean that they do not act. It means that a considerable portion of their activity may be disruptive and disintegrative, and it must be carefully guided by the staff.

Consequently the staff's role in integration is a major one. In most internats, most of the integrative action is done by the staff; in others, gradual sharing with the wards is possible and even desirable. Differences among internats in this respect stem from population characteristics or from the theory/philosophy that underlies everyday activity. In the Glen Mills School in Pennsylvania, for example, delinquent inmates' integrative ability was developed by guided group interaction [Sherer 1983].

At Summerhill, Neill [1960] attempted to build an integrated internat with an emotionally troubled population by organizing an almost completely permissive environment. Cohen and Filipczak [1971] report on integrative action achieved with delinquents through a token economy, and Makarenko [1955] did the same through ideology and charismatic leadership. These examples—and more could be mentioned—illustrate that whatever the population and/or the theory/philosophy may be, coherent planning by the staff plays a crucial role in establishing integration.

Responsibility for the internat's integration is not equally distributed. Those who have more power have more responsibility, but every staff member has an integrative role. The cook who does not consider the eating habits of the wards together with the nutritional value of the food he or she prepares acts against integration. The teacher who punishes or rewards a pupil against the internat's policy acts against integration. The child-care worker who relates to a youth according to his or her own personal sentiment rather than in accordance with the prescribed program regimen also undermines integration.

Supporting the Integrative Role of the Staff

In essence, therefore, an internat must have a clear-cut modus operandi based on a clearly declared belief system, and a mechanism that guides and enables staff members to act accordingly. Thus, in any discussion of internats, an important matter to deal with is that of staff training and development, yet this is, unfortunately, relatively neglected. Anyone who is close to internat work will undoubtedly confirm that the success or failure of an internat is largely determined by the behavior of the staff.

The staff of an internat is unlike most other groups of workers in its dependence on a relatively small group of people who live in the setting for most of the social inputs that a human being requires to function effectively. Thus, the relatively closed nature of the internat environment affects staff members, obligating them to develop interpersonal relationships that are not always satisfying. This type of environment is liable to breed latent and/or manifest envy, intrigues, and mutual hostility. It may, however, also lead to unusually close cooperation and highly satisfying and constructive interpersonal relationships, provided that most of the members of the staff share the same goals and that the overall direction of the internat is collectivist.

Staff members in an internat live in an atmosphere of tension among several elements:

The Residents

Staff members are viewed by the residents as the persons in authority who are usually charged with getting them to perform. By virtue of this role, staff members depend on the residents to some extent, since the behavior of residents may sometimes serve as a gauge of staff members' effectiveness.

The Staff

Staff members enjoy a certain standing among their fellow workers in the internat. They are in continual interaction with them and must retain their status; in fact, it is only natural to try to improve it. Thus, workers are under continual pressure from fellow workers to conform, on the one hand, and to compete, on the other.

The Family

Work in an internat necessitates a major investment on the part of staff members, but, in addition to dedicated work there, they must also function at home as members of family units. Families' needs may sometimes run counter to those of the internat, and workers must cope with tensions created by the conflict of interests between these two needs and must find effective ways of resolving them.

The Management

The internat management requires that staff members perform certain roles, and the workers, in turn, wish to make a favorable impression on the management. This may lead to complications in relations with fellow workers, with the residents, and with one's own family.

The Staff Member's Professional Group

Most staff members are affiliated with some outside professional group that dictates the norms of their profession. Since this group may be unfamiliar with the demands of work and life in an internat, or in this particular internat, conflict may arise between the professional group's norms and those of the internat. Once again, workers find themselves in a conflict situation as persons on the periphery.

The "Personal" Factor

Every individual has his or her own truths and pet theories. Working in a closed community, staff members may be unable to find a way of airing a personal grievance or disagreement; that too, may interfere with one's intra-internat relationships.

The foregoing six pressure points also exist for workers outside internats, but within the internat setting they are concentrated in a relatively confined space to create a tension-packed social climate that can have a destructive effect on the residents as well as the staff. There are several ways of alleviating this tension, however, some of which may need to be applied more widely and effectively. "Staff development" is a general term that encompasses various activities to reduce tension and to foster desirable interrelationships among the staff members. Several examples follow.

Cultural-Intellectual Activity

In some internats, cultural events are organized from time to time for the staff members by inviting performers to the internat, using people from within, or planning group outings into the community. Programs are also organized on subjects related to the day-to-day work of staff members or on other topics that may interest them.

Group Dynamics

This activity usually takes place in small groups and is meant to enable the participants to express themselves and to work through their feelings toward themselves and others under controlled conditions. These frameworks also provide staff members with an opportunity to receive feedback and to incorporate it into their future behavior.

Personal Counseling

In some internats, each worker is assigned a personal counselor with whom he or she meets at fixed intervals. During these sessions, the staff member and the counselor discuss subjects that are connected with work and that may also affect fellow workers or family.

Ensuring Physically Adequate Living Conditions for Workers and Their Families

Most internats fail to appreciate the importance of this requirement for the improvement of the worker's psychosocial condition. Ways should indeed be sought to satisfy the existential needs of workers and their families as fully as possible. Too often, the upper echelons of management are not sufficiently aware of the need or may even regard the entire subject with a touch of disdain.

Each of these four activities has advantages and difficulties. It would be difficult to make a case for one over another, but it seems clear that a combination of these approaches can be conducive to creating a social climate that will improve the level of operation of the internat. Child and youth care workers can take the lead in promoting opportunities where they do not yet exist.

Training

Another area involving staff members is, of course, the training for their particular type of work. This offers an especially difficult challenge, because relatively few trainers are sufficiently familiar with the unique requirements of work in an internat. Many are specialists in their particular fields, who may be inclined to believe that whatever training they have had is applicable to internat working conditions as well—which is frequently not the case. Work in internats requires a greater degree of functional flexibility, for example, than is required in many other kinds of settings. The quality of one's work is appraised not only in terms of direct output, but also, and perhaps mainly, in terms of indirect output, that is, influence on the residents. Moreover, staff members who have been in an internat for a long time are often unable to keep up with broader developments in their fields, whether because of the closed nature of the internat setting or because of the rigid work schedules and routines that prevail in many of them. These workers need continual opportunities for training and orientation.

It is important to distinguish between what I have called *staff development* and *staff training* and to allot the necessary resources to each in its own right.

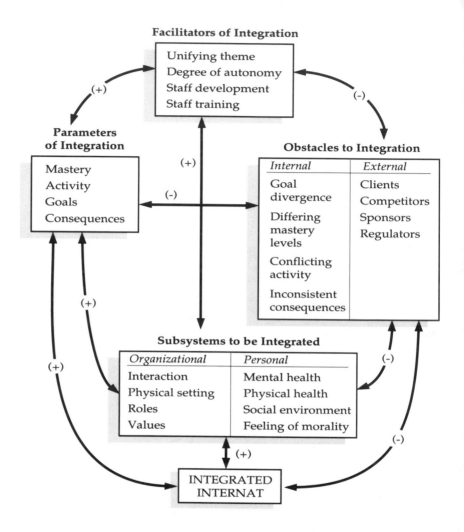

Figure 1. Components of the Integrated Internat.

Note: This is an ever-growing (morphogenic) system. The plus sign (+) means that, when one component grows, the other grows in the same direction. The minus sign (−) means that when one component grows, the other grows in the opposite direction [Maruyama 1963]. That is to say, the stronger the Facilitators, the weaker the Obstacles; the weaker the Obstacles, the more Integration; the more Integration, the stronger the Parameters; the stronger the Parameters, the stronger the Facilitators and the weaker the Obstacles, and so on.

Staff development entails all those steps taken to make it easier for staff members to withstand the day-to-day pressures of living and working in an internat. Staff training comprises those activities designed to teach staff members—before they begin work or thereafter—how to perform their tasks. The tendency to confuse the two terms may detract from the achievement of their differing objectives and of the overall goal.

Conclusion and Summary

In this chapter, integration is described as a major condition in making the internat an effective instrument of direct care. An internat must be organized in an integrated way to become an effective instrument of therapy, change, or any other function it purports to fulfill. Readers seeking to learn more about this may want to reread Bettelheim [1950], Redl and Wineman [1951, 1952], Jones [1953], and Cumming and Cumming [1962], to name just a few who have presented similar views, usually in the context of their psychological theory or belief system. These classics are cited here to remind us all that ideas for good internat care have been present for a long time; it is in their implementation that many programs have fallen short. Perhaps the elaboration here of some of the difficulties and complexities will facilitate understanding of the internat's organizational infrastructure, which needs to be integrated with a psychological and/or humanistic ideology. The concepts that have been presented are portrayed with their interrelationships in Figure 1, which can serve the reader as an overview.

NOTE

[1] "Internat" is a generic name for institutions, residential care or treatment centers, training schools, boarding schools, hospitals, and so on [Wozner 1972; Wolins and Wozner 1982]. More generally, an internat is an organization where people who have no kinship relations live together for the 24-hour sequence of the day under the governance of a central authority for a definite or indeterminate period of time.

REFERENCES

American College Dictionary. 1969. New York: Random House.

Bettelheim, B. 1950. Love Is Not Enough: The Treatment of Emotionally Disturbed Children. New York: Free Press.

Cohen, H., and Filipczak, J. 1971. A New Learning Environment: A Case for Learning. San Francisco, CA: Jossey-Bass.

Cumming, J., and Cumming, E. 1962. Ego and Milieu: Theory and Practice of Environmental Therapy. New York: Atherton Press.

Goffman, E. 1961. Asylums: Essays on the Social Situation of Mental Patients and Other Institutions. New York: Doubleday.

Jones, M.   1953.   *The Therapeutic Community*. New York: Basic Books.

Krause, M.S.   1969.   Construct validity for the evaluation of therapy outcomes. *Journal of Abnormal Psychology* 74: 524–530.

Lambert, R., and Milham, S.   1974.   *The Hothouse Society*. Hammondsworth, Middlesex, England: Pelican Books.

Makarenko, A.S.   1953.   *Learning to Live*. Moscow, USSR: Foreign Languages Publishing House.

Makarenko, A.S.   1955.   *The Road to Life: An Epic of Education* (3 volumes). Moscow, USSR: Foreign Languages Publishing House.

Maruyama, M.   1963.   The second cybernetics: Deviation-amplifying mutual causal processes. *American Scientist* 51: 161–179.

Neill, A.S.   1960.   *Summerhill: A Radical Approach to Child Rearing*. New York: Hart.

Polsky, H.W.   1962.   *Cottage Six*. New York: Russell Sage Foundation.

Redl, F., and Wineman, D.   1951.   *Children Who Hate*. New York: Free Press.

Redl, F., and Wineman, D.   1952.   *Controls from Within*. New York: Free Press.

Sherer, M.   1983.   The incarceration period and educational achievements of juvenile delinquents. *Criminal Justice and Behavior* 10: 109–120.

Shye, S., and Wozner, Y.   1978.   Organizational Quality: A Conceptual Framework and Empirical Study. Jerusalem, Israel: Israel Institute of Applied Social Research (mimeographed).

Spitz, R.A.   1945, 1946.   Hospitalism: An inquiry into the genesis of psychiatric conditions in early childhood. *Psychoanalytic Study of the Child* 1: 53–74; 2: 113–117.

Street, D., Vinter, R.D., and Perrow, C.H.   1966.   *Organization for Treatment*. New York: Free Press.

Thompson, J.D.   1967.   *Organizations in Action*. New York: McGraw-Hill.

Wolins, M., and Wozner, Y.   1977.   Deinstitutionalization and the benevolent asylum. *The Social Service Review* 51: 604–623.

Wolins, M., and Wozner, Y.   1982.   *Revitalizing Residential Settings*. San Francisco, CA: Jossey-Bass.

Wozner, Y.   1972.   *The Modifying Milieu*. Unpublished doctoral dissertation, University of California, Berkeley.

Wozner, Y.   1979.   Positive control in institutions. *Residential & Community Child Care Administration* 1: 187–205.

Wozner, Y.   1982.   Assessing the quality of internat life. *Human Relations* 35: 1059–1072.

PART 4

Broadening the Scope of Residential

Child and Youth Care Work

14

The Child-Care Worker as Ethnographer: Uses of the Anthropological Approach in Residential Child and Youth Care Education and Practice

During our weekly team meetings, I would take a few minutes to read some of my field notes to the team members for correction and feedback. Here are some typical reactions:

"Is this really what we sound like?"

"Could all this make sense to an outsider?"

"Isn't that ridiculous how much time we spent on her?"

"He was speaking all the time, taking all the decisions."

Gradually they started using my field notes to evaluate their group process. These both stimulated them and provided that minimal distance necessary to contemplate their own actions.

R. Eisikovits [1980: 159]

This excerpt from "The Cultural Scene of a Juvenile Treatment Center for Girls: Another Look" illustrates some ways in which anthropological data can be used by child-care workers. This chapter, based on the writer's experience of having carried out an 18-month ethnographic study in a residential treatment center for girls, explores the potential of the anthropological approach for the socialization and professional enhancement of child-care workers. It analyzes the stereotypes and prejudices concerning researchers held by institutional workers as a prelude to understanding the particular nature of the ethnographic researcher/child-care worker relationship to be discussed.

Following a presentation of the major characteristics of anthropological inquiry and its basic conceptual tools, it applies them to the analysis of interaction in child-care settings on various levels of specificity—from the intra-cottage level through the intra-organizational and inter-organizational level to considering their possible effect on the future of child-care work as a profession. A brief historical overview of images of child-care workers in the literature precedes the introduction of the child-care-worker-as-ethnographer model of professional socialization in order to facilitate the logical transition from the idiographic (particularistic) to the programmatic level.

Here are a few explanatory notes about the site where this particular project was conducted and the organizational roles assumed by the researcher during the study. The residential treatment center is a private, non-profit organization for 55 residents, operated by a religious order of sisters. The client population comprises adolescent girls aged 12 to 18 with a range of emotional, behavioral, and social adjustment problems. The residents are referred through the juvenile courts and other social service agencies.

The facility is a modern one in a suburb, with a private lake and a variety of indoor and outdoor recreational facilities. The girls live in five cottages, and each has a separate room. The cottages are designed and decorated to create a homelike atmosphere. A small public school offering a special education program to residents as well as to neighborhood youngsters is located on campus.

While doing fieldwork in this treatment center, I was working in the setting as a part-time "youth counselor" (the local term for direct care worker) and communication consultant. Both roles gave me the opportunity for a firsthand study of the cottage world.

Researchers as "Bad Guys"

The negative or even hostile attitude toward researchers that workers in this setting share with many other practitioners in the human service field [Argyris and Schon 1974; Beker and Baizerman 1982; Bloom 1975; Garduque and Peters 1982; Lindblom and Cohen 1979; Rein 1976; Rothman 1980] constituted a major stumbling block that had to be overcome before rapport could be established. Child-care workers tend to view research activities as investigator-oriented and feel that the researchers usually "conjure up" the research topic to satisfy their own interests: "They use the institution to satisfy their curiosity." Hence, their endeavors are regarded as exploitative and often referred to as hit-and-run activities. "They come, or often just send their students along, have their questionnaires filled out, and vanish."

One frequently voiced complaint concerns the applicability of findings: "They don't care about our problems in the first place. Do they have to stay here to battle with the everyday reality of residential education and care?" Another pertains to the process of feeding back the findings: "That is, when they bother to let us know about them at all. Mostly they end up sending a brief report or a copy of some journal article months or even years later. That, too, is kept up in the office. Never mind the time we put into the stupid project."

Encounters with representatives of the evaluation research world seldom constitute positive experiences for direct care workers, either. Although the research topic might be relevant, the researcher's presence usually connotes change and control, since the researcher is normally asked to come in by the administrative echelons of the organization "when things don't seem to be going all that well." The workers are aware of the fact that the "implementation of findings" means change in their everyday routine, and that is inherently threatening. A general sense of latent suspicion accompanies the workers' experience of cooperating with the outside evaluator, which often entails answering probing questions without the assurance of complete confidentiality.

The line staff members spend long hours in the setting, as a result of which they come to see the world from within the institution, identifying with the residents' perspective. This view in itself is an asset that enables them to form trusting and lasting relationships with their charges. Yet at the same time, it evokes antagonism toward a generalized blanket category of "outsiders" that, in addition to researchers, includes representatives of various social welfare and counseling service organizations. What all these outsiders are considered to have in common is their membership in groups invested with policy- or decision-making power related to the future of these young people whom only they—the direct care workers—claim truly to know.

A Different Approach: The Anthropological Method

What helped to overcome the sense of suspicion was the workers' gradual realization that the anthropologist, for the strange species of researcher he or she is, does not look at the world from the "opposite angle," as Garduque and Peters [1982] put it in their article analyzing the mutual perceptions or respective stereotypes of researchers and practitioners in child-care work.

Instead of taking the atomistic route, whereby complexity is analyzed and broken down into its constituents to produce units amenable to research (as in the neopositivist approach), the first characteristic of anthropological inquiry is the adoption of a holistic approach to any topic studied. Descriptive and analytical in nature, this genre of research favors the mapping of an entire culture-bearing unit before the formulation and testing of hypotheses or the analysis of relationships among clearly defined variables.

The underlying assumption, stemming from the long tradition of studying foreign cultures, is that the investigator is not equipped to ask specific questions before having acquired a plausible level of familiarity with the whole of a culture. The ability to ask intelligent questions develops in the course of long-term, intimate association with the setting, through learning the local language, the social structure, basic life routines, the meanings attributed to major cultural events, and so on. In other words, the investigator is being socialized to do and see things the local way.

For the purpose of this study, the treatment center is defined as just such a culture-bearing unit, with language, norms, values, and social structure of its own. Like most cultural systems, it can be further subdivided into smaller cultural entities according to its various members' major organizational reference groups, all of which are to be gradually uncovered by the outsider [Eisikovits 1980]. According to the anthropological paradigm, the members of a culture (in our case, child-care workers, consultative and administrative staff members, clients, and other actors in the setting) are treated as informants—partners without whom the study would not have been possible—rather than as research subjects. Only through their willing cooperation can the investigators gain access to the kind of in-depth information that they are seeking.

Thus, anthropologists do not play the role of the omniscient researcher who knows in advance the precise object of the study, but rather assume the stance of the culture learner guided by the natives throughout the exploration. Knowledge of the culture is acquired through a combination of participant observation and interviewing of all pertinent categories of informants, both as a validity check on their own insights and to gain an insider's perspective or definition of the cultural experience they came to uncover. The result is a composite picture made up of the views of all members. Only by understanding and portraying this diversity can anthropologists do justice to their scientific mandate: to produce an ethnographic description of the cultural scene studied.

Ethnographers are interested in the subjective realities of all actors; therefore, synthesizing their various positions is impossible. Thus the multiplicity of opinions, beliefs, "truths" that characterizes even such a small cultural setting as a treatment center is given visibility. Since negotiation and transaction of meanings is at the core of all interaction, the importance of discovering the meaning-attribution processes adopted by various participants is underscored.

In the existentialist phenomenological philosophical orientation underlying the anthropological research paradigm, all documented positions are accepted as legitimate. The ethnographer's efforts are concentrated on accounting for them in "emic" terms—an in-house expression for the insider's perspective or the native's point of view—even if in this particular culture the end goal is intervention aimed at changing many of these documented positions or behaviors.

The experience acquired through working with foreign cultures makes anthropologists highly tolerant of diversity. This cross-cultural wisdom teaches them that there are several ways to achieve the same goal, none more valid than the other by any absolute moral canon, as they are all adaptive strategies devised by people to suit their needs and dictated by their ecological conditions—in other words, a stance of cultural relativism.

Like many other small-scale cultures, institutions tend to be highly normative. Their combined correctional and educational ethos presupposes that bringing about changes in clients in narrowly defined, behaviorally specified ways is at the core of their social mandate. Therefore, the importance of the above-mentioned tolerance cannot be overemphasized, particularly in the context of working with culturally pluralistic client populations.

Due to the highly interactive nature of this research venture, in the course of which the ethnographer constantly fed insights back to the informants for verification, the research process itself became a developmental experience for the staff, as the excerpt quoted in the introductory section demonstrates. I gradually became a welcome member of the cottage world as the workers realized that I had grown sufficiently acquainted with their everyday life to be able to grasp their problems in their actual context. Whenever I offered a theoretical reformulation of some question that arose, I always made sure to recast it into the original framework. Thus, the theoretical perspective came to be regarded as a practical alternative way of looking at actual events. This was made possible by the inductive approach to generating abstractions underlying anthropological research, which constantly refers us back to the idiographic or particularistic level as its primary data base.

In my communication consultant capacity, I was present at most team meetings and made a point of explaining how I reached my generalizations, trying thereby to bridge the different conceptual levels. Over time, as the ethnographic perspective took over, it resulted in an upgrading of the level of analysis used in case conferences as well as the level of group discussions during team meetings.

Literature Review

Since there is a qualitative leap between merely describing one such co-operative research venture and putting it forward as an inductively derived model of professional socialization and enhancement, I looked for other studies that highlight the research partnership of child-care workers as an intrinsic developmental goal of the research. To this end, I applied the following questions to the material surveyed.

Who mandated the research?

How did the mandate affect the scope of the research?

What view of child-care workers does the author hold in terms of personality and educational level?

For whom is the author writing? Are line workers the target audience?

What proportion of the information is obtained from child-care workers?

To what extent is the process described as it is seen through the eyes of child-care workers?

Are child-care workers active partners in the research process or just one category of research subjects?

Does the researcher see the results as applicable to child-care workers' everyday activities?

Is the work research-based? If not, on what is it based?

Although only a few illustrative studies are cited here in relation to which these questions will be tackled, one can state in advance that the literature faithfully reflects the history of the field. The dichotomized, elitist view of researchers as knowledge generators and of practitioners as knowledge utilizers [Guba 1968] predominates in the literature, and the overall treatment of child-care workers substantiates some of their previously described prejudices against researchers.

In the 1960s, much research portrays child-care workers as ignorant and non-professional, being "blamed" for that status. Hence, they are seldom addressed as potential knowledge utilizers and are mostly treated as research subjects rather than as partners in the research process. During the seventies, child-care workers are viewed as perfectible. Thus, professional training is increasingly viewed as desirable and, in the 1980s, became more and more a reality, with more than 60 universities in the United States and Canada offering a range of undergraduate and graduate degree programs in child care, youth studies, and related fields.[1]

One of the best-known early examples of qualitative studies in an institutional context in the sixties is Howard Polsky's [1962] *Cottage Six*. Polsky's research mandate, as stated by the institution's administrator [p. 9] was to research a particular cottage that the administration found most problematic and oppositional toward its reorganization plans to "improve their therapeutic endeavors." Cottage parents and counselors were treated as one low-status category made up of individuals with personal histories of occupational failure. Polsky made a clear distinction between the clinical staff members, who interacted with clients outside the cottage context, and the non-professional cottage staff. The integration of professional and non-professional staff members into a unified therapeutic team is the study's message.

The study's overall purpose is given as making "more effective use of the social sciences in the institution's therapeutic program." It is further posited by L.S. Cottrell, Jr., author of the foreword, that "Sophisticated analysis of the social and cultural processes in a given institution is a basic requirement for any intelligent planning for the development of a therapeutic milieu." Reference here is not to cottage staff, as he does not consider this "a job for amateurs" [p. 6].

The research style Polsky adopted did not make the staff members into active partners in his study. He observed and interviewed them as he did the residents. In other words, no direct developmental gains for the staff were expected from the research process. The researcher was invited on the understanding that the findings would be reported to the administration, which would, in turn, implement recommendations according to its own judgment. How this predefined mandate influenced the formulation and scope of the research problem—whether studying the administrative system, for example, as part of the ecology of the institution was at his discretion—we do not know.

The Other 23 Hours, by Trieschman et al. [1969], is another famous volume from the sixties. Although the book is not formally research-based, arising primarily from the authors' extensive experience in residential care, some child-care workers did provide them with notes on their daily activities. Here, too, the authors have in mind a non-professional, low-skilled child-care worker who needs task-specific directions for "managing wake-up behavior," "managing mealtime behavior," "bedtime behavior," and the like, rather than analytically presented abstract materials. In the authors' words:

> Such topics may be useful as supplements, but they can no more tell us how to do our job than the analysis of cement tells us how to construct a building [p. 233].

The child-care worker's intellectual capacity is not the only domain about which the authors are skeptical:

> In much the same manner as a former alcoholic may become an activist in temperance work to regulate his own drinking behavior, so too a child care worker may hold his own antisocial impulses in check by exercising control over impulsive children [p. 227].

Or, even more extremely formulated:

> It is sometimes a moot question whether the child care workers change the behavior of disturbed children more than the children change the behavior of the child care workers [p. 228].

This is a surprising position to be found in a book whose message is to elevate the therapeutic effect of the overall residential experience, yet it finds support in the conclusions reported by Polsky as well.[2]

In the late sixties, more clearly optimistic approaches to the role and education of child-care workers also appear. Polsky and Claster [1968: 177] conclude that the objective should be to upgrade the child-care worker's position by developing in these directions:

> A new concept of child-care work that transcends the custodial emphasis but does not deny its crucial importance
>
> A training program in which workers can develop practical group and community skills and a deeper theoretical understanding of working with residents so as to constantly increase their decision making and autonomy
>
> Recruitment of more competent workers who can be trained to assume these new tasks in child care

They do not, however, spell out the locus (within the agency or in an unrelated, outside institution such as a college or a university), the timing (pre-service or in-service), or the curriculum necessary for attaining these goals.

In their comprehensive and systematic review of evaluation studies on residential treatment programs for disturbed children, Durkin and Durkin [1975] highlight several—Goldenberg [1971], Monkman [1972], Thomas [1972]—that do have staff development for child-care workers among their main objectives. Although they all emphasize the process aspect of research and aim at improving staff performance, they are all considerably pre-structured in program orientation and prescriptive in staff role perception, since they provide "optimal" models for child-care worker intervention. None envisages the possibility of open-ended skill development that can result in changes in all the foregoing areas—which is the promise (or peril?) of the ethnographic model of child-care work offered in this chapter. Tripodi and Epstein [1978] and Thomas [1978] both talk about developmental research, but social workers rather than child-care workers are their target audience, and they do not really envisage an active partnership between researchers and practitioners.

In the 1980s, concern with professionalization, child-care worker education and training, and future trends for the profession were some of the major issues, as reflected, for example, in *Child and Youth Care Forum* (formerly *Child Care Quarterly* and *Child and Youth Care Quarterly*), the main U.S. journal in the field. This chapter can be considered as part of that general effort.

The Ethnographic Model

What do the basic theoretical tenets of the anthropological perspective and the anthropological method—the way the anthropologist goes about obtaining cultural knowledge—as applied to the analysis of interaction in residential settings—contribute to the professional functioning of the child-care worker? The uses of this approach will be demonstrated on several levels of application, from the specific to the more general, in the following order: the intracottage level, the intraorganizational level, the interorganizational level, and the future of child-care work as a profession.

Intracottage Application

We have already discussed what can be gained by applying the concepts of culture, cultural relativism, and the holistic approach to the institution and the various subpopulations of clients and workers within it. Let us now turn to a further elaboration of the anthropological method in its application within the cottage. The reason for starting here lies in the fact that, unlike the bulk of research on residential care (which is addressed primarily to those at the higher echelons of the organization, such as supervisors, administrators, program developers, and evaluators), the anthropological model presented here addresses line workers as its primary target audience. Naturally, this approach does not exclude administrators and others as potential beneficiaries.

The child-care workers in the cottage operate in a highly dynamic universe made up of the intricate interplay among several constantly negotiated and re-negotiated realities, which are characterized in different terms by members of each of these reference groups. They have to be attuned to all these nuances and to be aware of the fact that every intervention affects a wider circle of members.

Therefore, child-care workers must first acquire the skill of "mapping" the various groups involved, their interrelationships, distinctive rules, and ways of attributing meaning and of operation. In other words, child-care-workers-as-ethnographers have to start out as non-participant observers until they gain sufficient cultural knowledge to engage successfully in more active participation. Unlike the ethnographer, whose main objective is to understand the studied culture and describe it through the eyes of its members, the child-care worker's goal is usually intervention as a change agent. Nevertheless, the necessary first step for both is careful and systematic documentation of observed behavior, with a clear distinction between factual description and interpretation.

The log, which serves as a written medium of communication among child-care workers in the cottage, can be turned into a reliable data base. Various techniques can be developed through a team effort to assure "intersubjective" note-taking, just as ethnographers often employ field guides and standardized observation sheets to maximize the accuracy of recording. Such guides serve as reminders of the behavioral areas to be covered and the degree of detail, background information, and verbatim reproduction of speech patterns desired, particularly in cooperative research projects [Whiting et al. 1968; Dobbert et al. 1989].

Elsewhere in this volume, Guttmann suggests that much of what child-care workers are called on to do involves on-the-spot reaction to crisis situations or "immediacies" that do not allow time for preintervention reflection and planning. Nevertheless, since the child-care workers may not be present at the scene of events when such crises occur (one would assume that their presence would often forestall the crises), it is quite feasible for them to start out by clarifying the occurrence and its antecedents before taking any action, unless they are facing an emergency.[3] This task is accomplished by soliciting accounts of the events from a large number of informants (participants) so as to gain a rounded, holistic picture. In addition, this strategy provides youths under their care with a positive model of adult decision making.

In spite of hectic schedules, the cottage work routine has built-in time slots for accomplishing various ethnographic tasks. "Quiet time" and night shifts allow for the child-care workers' own note-taking and analysis, as well as for catching up on the "news" and comparing one's own reading of individual residents' behavioral patterns with that of other team members through the log. Team meetings serve as occasions for more thorough interpretation and collaborative planning.

Intra- and Interorganizational Implications

The cottage and its team constitute a universe unto itself. Its various members develop, as we have seen, a common language and a shared set of values. Due to the amount of time they spend together, there emerges a strong cottage identity that can easily outweigh the sense of identification with the institution at large. This dysfunctional tendency toward closure is exhibited by many human systems upon the reduction of information exchange with other systems, and it is often expressed in unreflective practice or routinization; the holistic view inherent in the ethnographic approach helps to counterbalance this tendency. The relevance of the institution at large, with its combined educational/treatment ideology as the proper frame of reference for effective direct practice, is reestablished.

This holistic vision gains further support from the organizational functions that the child-care-worker-as-ethnographer fulfills outside the cottage, coordinating the residents with the various institutional subsystems, such as school, recreation, health care, administration, and maintenance, as well as with outside agencies [Eisikovits and Eisikovits 1980]. In all these contacts they are, in fact, called on to engage in intercultural translation.

The comparative method, another anthropological instrument, can also be put to use to maintain this wider perspective, by working out a schedule of temporary rotation—an intercottage exchange program—for child-care workers. This arrangement would carry further organizational advantages; it could create an atmosphere of openness and sharing that would encourage the child-care-workers-as-ethnographers to look upon their experiences as a valuable resource from which co-workers can benefit as well, particularly since the experiences will have been carefully documented and systematically recorded. The rotation would also be liberating, because it would free the direct care worker from the isolation of the single cottage, perhaps thereby reducing the notoriously high burnout rate among these workers.

The comparative perspective offers a new paradigm within which one learns to think of one's everyday work in more universalistic categories. A more reflective, flexible, and innovative worker is the end result. In other words, this technique is one possible avenue for unlocking the much-discussed "tacit knowledge" [Polanyi 1967] of practitioners, as is elaborated below in the section on training.

Although it may be self-evident, it should nevertheless be pointed out that the organizational cost of the model is considerable. Layered or hierarchical organizational structure and the child-care-worker-as-ethnographer model are largely incompatible. The latter presupposes a confident and flexible administration that will take the risk of encouraging its direct care workers to become "reflective practitioners" [Schon 1983]. This attitude means being open to grass-roots-initiated change, since the hallmark of reflective practice is ongoing assessment of worker performance and client needs. The direct implication of such a practice modality is a pro-change orientation constantly seeking ways to enhance the quality of care. To keep the staff loyal and motivated, however, the administration must also be willing to invest in higher wages and to provide career advancement opportunities.

Implications for the Future of the Profession

The broadening of horizons that child-care-workers-as-ethnographers experience in the foregoing scenario prepares them to transcend narrowly drawn, task-specific role definitions as well as organizational boundaries. The anthropological skills thus acquired equip them for professional work in a rapidly changing social context. In such a framework, institutional arrangements are viable only as long as they provide the most adaptive organizational response to constantly emerging needs. Hence evaluation—essentially, self-evaluation of performance on all levels outlined above—becomes a sine qua non, an essential condition for continued professional development of individuals and of the field as a whole.

The principal advantage of this model in the context of knowledge utilization is that it offers an organic continuum between raw experience at one end and conceptual practice at the other. The anthropological approach acts as a prism or filter that organizes haphazard child-care work experience into a body of systematized or patterned information, which thus qualifies it to be treated as knowledge. From the latter, culturally informed practice flows.

Although analyzed here in terms of the skills it provides for child-care workers, the ethnographic model cannot be reduced simply to a practice technology. It is a humanistic world view from which a humanistic practice ideology can be derived.

Beker and Maier [1981: 200–201] have written that:

> A major theme that the field will need to confront, one that seems poised to take center stage with regard to a host of public issues and private agendas in the 1980s and holds much promise for our work, is interconnectedness. More precisely, what is new is not the fact of interconnectedness, but the recognition that it exists and must be harnessed in the service of our work.

and

> The awareness of interconnectedness is reflected in changing practice expectations and constraints. The focus has shifted from the boundaries between traditional professional disciplines to highlight multidisciplinary or generic approaches that focus on what needs to be done to ease a particular kind of problem or best serve particular client groups.

With its emphasis on holism, on the importance of context for the interpretation of acts and events, and on the interplay among multiple identities due to simultaneous membership in several culture-bearing units, the ethnographic approach that has been described promises to promote these perspectives, and it offers an operational training model for this emergent type of child-care worker. Anthropology's broad perspective and interest in things human makes it a suitable theoretical umbrella for such eclectic, integrative practice.

Training

Let us now examine the circumstances under which this perspective can best be transmitted: when, where, for whom, and how.

When and Where

Naturally, this perspective is most conveniently taught at the pre-service stage, as part of a formal educational program where curriculum content can be structured into desirable units, and supplementary practicum or fieldwork experiences can be pre-planned and coordinated with theoretical learning. But as the research experience described in this chapter has demonstrated, it can be at least partially transmitted even informally on the job. Needless to say, a series of more formalized in-service training sessions combined with supervised practice and evaluation can maximize on-the-job acquisition of the model.

Blase and Fixen [1981] fault the lack of coordination between pre-service and in-service training in child-care education for many of the shortcomings of the field. The anthropological model can serve as a vehicle for integrating the two. Professionally directed longitudinal field projects for individuals or teams are only one illustration of its potential.

For Whom

The model can be adapted to suit the needs of direct care workers with a variety of educational backgrounds. Like all learning material, it can be dealt with at different levels of terminological and conceptual sophistication. Appropriate field projects can assist all child-care workers to optimize their learning so as to benefit from the model according to their ability. As a result, it is applicable to both the university-educated and the paraprofessional worker. My personal experience in the setting described was with child-care workers of both categories as research collaborators. They all reported this involvement to have been an opportunity for professional development, although that was not one of the original goals of the ethnographic research I was conducting in the institution.

How

The theoretical concepts as well as the field methods lend themselves to experiential transmission and acquisition. Child-care settings provide ample opportunities for illustration (e.g., see above concerning intercottage exchanges of staff members) and experimentation. To achieve the distancing necessary for the ethnographic stance, however, and to allow trainers to experience new cultures, it is advisable to send them to conduct fieldwork exercises in other settings.

They could carry out cultural mappings of social service agencies, such as schools, hospitals, churches, or prisons, or of completely different kinds of institutions such as banks, factories, or retail businesses, to name only a few. Through comparative study of their language, symbolic structures, value systems, and social organizations, trainees grasp the meaning of cultural patterning of behavior.

Simultaneously, they should be introduced to classical anthropological studies of territorially bounded cultural groups such as tribal societies, religious communities, or ethnic enclaves [e.g., Spindler and Spindler] or street corner gangs [Liebow 1967; Whyte 1955] to gain a broader understanding of culture theory. Ethnographic films are another effective didactic tool; discussing the films provides a good context for elucidating ethical dilemmas arising in the field, as well as fieldwork styles and methods.

Conclusion

The ethnographic model equips workers with skills that enhance their on-the-job effectiveness with clients, co-workers, and supervisors, and provides a means of more conceptually sophisticated interorganizational communication with other child-care work professionals. In short, it helps prepare child-care workers to face the challenges of a dynamic, emergent profession.

NOTES

[1] Professional education and status of child-care workers in Europe predates that in the United States [Linton 1971].

[2] All of these authors later emerged as strong advocates for the professional enhancement of child and youth care personnel, and both books remain among the landmark early contributions to this process.

[3] In such a case, if the child-care worker's reaction is later judged as inappropriate (by self, team, or supervisors), it can be amended on the basis of information gathered subsequently.

REFERENCES

Argyris, C., and Schon, D.A.   1974.   *Theory in Practice: Increasing Professional Effectiveness.* San Francisco, CA: Jossey-Bass.

Beker, J., and Baizerman, M.   1982.   Professionalization in child and youth care and the content of the work: Some new perspectives. *Journal of Child Care* 1(1): 11–20.

Beker, J., and Maier, H. 1981. Emerging issues in child and youth care education: A platform for planning. *Child Care Quarterly* 10(3): 200–208.

Blase, K., and Fixsen, D. 1981. Structure of child care education: Issues and implications for educators and practitioners, *Child Care Quarterly* 10(3): 210–255.

Bloom, M. 1975. *The Paradox of Helping*. New York: Wiley.

Dobbert, M., Eisikovits, R., and Pitman, M. 1989. Culture acquisition: Operationalizing a holistic approach. In Pitman, M., Eisikovits, R., and Dobbert, M., *Culture Acquisition: A Holistic Approach to Human Learning*. New York: Praeger.

Durkin, R., and Durkin, A. 1975. Evaluating residential treatment programs for disturbed children. In Guttenberg, M., and Struening, E. (eds.), *Handbook of Evaluation Research* (Vol. 2). Beverly Hills, CA: Sage Publications: pp 275–339.

Eisikovits, R. 1980. The cultural scene of a juvenile treatment center for girls: Another look. *Child Care Quarterly* 9(3): 158–174.

Eisikovits, R., and Eisikovits, Z. 1980. Detotalizing the institutional experience: The role of the school in the residential treatment of juveniles. *Residential and Community Child Care Administration* 1(4): 365–373.

Garduque, L., and Peters, D. 1982. Toward rapprochement in child care research: An optimistic view. *Child Care Quarterly* 11(1): 12–21.

Goldenberg, I. 1971. *Build Me a Mountain: Youth, Poverty, and the Creation of New Settings*. Cambridge, MA: MIT Press.

Guba, E. 1968. Development, diffusion, and evaluation. In Eidell, T., and Kitchel, J.A. (eds.), *Knowledge Production and Utilization in Educational Administration*. Eugene, OR: Center for the Advanced Study of Educational Administration, University of Oregon.

Liebow, E. 1967. *Tally's Corner*. Boston, MA: Little, Brown.

Lindbloom, C., and Cohen, D. 1979. *Usable Knowledge*. New Haven, CT: Yale University Press.

Linton, T. 1971. The educateur model: A theoretical monograph. *Journal of Special Education* 5: 155–190.

Monkman, M. 1972. *A Milieu Therapy Program for Behaviorally Disturbed Children*. Springfield, IL: Charles C Thomas.

Polanyi, M. 1967. *The Tacit Dimension*. New York: Doubleday.

Polsky, H. 1962. *Cottage Six*. New York: Russell Sage Foundation.

Polsky, H.W., and Claster, D.S. (with C. Goldberg). 1968. *The Dynamics of Residential Treatment*. Chapel Hill, NC: University of North Carolina Press.

Rein, M. 1976. *Social Science and Public Policy*. New York: Penguin Books.

Rothman, J. 1980. Harnessing research to enhance practice: A research and development model. In Fanshel, D. (ed.), *Future of Social Work Research*. Washington, DC: National Association of Social Workers, Inc.: pp 75–90.

Schon, D. 1983. *The Reflective Practitioner*. New York: Basic Books.

Spindler, G., and Spindler, L., (series eds.). *Case Studies in Cultural Anthropology Series*. New York: Holt, Rinehart, & Winston.

Thomas, E. 1978. Generating innovation in social work: The paradigm of developmental research. *Journal of Social Service Research* 2(1): 95–115.

Thomas, G. 1972. Community-oriented care in children's institutions. Second Year Interim Report, U.S. Office of Child Development Project No. OCD-CB-106 (as cited in Durkin and Durkin, 1975).

Trieschman, A., Whittaker, J.K., and Brendtro, L.K. 1969. *The Other 23 Hours*. Chicago, IL: Aldine.

Tripodi, T., and Epstein, I. 1978. Incorporating knowledge of research methodology into social work practice. *Journal of Social Service Research* 2(1): 65–78.

Whiting, J., Child, I., Lambert, W., et al. 1968. *Fieldguide for the Study of Socialization*. New York: Wiley.

Whyte, W. 1955. *Street Corner Society*. Chicago, IL: University of Chicago Press.

15

The Development of Effective Child and Youth Care Workers

DONALD L. PETERS
RONALD A. MADLE

Mindy is 23. She has just graduated from the university with a degree in family and child development and she considers her specialty to be youth development. She has studied hard and has achieved a B+ average in her major, though her cumulative overall average was much lower; she did so badly in math and statistics that it really pulled her down. She was an active volunteer while in school, having headed the canned food drive for homeless families, worked with the elderly at a nearby nursing home, and participated at the campus day care center three afternoons a week during her last year. If asked what the most valuable part of her college experience had been, she would not hesitate to tell you about her field practicum course at the Pine Tree Youth Center. There she had the opportunity to confirm her desire to work with problem teenagers, and it led to her current job as a youth care worker at the P.J. Marshall Residential Treatment Center.

Ralph is a six-foot, two-inch, 220-pound balding veteran. He had bounced around from job to job in construction for several years before finding a community where he wanted to stay for a while. To this day, he can't say whether it is the community that holds him, his job as a youth worker, or whether he just got tired of traveling. Anyway, at 35, he has now been here seven years and in his job, four. He laughs about the fact that that's longer than any other job has kept him, including the army.

Sarah is 48, divorced, and the mother of three children. The children are pretty independent: Mary is married, Brad is in the army, and Lee is at the vocational high school. Sarah's neighbor suggested that she apply for the job at the group care center, telling her it was perfect for her; it was close and required only that she cook, clean, and mind the children, in which she was certainly experienced.

In spite of their apparent differences, these three persons have one thing in common. They are all employed as group care workers. Mindy is the most typical of those entering the child and youth care field in the United States at present. Surveys tell us that most beginning group care workers fall in the 23- to 28-year age bracket. About half are female; most are single. About 60 percent have a bachelor's degree [Krueger 1982], but Ralph and Sarah are not atypical. Indeed, Sarah may represent an important aspect of the child and youth care labor force in the next decade or two. This kind of mix of people in group care work seems to be representative nationwide [Ainsworth and Fulcher 1981].

What makes an effective group care worker? Are Mindy, Ralph, and Sarah effective? What knowledge and skills do they need to have? How will they get them? How can we make sure that the knowledge that has been gained in the child and youth care field is used in the work done by these three individuals? How shall we make sure that there is a steady stream of the right kind of recruits for this work?

These are not easy questions to answer, but we will try to provide a developmental perspective (thus consistent with the overall themes of this book) for thinking about the recruitment and development of effective group care workers, as well as a model for their educational and training needs, considering both the individual worker's development and the multiple settings within which that development takes place.

A Developmental Perspective

The three sketches above portray real persons currently working in the child and youth care field. They remind us that when thinking of recruitment and training, we must take a life-span perspective [Peters and Getz 1986]; that is, we must attend to the differences in individual characteristics, abilities, traits, talents, and skills that the workers bring to the work and training situation. Equally important are the changes that take place in these characteristics over time, as a result of employment, training, or other events in their lives.

A developmental perspective involves a holistic view of individuals and the environmental settings within which their development occurs in a complex, changing world over which the individual has some influence. Developmental changes can happen in many aspects of the individual's life, and changes in one aspect of development affected by one part of the environmental setting may proceed differently from other aspects affected by other environmental influences. The reciprocal nature of person-environment influence is implied.

For the first-line supervisor or other person responsible for training, it is useful to think of group care workers as having two concurrent and related patterns of development: one that relates to their work in the residential or community setting and one that relates most closely to their personal development in their home, family, church, and social lives. That is, the work lives of group care workers are defined by their employment environment, both immediate and distal. In this sense, we may talk of their developmental pattern, using the terminology caregiver-as-caregiver. In contrast, the term caregiver-as-person is used when discussing other, more general aspects of personal development. This distinction helps in thinking about the potential and actual reciprocal interaction patterns typical of the life course.

Each individual's personal history and development affect his or her readiness and receptivity for training and work, while at the same time professional development and work experience affect his or her personal development in other aspects of life. We recognize these relationships when preparing a treatment plan for a client, and we need to consider them when planning staff training. We also recognize that, when personnel live on the premises of a group care center, boundaries between personal and work activities are often blurred [Maier 1987].

The life-span perspective focuses attention on the changes that do and/or must occur in the group care worker rather than on the stability of individual worker characteristics. That is, the concern is for inter-individual differences in intra-individual development changes [Baltes 1973; Baltes and Schaie 1973] and the causative factors in these changes, rather than the more typical search for desirable, presumably stable worker characteristics.

It is also important to adopt an ecological perspective for conceptualizing and describing the changing environmental settings of the developing worker, recognizing a hierarchy of settings from most immediate influences to the broadest context of society [Bronfenbrenner 1977].

Finally, we must be concerned not only with the recruitment, selection, and initial preparation of group care workers, but also with promoting their continuing education and development throughout their personal and professional lives.

Approaches to Developmental Theory and Research

Two dominant approaches that are important for supervisors and trainers planning the recruitment and training of care workers are discussed in the literature: the life-task approach and the developmental construct approach.

The Life-Task Approach

This approach investigates the universal tasks that people must accomplish at more or less particular times of their lives if development is proceeding normally. For example, Erikson [1950] has described eight issues or tasks to be resolved by an individual during the life course. The primary tasks from young adulthood to older age are the resolution of identity versus role confusion, intimacy versus isolation, generativity versus stagnation and self-absorption, and integrity versus despair. The individual's resolution of these issues take place within a multi-level environmental context, both as individual development and as historical, societal, and cultural changes that produce cohort and generational effects. Thus, there are identifiable patterns of normative development and inter-individual variations in them.

Mindy seems to have emerged into young adulthood with what Erikson would call a well-resolved sense of identity. She has an awareness of who she is, where she has been, and where she is going. Ralph, though older, seems to be still involved (or reinvolved) in an identity conflict, less sure who he is or where he belongs. At the same time, Ralph's pattern of personal development is more typical (normative) for his cohort, and Mindy's is more typical for hers.

Viewing Mindy and Ralph in terms of their patterns of personal development (caregiver-as-person) can be extended to taking a normative view of typical patterns of events within the life cycle [e.g., Levinson 1977a, 1977b]. Certain personal life events happen more typically within certain age spans and have different meanings or stresses associated with them if they occur outside the typical age span. For example, Mindy is taking her first "serious," paying job after completing her schooling—a typical or normative event.

It is also important to consider the possibility of normative patterns of development associated with work, particularly in the helping professions [Vander Ven 1981, 1988]. In our terminology, this refers to caregiver-as-caregiver development. The work of Fuller [e.g., Fuller 1969; Fuller and Brown 1975], dealing with teachers, typifies an issue or conflict resolution approach in the domain of work similar to that of Erikson in the domain of personal development.

Within either the personal or professional developmental stream, certain characteristics of a person's placement are considered important [Danish et al. 1980].

> *Timing*: Is the timing of life or work events congruent with either personal or societal expectations? This question leads to the notion of being "on time" and "off time" in development.
>
> *Duration*: What is the temporal extent of the event, including anticipation, the event itself, and the post-event influence?
>
> *Sequencing*: Does the event appear in a personally and societally normative order?
>
> *Specificity*: Is the event unique to the individual or cohort group?
>
> *Contextual Purity*: To what extent do the various life and professional events interact and support or interfere with each other?

Understanding these characteristics in both the personal and work domains is important to designing training activities that are developmentally appropriate. For example, Sarah may be considered by herself and others to be "off time" for her initial entry into the work force, and if, after working for a period of time, she sought a bachelor's degree the better to prepare her for her new-found field, her education and work experience would be out of sequence from the norm in the child and youth care field. It would, however, not be entirely unique, since many of her female cohort group are doing the same thing.

Ralph's story can illustrate contextual purity. Ralph might be viewed as falling into a stage of life that Keniston [1971] has called "youth." He has not settled fully his relationship to existing society, his vocational direction, his social role, or his lifestyle, although he seems to be getting close. One of the key sources of difficulty in having youths treat adolescents is the great degree of similarity between the two groups. As a result, youth-stage workers (like Ralph) often decline to take what they consider to be an adult, authoritarian role in setting limits and providing guidance [Sobesky 1976]. Over time, however, group care work and the workers' relationships with the adolescents who need them tend to push people like Ralph toward commitment and responsibility, toward being more effective care workers and more mature individuals. That is, the nature of the work forces development in the caregiver-as-caregiver, which, in turn, produces changes in the caregiver-as-person.

The Developmental Construct Approach

The second and, actually, the most common, approach in the developmental literature deals with psychological, sociological, and biological constructs and studies changes in them over time. Hultsch and Plemmons [1979] have pointed to the wide range of constructs studied, which they have termed resources. For our purposes, these are considered to be the resources that the individual brings to the learning and work situation, including (a) biological factors such as general health or physical impairments; (b) psychological factors such as cognitive abilities and accumulated knowledge, attitudes toward the self, ability to cope with the environment, time perspectives, and general personality traits; and (c) sociological factors such as personal support systems, supportive frameworks of familial and interpersonal relationships, and societal and cultural supports.

Several bodies of literature suggest desirable or essential characteristics for group care workers. Some of these are based upon empirical research, some on experience and common sense. The most common physical characteristics include physical health, stamina, and a high energy level. Psychological characteristics include patience, warmth, nurturance, openness to new ideas, tolerance for ambiguity, flexibility in thinking, maturity of judgment, a positive self-concept, positive attitudes and expectations regarding children's achievement, an understanding of child development, and the ability to translate that knowledge into a consistent pattern of behavior. The sociological characteristics include connectedness to a familial or interpersonal support network (i.e., an outside personal life), sufficiency of economic support, and opportunities to gain recognition and approval.

These factors are likely to affect the degree to which the individual (a) adapts to new situations and is motivated to learn; (b) accepts innovation and training suggestions; (c) uses flexibly the child and youth care skills and strategies taught; (d) functions on a team; and (e) handles work-related stress, including the sometimes conflicting and often draining demands placed upon the worker. In essence, they determine the capability of the individual to function as an integrated human being in both the personal and the professional domains. They are the same characteristics that contribute to or are lost when workers burn out.

To argue that individual characteristics or personal resources are important is not to argue that good youth care workers are born, not made. Indeed, the research on stress and burnout [e.g., Freudenberger 1975, 1977; Maslach and Pines 1977] and the research on the relation of work environment to psychological functioning provide convincing evidence otherwise. It appears that one's current work environment has a definite effect on one's future personality and intellectual functioning, for better or worse.

The sketches of Mindy, Ralph, and Sarah are too brief to give more than a hint of the personal resources they bring to the group care and training situations. They are, however, sufficient to suggest that we could expect considerable, important variability among the three on factors that would be important for planning training.

Curriculum for Group Care Worker Education

We can address group care training with the question, "What does the group care worker need to know?" This is the curriculum content question. We can then go on to two highly related questions: "How will the group care workers best learn it?" "How can we best teach it?" The former requires that we know something about the learner, a matter already extensively discussed; the latter requires that we know something of the options available for curriculum organization and delivery. Finally, we must ask the question, "What should be the criteria of success?"

Foundations of the Curriculum

Child and youth care work is an emerging profession that may be defined functionally. That is, we may consider the functions to be performed by the group care worker in relation to the children and youth in care, in relation to other associated professionals, and in relation to oneself. Some functions are site- and clientele-specific; most are generic to helping relationships with children.

Children under the guidance of adults other than their own families need the same basic nurturance, care, and support as all other children in order to enhance their full potential for growth and development. Child and youth care workers are pivotal persons in their young charges' daily lives. The provision of support for normal development through the application of group care knowledge is at the heart of group care work. Using everyday life events as occasions for social learning, group care personnel seek opportunities for positive interactions to promote personal and social development in members of their group [Ainsworth and Fulcher 1981]. To do so requires full knowledge of how physical environments and group dynamics affect behavior and the active utilization of that knowledge intelligently and consistently, with a particular group in a particular setting.

The task approach discussed above reminds us of the necessity of considering the various aspects of the ecological environment in which development takes place. When considering the development of the caregiver-as-caregiver, the immediate work setting should be viewed generically. The caregivers' role is extremely broad, allowing extensive group and individual interaction with the children and youths in their charge. The responsibilities range from teaching daily living, social, recreational, and self-management skills to carrying out the plans of other professionals, and involve observing and recording behavior firsthand and communicating effectively with other team members. The extent of involvement is relatively unlimited when compared to that of the many other specialists in the children's lives.

In their day-to-day work, group care workers also have a great deal of autonomy. They must and do deal with situations as they arise. They are frequently called upon to carry out their own ideas for individual and group management. They must be able to plan and accomplish a consistent program, select their methods of interaction case by case and situation by situation, and organize materials and their environment to meet the needs of the children in their charge in a consistent, positive, and effective manner. Ideally, they should be planful, flexible, and independent and should act on the basis of a firm understanding of developmental theory. Their effectiveness or lack of it is usually immediately apparent to themselves and others.

In addition to autonomy and immediate feedback, the group care work environment has several other important characteristics. The first is the mix of the children or youths whom it serves. Developmental variability among children is great, even within a single sex and chronological age group. Within most group situations, however, what is most obvious is the heterogeneity of the children and their problems. Yet it is the goal of the child and youth care workers to meet each child's needs—not just in a single academic subject area as might a school teacher, or for just one hour as might a psychiatrist or psychologist, or one at a time as might a speech or physical therapist. Rather, group care workers have traditionally taken on the responsibility for the whole child (and, in some cases, the whole family). This task is, indeed, a formidable responsibility even for one child at a time; multiply it by the number of children or youths in the group and expand the conception across 24 hours a day, seven days a week, 52 weeks a year.

Second, group care workers work more directly with other adults than do many professionals whose focus is children. Not only are there multiple caregivers, specialists, teachers, and the like, involved, but they are generally expected to act as a smoothly functioning team. Frequently, the caregiver will have responsibilities to, and contact with, parents as well. Thus, the caregiver's work environment is exceptionally complex interpersonally; it requires flexibility, openness, and social, communication, and mediation skills, as well as a great deal of personal strength.

Third, certain characteristics of the agency, service system, and broader society impinge on the work situation, such as agency policy, administration and supervisory structure, the relative connectedness or isolation of the setting with regard to the larger community, and the respect and esteem that the group care field is accorded. All bear on the opportunities that group care workers have for personal and professional development and the stress that they may experience during the course of development [Mattingly 1977].

Fourth, quality care requires both skills and knowledge, as well as the willingness constantly to test and extend the validity of the knowledge and skill base.

Fifth, group care workers must understand and protect themselves as persons and as professionals.

Curriculum Content

Even this somewhat superficial functional analysis suggests the range of curriculum content needed by group care workers. Included are the following elements:

Human Development

Human development as intended here is the life-span, interdisciplinary study of the individual from conception to death, within familial, social, cultural, and physical contexts. Central, however, is a concentrated knowledge of development within a particular age range (e.g., child and adolescent development). At the beginning of training, fundamental principles and landmarks in development are emphasized, as are techniques for observing behavioral development. At more advanced levels, consideration of different theories and their support, as well as developmental trends in the areas of physiological, intellectual, emotional, and social development are stressed, along with an appreciation of variations in patterns of development as this relates to both normal and exceptional populations [Ainsworth 1981; Peters et al. 1974].

It is also essential to incorporate consideration of family development and functioning. Teaching sequences that portray the family in all its cultural diversity as a major socialization influence and foundation of individual development are important.

Intervention

Included with intervention is a range of historical, programmatic, and policy considerations that allow group care practitioners to see themselves within the larger framework of human services helping professions: study of the organizational structure of human services delivery; the underlying political, social, and economic concerns; the history of services; the principal programs and methodologies; the key figures in the field; and the observable evolution and trends. Also considered are such areas as legislation, ethical issues and concerns, geographical and organizational diversity, as well as the range of interventions—for example, informal to formal; private sector, public sector; primary, secondary, and tertiary prevention—from least to most restrictive alternatives.

Until this point, we have been talking about what may be called the substantive knowledge base within the group care worker curriculum. This aspect is only half the story. The other half is skills.

Interpersonal Skills

In the work environment of the child and youth care worker, caregivers work with and through people in their roles as change agents. They also need people for their own personal and professional development. To be successful requires skills as a listener as well as a talker; knowledge of and skill in the manipulation of group dynamics; flexibility in using interpersonal skills to be a friend and a manager, a supervisor and an advisor. These skills can be taught and learned.

Group Care Skills

The potential range of specific and general group care skills that a child and youth worker might need or like to know is extraordinarily large. Indeed, most of this volume deals with just those skills, understanding their basis, and knowing how to use them and how to adapt them to different individuals and situations. Table 1 provides one listing of the kinds of skills and methods deemed important [Peters and Kelly 1982].

Knowledge-Generation Skills

To provide a means for their personal and professional development, group care workers also have to know how to acquire new ideas and new information. This process includes using library resources; reading professional journals; participating in workshops and professional seminars; and gathering, interpreting, and using empirical data for decision making. The level of sophistication varies from worker to worker, but these skills, at some level, are essential for all.

Child and Youth Care Worker
Preparation Activities

Although there is general agreement about what child and youth care workers need to know, there is less certainty about how to ensure that they have the requisite knowledge and skills. Curriculum content, curriculum organization, and

TABLE 1
Child Care Skills and Methods

1. Caregiving and teaching methods, including but not limited to:
   Communication skills (e.g., verbal and non-verbal communication, listening, reflective listening)
   Modeling
   Contingency management and discipline
   Structuring the environment and routines
   Play and play techniques
2. Program planning and implementation, including but not limited to:
   Analysis and critique of the philosophical and theoretical bases of activities and plans
   Client-needs assessment
   Establishing goals, implementing plans, and evaluating goal attainment
   Short- and long-term program planning (selecting, organizing, and sequencing materials and experiences)
   Varieties of program content (e.g., language and communications, creative endeavors, self-help, life skills)
3. Alternative modes and levels of intervention, including but not limited to:
   a. Therapeutic or remedial
      Individual (e.g., behavior modification, psychodynamic, humanistic, cognitive therapies)
      Group (e.g., self theory and gestalt, transactional analysis)
      Family (filial therapy, family counseling)
   b. Preventive and educative
      Individual (e.g., behavior modification, peer tutoring, and the like)
      Group (e.g., Head Start, Follow-Through)
      Family (e.g., home-based programming, parent involvement)
   c. Psychobiological and medical
4. Administration and supervision, including but not limited to:
   Policies, regulations, and the law
   Public relations
   Personnel management, team collaboration, and staff development
   Budget planning and management
   Program and personnel evaluation
5. Advocacy, including but not limited to:
   Understanding the political process, governmental structure and function
   Organizing, lobbying, and networking
   Laws and regulations affecting children and families

methods of curriculum delivery are all interrelated. The way we approach these matters is often based upon our beliefs about the nature of the client's individual development, the substantive focus of the group care field, and what constitutes high-quality group care. Less often is the nature of the group care workers' development considered in designing a curriculum. A consistent overall framework is needed, however, for understanding the relationships between individual client development and the developmental status of the group care worker. As has been noted previously, understanding of the ecological settings in which group care workers function can also be critical in establishing effective training and educational activities for the workers that will carry over into day-to-day application. This is particularly evident when training is taking place within an existing group care program, or when the group care worker has previously learned content different from that which is now being taught.

Preparation occurs at multiple levels, from a virtual absence of formal preparation to highly structured educational programs resulting in credentials ranging from certificates to doctorates. Although some in the field believe that the use of individuals without credentials should be minimized, untrained workers and volunteers entering the group care field will probably continue to be needed, as is evident in the substantial number of job titles representing aide-level functioning under the direct supervision of professional workers. Program administrators should provide for explicit, sequenced career ladders based on the principles of adult education, rather than the more rigid credentialing approaches that have traditionally existed in professions such as law, psychology, social work, and elementary and secondary education. Another contributing factor is the increasing tendency toward second (or even later) careers and the effect that this trend will have on the group care field.

Adult-Centered Continuing Education and Training

Group care workers such as Mindy, Ralph, and Sarah have already participated in various types of training and educational activities. Mindy, for example, graduated from a bachelor's degree program in child and family studies. This kind of educational preparation has typically been referred to as pre-service training— preparation received by those not yet working in the field to prepare them for entry-level positions—a requirement for virtually all professional careers.

Ralph and Sarah did not receive this type of educational preparation before actually beginning work in the group care field. They will presumably obtain the knowledge and skills needed to function effectively in their positions through educational and training activities that take place after they begin work, commonly referred to as in-service training. These agency-based activities do not usually afford academic credit, but community-based training during the course of work, tailored to agency personnel, may carry degree-oriented academic credit.

In all cases, though, it is evident that group care workers can expect to receive various educational experiences at different points in their work and personal development. We will be focusing our discussion of education and training activities primarily on the in-service and during-service [Peters 1988] components of group care worker development.

The purpose of a preparation activity also merits attention [Madle 1980]. Preparation efforts can be viewed as falling on a continuum from the transmission of a basic set of knowledge and problem-solving methods (education) to information and job skills specific to the agency that are needed in day-to-day work with clients (training). This is not an arbitrary distinction, but one that can have a significant influence on the receptivity of adult learners, especially as related to stages in life tasks in adult development.

Many adult learners feel threatened by activities perceived as "school," which they regard as for children and youths, not adults, a perception often heightened by the traditional trappings of academia found in many educational programs: classrooms, prestigious instructors, highly structured curricula, and so forth. Some of this reaction can be traced reasonably to the usual sequencing of developmental life events. Many adults feel that the preparation for a career should take place before obtaining a job. In addition, group care workers who have had personal experience similar to their present work often react negatively to the timing of formal preparation; they may feel that it is inappropriate to receive instruction in caring for children or youths similar to those they have already cared for in their families. Requiring additional training is often interpreted as an implicit indictment that their past performance may have been inadequate. Sarah might be a prime candidate for this type of reaction, since she has previously been involved in child-care activities.

These reactions of adult learners can be modified significantly if adult development principles are considered in program design. Three characteristics of education and training are particularly important in determining what the adult learner might see as the perceived relevance and advantages of the training and education [Peters and Kostelnik 1981].

> The degree to which the content of the instruction is generated or at least endorsed by the adult learner
> The degree of independence versus structure afforded the learner in acquiring the knowledge and skills
> The degree of correspondence between what is learned and what is demanded in the work setting

Group care workers, as adult learners, quickly begin to weigh whether the material and skills learned in an educational activity will contribute to their effectiveness on the job and in future positions or learning, and whether these activities will affect personal as well as occupational development.

Educational and Training
Needs Assessment

One of the earliest stages in the development of any overall plan for group care worker training and education should be the completion of a thorough training needs assessment. Although for many agencies this stage means asking employees what coursework they need or having a director dictate what is needed, it should actually be a much more involved process that examines needs from three perspectives: the organization, the job, and the person [Goldstein 1974]. An assessment that adequately covers these areas will begin to involve the adult learner and address the concerns brought out by Peters and Kostelnik [1981], as noted above.

Organizational Assessment

This level of assessment requires a thorough analysis of the needs of the employing organization (day treatment center, institution, and the like). What types of problems are encountered in delivering services to the clients? Are they due to human performance problems? If so, do the staff members have the needed skills and knowledge to perform the tasks expected of them? If they do, then do supervisors have the needed skills to make the most of the group care workers' talents? This type of analysis develops a picture of the organization's performance problems and strengths and points up what types of additional knowledge and skills the staff may need in order to improve the overall effectiveness and efficiency of the organization.

Job Assessment

A traditional analysis of the knowledge, skills, and abilities needed by workers in specific positions is the second task. It involves examination of the job tasks to be performed and the competencies needed by the existing staff in order to perform them. This stage is particularly critical because person assessment amounts to little without a job assessment.

Person Assessment

The third component of training needs assessment considers the current developmental and skill levels of each worker and how these relate to the job to be accomplished. Although this assessment is often done for new staff members, especially those such as Ralph and Sarah who lack formal educational credentials, it is needed for all staff members periodically. Positions change over time. New skills are needed. Existing skills become weakened or out of date. Perhaps somehow the formal educational program never really taught a skill that has been assumed to be present. In addition, individuals are promoted to positions for which they are not fully prepared. Probably the most common example of this situation is the youth care worker who becomes a supervisor or program manager. Here is where the notion of career development comes into play; that is, education and training must accomplish more than enabling a person to perform certain job tasks; they must provide for a sequence of activities, planned with the worker, optimizing the professional and personal development of the worker.

The training needs assessment is particularly germane to the first characteristic listed by Peters and Kostelnik [1981]: the degree to which the content of an activity is generated and/or endorsed by the adult learner. Although this factor is typically considered in person assessment, it is often ignored in job and organization assessments. It need not be, however. Youth workers can be asked for input into these assessments or, consistent with current "participative management" concepts [e.g., Pascale and Athos 1981], the assessments can actually be conducted at stipulated intervals by groups of workers, with appropriate guidance. This approach significantly increases the perceived relevance of the training.

Structure and Delivery of Education and Training

Certain types of educational programs directed at children can have a substantial negative effect if they are used with adults who have not satisfactorily resolved their identity/role-confusion conflicts. Program delivery must deal effectively with this difficulty. A frequently encountered issue here is that highly directive learning experiences, where the method of learning is dictated by the instructor, increase the similarity of the education and training program to pedagogical models of instruction. Adherence to the adult education model initially posed by Knowles [1970] gives increased control to the participants, under appropriate guidance, in determining program content and structure, and creates a less didactic, more group-oriented delivery. This model recognizes that adult learners are independent and able to make and carry out decisions; have varying responsibilities, backgrounds, experiences, needs, and interests; and respond best to learning that is centered on real-life problems rather than "subject matter" [McLagan 1978]. Another factor that capitalizes on adult status is individualized learning [e.g., Johnson and Johnson 1975], which tailors objectives and learning methods to the learner's needs.

Daily Application of Education and Training

Strategies for group care worker development are also important in their linkage to the overall problems of developing and administering group care programs. When program administrators install new methods or ideas and, as part of this change, train their staff members accordingly, the staff members frequently fail to use the new knowledge and skills when they return to the group care setting. What can be done about this problem, which exists in virtually all types of programs? How can the outcome of a training program be translated into job behavior?

Here we will consider some of the factors mentioned by Allen and Silverzweig [1976] under the concept of group norms; similar ideas can be found in most discussions of transfer of training to the actual work environment. The point should first be made, however, as stressed by Gilbert [1978], that while the immediate cause of a problem (e.g., failure to use training provided) may lie primarily with the person or in the work environment, the ultimate cause will always be a deficiency in the management system. That is, the responsibility for transferring trained skills into practice rests unequivocally on the shoulders of those running the group care program.

Leadership Commitment

The first important consideration is the role and commitment of the supervisory staff, which requires that the administrators must be committed to more than the training program alone. Too often, administrators support training as a substitute for effective supervision [Madle 1982]. Without leadership commitment, the learning is likely to remain intellectual, with little or no carryover to the learner's functioning. Training programs exist as methods of developing new behaviors and skills that must be supported on the job, not as independent activities.

Modeling of Desired Behavior

Prestigious members of a group usually serve as effective models; others readily copy the behaviors they exhibit. The modeling may not be a planned part of the formal training program (although it probably should be), but it is an essential element in obtaining functional transfer. Yet the absence of modeling by experienced and supervisory staff members is frequently one of the obstacles to translating new approaches into the program. Many supervisory staff members, selected for their positions because of past technical competence in direct practice roles, tend to cling to their past behaviors. This tendency results in modeling behaviors that may conflict with those being taught in a training program. What is implied here is that both supervisors and experienced workers must accept the training prior to the line staff, so that both the former groups will feel committed and secure enough to be good models. Clearly, they need to receive training in the same skills being taught to the rest of the program staff very early in the implementation of a new program.

Feedback of Information

If new forms of behavior are expected as a result of a training program, then the educational component within the supervisory process has to reflect the importance of this behavior [Blanchard and Johnson 1982], such as through frequent supervisory conferences and posting of the number of training sessions held. Program staff members need regular, systematic information on the degree to which their behavior in the program setting is meeting the expectations of the administration. Numerous factors must be considered in determining whether feedback should be given on individual and group performance, who should give it, how often it should be given, and so forth [Fairbank and Prue 1982].

Recognition and Reinforcers

Group care workers require motivation to take the time and effort to change their behavior. In addition to information feedback, they need to receive frequent and regular reinforcers, such as recognition of performance, supervisor praise, and the opportunity to participate in program decision making, for incorporating learned behaviors into the job setting.

Work-Group Support

Fragmented training efforts directed primarily at individual workers often result in little more than a rapid loss of skills when the group care worker returns to the work setting, because the lack of work-group support for the trained behaviors prevents, or at least inhibits, new skills from being regularly displayed. This result is most often observed when one or two staff members attend isolated courses, as opposed to a situation in which a group-oriented training program is designed to introduce changes into the whole system. When a sufficient number of individuals in the same work setting are trained, changes in their behaviors are much more likely to occur. It has been estimated that training of at least 30 percent of the individuals in a setting is required to achieve this type of "critical mass" [Keller 1983]. Training directed at on-the-job teams of workers is typically considered the most valuable in promoting transfer of new skills to a job; work-group members are able to provide support (above and beyond the supervisors' efforts) for using new skills on the job. The need of supervisory staff members for a formal program preparing them for their positions, which is often overlooked, is critical as well.

Professionalization of the Group Care Field

It has increasingly been pointed out [e.g., Spodek et al. 1988; Almy 1982] that group care work has been a relatively low-status field, lacking some of the defining features of a profession [cf. Bayles 1982]. Movement toward the establishment of group care (under a number of titles, such as human services) as a fully professionalized field has been taking place over the past several years, as may be seen in the growth of college- and university-level training programs, efforts at credentialing (such as the Child Development Associate program), and registration or certification. A need exists for a consistent and uniformly accepted code of ethics. One of the difficulties in generating this professionalism is that group care has usually been perceived as a subspecialty of various other professions such as education, social work, or nursing.

The movement toward professionalization has not, however, been universal. Dissenting voices have asserted that professionalization will inhibit the warm, caring relationship between the worker and the client. Others feel that this movement will greatly increase the costs of group care programs. Arguments analogous to these can be found in any field moving in a similar direction. Indeed, psychologists in the United States are currently experiencing similar difficulties in the move to make psychological practice an independent profession. Herein, though, may lie the dilemma with which professionalization efforts in group care work must grapple. Professionalization of a field of practice does not necessarily require that all workers within the field be recognized as professionals capable of independent functioning. Some have suggested that professional credentialing should occur only at the program director or supervisory level. Perhaps a refined system of multiple levels (e.g., a registry through a certificate to a credential reflecting high competence) would be desirable in this arena. It seems that any attempts at professional credentialing will need to acknowledge that many group care workers enter the field at relatively untrained levels and function as para-professionals for a significant period of time.

The Dilemma of the Reward Structure

Given the current economic and social climate in most countries and the incongruity that exists between lip service to the importance of child and youth care and the reality of the reward structure for child and youth care workers, in all likelihood the field will continue to experience the recruitment of the untrained and the relatively rapid loss of the experienced. Therefore, we are faced with the continual need (a) to find the most able and most trainable, (b) to provide individualized and effective (though inexpensive) training, and (c) to develop internal reward structures that provide for the personal and professional development of workers without the tangible resources and contextual supports of the larger society. That is, we need to work constantly toward what Erikson [1950] calls *community* (the sense of belonging and of being part of a shared enterprise with common values and goals), and *diversity* (encouraging individuals to continue to grow and explore by providing a variety of opportunities and challenges that encourage self-actualization). Yet we must also operate within institutional and societal structures that are principally concerned or preoccupied with matters of fiscal accountability and self-preservation.

To meet the needs of group care workers and, ultimately, those of the children and youths they serve, requires careful adherence to a developmental perspective that recognizes individual differences in personal and professional development. To meet the needs of economy and efficiency requires equal care in the design of training that "takes" and will be carried forth in the work setting. Both concerns require careful planning.

REFERENCES

Ainsworth, F. 1981. The training of personnel for group care with children. In Ainsworth, F., and Fulcher, L.C. (eds.), *Group Care for Children: Concept and Issues*. London, England: Tavistock.

Ainsworth, F., and Fulcher, L.C. (eds.) 1981. *Group Care for Children: Concept and Issues*. London, England: Tavistock.

Allen, R.F., and Silverzweig, S. 1976. Group norms: Their influence on training effectiveness. In Craig, R.L. (ed.), *Training and Development Handbook: A Guide to Human Resource Development*. New York: McGraw-Hill.

Almy, M. 1982. Interdisciplinary preparation for leaders in early education and child development. *Advances in Early Education and Day Care 2*: 61–89.

Baltes, P.B. 1973. Prototypical paradigms and questions in life-span research on development and aging. *Gerontologist 13*: 458–467.

Baltes, P., Reese, H., and Lipsitt, L. 1980. Life-span developmental psychology. *Annual Review of Psychology 3*: 65–110.

Baltes, P.B., and Schaie, K.W. 1973. On life-span development research paradigms: Retrospects and prospects. In Baltes, P., and Schaie, K. (eds.), *Life-Span Developmental Psychology*. New York: Academic Press.

Bayles, M.D. 1982. *Professional Ethics*. Belmont, CA: Wadsworth.

Blanchard, K., and Johnson, S. 1982. *The One-Minute Manager*. New York: Morrow.

Bronfenbrenner, U. 1977. Towards an experimental ecology of human development. *American Psychologist 33*: 513–532.

Danish, S., Smyer, M., and Novak, C. 1980. Developmental intervention: Enhancing life event processes. In Baltes, P., and Brim, O. (eds.), *Life-Span Development and Behavior* (Vol. 3). New York: Academic Press.

Erikson, E. 1950. *Childhood and Society*. New York: Norton.

Fairbank, J.A., and Prue, D.M. 1982. Developing performance feedback systems. In Fredericksen, L. (ed.), *Handbook of Organizational Behavior Management*. New York: Wiley.

Freudenberger, H. 1975. Staff burn-out. *Journal of Social Issues 30*: 159–165.

Freudenberger, H. 1977. Burn-out: Occupational hazard in child care work. *Child Care Quarterly 6*: 90–99.

Fuller, F.F. 1969. Concerns of teachers: A developmental conceptualization. *American Educational Research Journal 6(2)*: 207–226.

Fuller, F.F., and Brown, D. 1975. On becoming a teacher. In Ryan, K. (ed.), *Teacher Education*. Chicago, IL: University of Chicago Press.

Gilbert, T.F. 1978. *Human Competence: Engineering Worthy Performance*. New York: McGraw-Hill.

Goldstein, I.L. 1974. *Training: Program Development and Evaluation*. Monterey, CA: Brookes-Cole.

Hultsch, D., and Plemmons, J. 1979. Life events and life-span development. In Baltes, P., and Brim, O. (eds.), *Life-Span Development and Behavior* (Vol. 2). New York: Academic Press.

Johnson, R.B., and Johnson, S.R. 1975. *Toward Individualized Learning: A Developer's Guide to Self-Instruction*. Reading, MA: Addison-Wesley.

Keller, G. 1983. *Academic Strategy: The Management Revolution in American Higher Education*. Baltimore, MD: The Johns Hopkins University Press.

Keniston, K. 1971. *Youth and Dissent*. New York: Harcourt Brace Jovanovich.

Knowles, M.S. 1970. *The Modern Practice of Adult Education: Andragogy versus Pedagogy*. New York: Association Press.

Krueger, M. 1982. *Professional Growth and Development of Child Care Workers*. Milwaukee, WI: Tall Publishing.

Levinson, D. 1977a. The mid-life transition: A period of adult psychological development. *Psychiatry 40*: 99–112.

Levinson, D. 1977b. Middle adulthood in modern society. In DiRenzo, G. (ed.), *Social Character and Social Change*. Westport, CT: Greenwood Press.

Madle, R.A. 1980, November. *Developing Training Structures for Child Care Personnel: Comments on Almy's Paper*. Paper presented at the Conference/Research Sequence in Child Care Education, Pittsburgh, PA (ERIC Document Reproduction Service No. 214 657).

Madle, R.A. 1982. Behaviorally-based staff performance management. *Topics in Early Childhood Special Education 2*: 73–83.

Maier, H.W. 1987. *Developmental Group Care of Children and Youth*. New York: The Haworth Press.

Maslach, C., and Pines, A. 1977. The burn-out syndrome in the day care setting. *Child Care Quarterly* 6: 100–113.

Mattingly, M.A. 1977. Sources of stress and burn-out in professional child care work. *Child Care Quarterly* 6: 127–137.

McLagan, P.A. 1978. *Helping Others Learn: Designing Programs for Adults*. Reading, MA: Addison-Wesley.

Nadler, L. 1979. *Developing Human Resources* (2nd ed.). Austin, TX: Learning Concepts.

Pascale, R.T., and Athos, A.G. 1981. *The Art of Japanese Management: Applications for American Executives*. New York: Simon and Schuster.

Peters, D.L. 1988, November. Current issues and future needs in staff training. Paper presented at the National Policy Conference on Early Childhood Issues. Washington, DC: U.S. Department of Education. Available through ERIC Clearinghouse on Elementary and Early Childhood Education.

Peters, D.L., Cohen, A., and McNichol, M. 1974. The training and certification of early childhood personnel. *Child Care Quarterly* 3(1): 39–53.

Peters, D.L., and Getz, S. 1986. Getting beyond the robot model of the child care worker. In Vander Ven, K., and Tittnich, E. (eds.), *Competent Caregivers—Competent Children*. New York: The Haworth Press.

Peters, D.L., and Kelly, C. 1982. Principles and guidelines for childcare personnel preparation programs. *Child Care Quarterly* 11(3): 222–234.

Peters, D.L., and Kostelnik, M.J. 1981. Current research in day care personnel preparation. In Kilmer, S. (ed.), *Advances in Early Education and Day Care*. Greenwich, CT: Jai Press.

Sobesky, W.E. 1976. "Youth" as child care workers: The impact of stage of life on clinical effectiveness. *Child Care Quarterly* 5: 262–273.

Spodek, B., Seracho, O., and Peters, D. 1988. *Professionalism and the Early Childhood Practitioner*. New York: Teachers College Press.

Vander Ven, K. 1979. Developmental characteristics of child care workers and the design of training programs. *Child Care Quarterly* 8(1): 100–112.

Vander Ven, K. 1981. Patterns of career development in group care. In Ainsworth, F., and Fulcher, L. (eds.), *Group Care for Children: Concept and Issues*. London, England: Tavistock.

Vander Ven, K. 1988. Pathways to professional effectiveness for early childhood educators. In Spodek, B., Saracho, O., and Peters, D. (eds.), *Professionalism and the Early Childhood Practitioner*. New York: Teachers College Press.

Epilogue: A Brief Conceptual

Integration

JEROME BEKER

ZVI EISIKOVITS

Given that the range of material in this volume represents essential areas of mastery for child and youth care workers today, readers may seek to identify the conceptual common denominators that tie the specifics together and guide effective knowledge utilization as new situations and needs arise. In this context, the editors would emphasize the importance of three basic perspectives—developmental, ecological, and experiential—in which practice should be rooted, as well as the need to be constantly alert to the implications of emerging knowledge and to the continuing flux of client needs and service system change.

A *developmental* perspective characterizes a setting in which, at least ideally, all structures, activities, relationships, program expectations, and the like are appropriate to the developmental level and needs of those involved. Within an *ecological* orientation, contextual influences encompassing the intrapersonal, interpersonal, organizational, and societal/cultural domains are taken into account in an effort to provide an integrative developmental experience that is relevant to post-institutional life as well as to the immediate situation. The *experiential* element emphasizes the importance of focusing not only on how young people in care perceive what happens to them, but also on how direct care workers experience their role and interactions. Only in that context can they exercise what we have described as educated intuition; only then can they fully exercise the "people-building" function that lies at the heart of their role.

The editors recognize that this book presents an ambitious challenge to a field that has too frequently fallen victim to both inadequate vision and inadequate knowledge, yet experienced child and youth care workers everywhere will agree, we believe, that it does not overstate the need. Most have taken up the challenge with great enthusiasm and faith, and the results of their striving have provided vast intangible rewards in the face of social structures that too often withhold commensurate material ones. Along with the authors, we hope that the book will contribute substantially to the effectiveness of the work and to the human sensitivity and technical expertise as well as the satisfaction and fulfillment of the workers. It is with this objective that the project was initiated, and this is the objective with which we now conclude, awaiting with interest and anticipation other works that will lead to even more sophisticated and effective practice in the years ahead.

About the Contributors

Co-Editors

Jerome Beker, Ed.D., is Professor in the Center for Youth Development and Research (which he directed for ten years) and the School of Social Work, and Adjunct Professor in the Department of Educational Psychology, University of Minnesota. He is a graduate of Swarthmore College and received his master's and doctoral degrees from Teachers College, Columbia University. Among his previous positions were faculty appointments at Syracuse University and the State University of New York at Stony Brook and research appointments with several leading child and youth care agencies. Earlier, Dr. Beker held direct and supervisory positions in child and youth care and related areas. He is Editor, *Child and Youth Care Forum* (formerly *Child and Youth Care Quarterly*) and *Child and Youth Services*, serves on the editorial boards of other journals in the field, and has authored several books and numerous articles and chapters. His professional interests include residential and community group care for youths and the development and professionalization of group care personnel. He is a former board member of the Association of Child Care Workers (New York State), a current board member of the Minnesota Association of Child and Youth Care Workers, and has been involved in the field in Canada, Israel, and South Africa, as well as in the United States.

Zvi Eisikovits, Ph.D., is Senior Lecturer in the School of Social Work and Director of the Center for Youth Policy at the University of Haifa in Israel. A graduate of the Hebrew University of Jerusalem, he completed his doctorate in education at the University of Minnesota, where he more recently received his M.S.W. Previous to his academic career, he worked extensively with troubled youth in community and residential settings as a gang worker and as director of youth services and director of a community center in Jerusalem. He is presently directing a program for graduate education of middle managers in youth services in Israel. Dr. Eisikovits, who is particularly interested in working with troubled adolescents in residential care, family violence, and practice-based knowledge, has published frequently in the field and in related areas and continues to be professionally active in the United States as well as in Israel.

315

Contributing Authors

Mordecai Arieli, Ph.D., an educational sociologist with wide experience in Youth Aliya and other group care agencies, is a Lecturer in the School of Education, Tel Aviv University.

F. Herbert Barnes, M.S.W., A.C.S.W., is President, Youthorizons, Portland, Maine, and Adjunct Assistant Professor, Center for Youth Development and Research, University of Minnesota. He directs the International Learning Exchange in Professional Youthwork (ILEX).

Diane Nelson Bryen, Ph.D., a specialist in communication, learning disabilities, and cross-cultural approaches to special education and rehabilitation, is Professor in the Special Education Program at Temple University.

Rivka A. Eisikovits, Ph.D., is an educational anthropologist who has focused much of her work in group care settings. She is Senior Lecturer and Director of Graduate Studies in the School of Education, University of Haifa.

Robert R. Friedmann, Ph.D., a sociologist, is Associate Professor and Chair of the Department of Criminal Justice, College of Public and Urban Affairs, Georgia State University.

Leon Fulcher, Ph.D., an American who has also had professional experience in Scotland before relocating to New Zealand, is Professor and Head, Department of Sociology and Social Work, Victoria University, Wellington, New Zealand.

Edna Guttmann, Ph.D., has specialized in developmental psychology and family studies and is a Lecturer, School of Education, University of Haifa.

Yitzhak Kashti, Ph.D., an educational sociologist who has focused much of his work on group care through Youth Aliya and other agencies, is Associate Professor, School of Education, Tel Aviv University.

Ronald A. Madle, Ph.D., is Director of Staff Development and Program Evaluation at Laurelton Center, Laurelton, Pennsylvania.

Henry W. Maier, Ph.D., a specalist in developmental approaches in group care, is Professor Emeritus, School of Social Work, University of Washington.

Anthony N. Maluccio, D.S.W., a specialist in child welfare and foster care, is Professor, School of Social Work, University of Connecticut.

Donald L. Peters, Ph.D., a specialist in early child development, is Professor and Chair of the Department of Individual and Family Studies in the College of Human Resources, University of Delaware.

Shunit Reiter, Ph.D., whose work focuses on the education of the retarded, is Senior Lecturer and Chair of the Department of Education, School of Education, Tel Aviv University.

Yecheskel Taler, Ph.D., a specialist in rehabilitation, is Senior Lecturer and Director of the Center for Rehabilitation Research and Human Development, School of Social Work, University of Haifa.

Karen Vander Ven, Ph.D., is Professor and former Chair, Program in Child Development and Child Care, School of Social Work, University of Pittsburgh. She is also Coordinator of the American Branch of the International Federation of Educative Communities (FICE).

Anita Weiner, Ph.D., is Senior Lecturer and Director of Continuing Education, School of Social Work, University of Haifa. Her work has focused on the history of group care in Israel and on the development of policy initiatives in this area.

Yochanan Wozner, Ph.D., is Senior Lecturer and former Dean, School of Social Work, Tel Aviv University. He has worked closely with the SOS Kinderdorf affiliate and other residential programs in Israel.

Indices

Subject Index

Name Index

Abrahamson, M., 239, 252
Adams, P., 116, 120
Adams, W., 161, 168
Adler, C., 45, 47
Aichhorn, A., 4, 20
Ainsworth, F., 159, 168, 177, 186, 189, 192, 251, 252, 292, 297, 299, 309
Ainsworth, M. D., 27, 35, 46, 87, 97
Akabas, S. H., 160, 161, 168
Alexander, F., 180
Allen, G. J., 103, 122
Allen, R. F., 306, 309
Allport, F. H., 222, 234
Almy, M., 308, 309
Anderson, J. A., 162, 168
Anglin, J., 176, 182, 189, 192
Angyal, A., 54, 62
Appelbaum, R. P., 5, 20
Argyris, C., 7, 20, 277, 288
Arieli, M., xvi, 27, 46, 124, 155, 195–211, 316
Ashen, B. A., 5, 20
Athos, A. G., 305, 311
Averbeck, D., 162, 169

Ayres, S., 174, 184, 192
Azrin, N. H., 161, 162, 168
Azumi, K., 240, 245, 246, 252

Baizerman, M., 10, 20, 277, 288
Bakker, C., 34, 46
Bakker-Rabdau, M. K., 34, 46
Balgopal, P., 186, 192
Baltes, P. B., 293, 309, 310
Baltes, P., 310
Bandura, A., 5, 20, 107, 120
Barker, R. L., 5, 20
Barnes, F. H., 27, 46, 58, 123, 316
Barrett, M. C., 75, 80
Bayles, M. D., 308, 310
Beker, J., xiii, xv–xvi, 3–23, 29, 46, 124, 155, 277, 286, 288, 289, 313–314, 315
Bell, B. M., 35, 46
Benn, K. D., 8, 20
Benning, R. J., 45, 46
Bennis, W. G., 8, 20
Bensman, J., 19, 20
Berdyaev, N., 71, 74, 80
Besalel, V. A., 162, 168